Rewire Your Brain

Rewire Your Brain

Think Your Way to a Better Life

John B. Arden, Ph. D.

WILEY

John Wiley & Sons, Inc.

Published by John Wiley & Sons, Inc., Hoboken, New Jersey

Published simultaneously in Canada

For general information about our other products and services, please contact our Customer Care Department within the United States at (800) 762-2974, outside the United States at (317) 572-3993 or fax (317) 572-4002.

Wiley also publishes its books in a variety of electronic formats. Some content that appears in print may not be available in electronic books. For more information about Wiley products, visit our web site at www.wiley.com.

Library of Congress Cataloging-in-Publication Data:

Arden, John B., date.
    Rewire your brain / John B. Arden.
        p.   cm.
    Includes bibliographical references and index.
    ISBN 978-0-470-48729-7(pbk.)
        1. Memory.   2. Neurosciences.   3. Brain.   I. Title.
    BF371.A595 2010
    153—dc22   2009028771

Printed in the United States of America

10 9 8 7 6

Contents

Preface

In the last few years, both *Time* and *Newsweek* magazines have published feature articles on the new advances in neuroscience. The concepts of neuroplasticity, mirror cells, neurogenesis, and the social brain have all been discussed on radio shows and in newspaper articles. The advances in neuroscience have dramatically affected our understanding of what occurs in psychotherapy. If you're like most people, you'll want to learn more about how these developments can be applied to your practical life.

This book is based on recent developments in neuroscience and evidence-based treatment (the types of treatment that have been found to work best). It is a less technical companion to my professional books *Brain-Based Therapy with Adults* and *Brain-Based Therapy with Children and Adolescents*. Those two books, written with my friend and colleague Lloyd Linford, address how the developments in neuroscience and evidence-based treatment can be applied to therapy. *Rewire Your Brain* is meant to be a practical resource book that describes how to actually change your brain based on well-researched principles that work. The book will guide you through the process of rewiring your brain so that you can change your life. You cannot change how you think and feel without changing your brain.

We all feel a little anxious or down in the dumps at times. You'll learn how to deal with normal levels of these feelings, how to minimize such periods, and how to get the most out of life. You'll also learn healthy habits to enhance your brain's longevity and to maximize a vibrant life free of self-imposed limitations.

Each chapter in this book addresses key components of the new developments in neuroscience and describes how to apply them to specific areas of your life in order to help you thrive.

In chapter 1, you'll learn about the major changes that have occurred in the field of neuroscience, including the discovery of neuroplasticity, which has been described by the saying "Cells that fire together, wire together." You'll learn how habits are formed and how to increase good habits and end bad ones. Since your brain is always developing new connections between neurons and killing off old connections that are not being used, you'll learn how to develop connections that promote good habits and shut off those that support bad habits. You'll learn the acronym FEED to help you remember the steps to rewire your brain: Focus, Effort, Effortlessness, and Determination. Through the practice of these steps, you can *feed* your brain to make the rewiring changes described in the rest of the book.

In chapter 2, you'll learn that the part of your brain called the amygdala can needlessly create fear. Since the amygdala can trigger a false alarm, it needs to be put in check by the frontal lobes. You'll also learn about the balance between the sympathetic and the parasympathetic nervous systems, which help you to become active when you need to be and to calm down afterward. I'll explain the concept of exposure from evidence-based treatment and the idea of a slow track versus a fast track and then make practical suggestions of how you can turn off a false alarm. You'll learn how to calm down your amygdala so that you can approach life courageously and with a sense of vitality.

In chapter 3, you'll learn that underactivation of the left frontal lobe has been associated with depression and that activation of this lobe is associated with the alleviation of depression and the promotion of positive feelings. I will explain how the techniques of *behavioral activation* (borrowed from evidence-based treatment) and *cognitive restructuring* (borrowed from cognitive-behavioral therapy) can shift your brain to a different *attractor state* (borrowed from neurodynamics) in your left frontal lobe. I'll also explain how light affects your biochemistry and your mood. You'll learn how to stay positive and enjoy life with optimism.

In chapter 4, you'll learn about memory skills that you can cultivate by wiring your brain to improve your memory. Various memory techniques have been used for thousands of years, and you can refashion them to enhance your memory capacity. You'll learn mnemonic devices to make your memory skills work optimally.

In chapter 5, you'll learn how to ensure that your brain creates the right biochemistry for making your brain cells communicate with one another so that you can be calm, energized, and focused. In addition to consuming the right amino acids, vitamins, and minerals, you'll need the correct essential fatty acids to ensure that your cell membranes are supple and flexible, enabling neuroplasticity to occur.

In chapter 6, you'll learn that exercise and sleep play a significant role in how your brain rewires and creates new neurons. Exercise is one of the most powerful ways to jump-start the neurochemical mechanisms of neuroplasticity and neurogenesis. You'll learn about the role of sleep in memory and how to achieve a healthy sleep cycle. The exciting field of psychoneuroimmunology (the links among the mind, the brain, and the immune system) is explained, and suggestions are made to achieve healthy and vibrant living.

In chapter 7, you'll learn about the research on the brain systems that are collectively referred to as the social brain. This system includes mirror neurons, spindle cells, the orbital frontal cortex, and the anterior cingulate. I'll describe how these neural systems help to build relationships and empathy. You'll read about research that has shown that people who maintain positive social relationships live longer and feel more satisfied with their lives. You'll learn how to expand and vitalize your relationships.

In chapter 8, you'll learn what factors increase your ability to be resilient and to approach life with vitality despite obstacles. You'll also learn how to make aging a gain instead of a loss. You can acquire wisdom by maximizing your brain's capacity to see the bigger picture and thus make your later years wise ones. Concepts from positive psychology, such as optimism and a positive focus on healthy ambition, offer an antidote to the passive and material focus that is endemic in contemporary society. In addition, the practice of compassion and nonattachment provides an antidote to needless tension and suffering. Since there are always bumps on the road of life, resiliency and openness allow you to rewire your brain to be flexible and accepting of the rich complexity of life.

In chapter 9, you'll learn about the calming yet vitalizing role of attention, your prefrontal cortex, and attitude. The subtle power of parasympathetic meditation can increase your tolerance of stress and your sense of peace. You'll learn how to increase your ability to be mindfully present and to maintain a sense of connectivity with others and the world you inhabit.

1

Firing the Right Cells Together

There is a revolution occurring in brain science. Not long ago it was thought that the brain you were born with was the brain you would die with and that the brain cells you had at birth were the maximum number you would ever possess. The brain was thought to be hardwired to function in predetermined ways. It turns out that this is not true. The brain is not hardwired; it's "soft-wired" by experience.

It has been a common belief that our genes dictate our thoughts, our emotions, and our behavior. Throughout the 1980s and the 1990s, the press was filled with stories on how genetics predetermine everything we experience. There were also stories about identical twins who were raised apart but who nevertheless had the same mannerisms or favored the same color. Popular culture saw these stories as evidence of the power of genetic hardwiring.

Neuroscientific research is now telling us that the brain is quite plastic. The brain you were born with is actually modified by your experiences throughout your life. Your brain is changing all the time. In fact, new brain cells can be born. Genes lay out potential and vulnerabilities, but they do not dictate your thoughts, your feelings, or your behavior. It turns out that behavior is not rigidly determined. You can even turn genes on or off with your behavior.

Two of my books, *Brain-Based Therapy: Adult* and *Brain-Based Therapy: Child*, were written for professionals to help them teach their patients to rewire their brains, and they were based on these new discoveries. *Rewire Your Brain* explains how this information can be used directly by you. This book tells you how you can make use of the new discoveries in neuroscience. I will define and describe the following areas and explain how they can be relevant to your life:

- Neuroplasticity
- Neurogenesis
- Social systems, such as mirror neurons
- Nutritional neuroscience

The new discoveries in neuroscience shed light on how you can maximize your potential and minimize your vulnerabilities. I will describe how to apply these findings to rewire your brain so that you can feel calm and positive. So much hinges on these two abilities: by learning to be calm and positive, you can improve your ability to focus, face challenges, reach your goals, and be happy.

Learning to be calm means feeling less tense, less anxious, and less easily stressed. There are parts of your brain that, when not tamed, tend to overreact and add to needless tension, anxiety, and stress. In this book I'll describe how to get those parts rewired. The bottom line is this: how you train yourself to think, feel, and behave on a regular basis will rewire your brain and allow you to be calm and focused.

Thanks to the new discoveries in neuroscience, we know much more about how the brain works and how you can rewire the parts of the brain that are out of balance with the others, having become either overactivated or underactivated. I'll describe how those specific parts of your brain tend to become overactivated and deregulated when you feel down in the dumps, lose your optimism, and look only at the dark side. Things don't look as bright as they could look, and the glass is half empty when it could just as easily seem half full. I will describe how to activate the parts of your brain that must be regulated and balanced so that you feel positive about your life and see the glass as (at least) half full. You'll learn to calm down in the face of stress and boost your mood when you're down. You'll also learn to improve your memory, have better relationships, and get a good night's sleep, all of which rewire your brain and thus enable you to be calmer and feel more positive.

Nurtured Nature

In order to rewire your brain, the first thing you should do is learn how the brain works. Your brain works in response to and in relation to the world around you. We have moved far away from the old debate on nature versus nurture; now we are able to "nurture nature." Since your brain is not hardwired but is really "soft-wired," your experience plays a major role in how you nurture your nature.

The brain weighs just three pounds, yet it's one of the most advanced organs in the body. It has a hundred billion nerve cells, called *neurons*, and many more support cells. That's equivalent to the number of stars in our galaxy.

Let's start with the brain's architecture. The neurons are clustered in the parts of the brain that have been called *modules*: the cortex (the outer layer, which has two hemispheres), the four lobes, and the subcortical (below the cortex) modules.

There has been a lot of hype about the character of the two halves of the brain. "Right-brain" people were said to be more creative, even more spiritual than "left-brain" people. The left-brain people were described as more rigid and picky. That hype, born in the 1970s, still exists, but many people who were instrumental in starting this fad have long since abandoned it. The truth is that the two hemispheres work together in everything you do. The brain contains a band of fibers called the *corpus callosum* that binds the two hemispheres together. It serves to connect distant neurons that fire together, adding dimension and depth to everything you do and think.

The corpus callosum of a woman is denser than that of a man. This means that the two hemispheres of a woman's brain work more evenly together. The female brain is more symmetrical. The male brain has an asymmetrical torque, which means that the right frontal lobe is larger than the left frontal lobe, and the left occipital (back of the head) lobe is larger than the right occipital lobe.

For both sexes, the right hemisphere processes visual and spatial information, enabling you to grasp the "big picture." The right hemisphere pays more attention to the context or the gist of a situation. The left hemisphere, in contrast, is more adept at details, categories, and linearly arranged information such as language. The right hemisphere is more active when you're learning something new. Once the knowledge becomes routine and overlearned, the left hemisphere comes more into play. This is another reason that language is processed by the left hemisphere.

The right hemisphere makes better connections with the parts of the brain below the cortex, so it is more emotional by nature. In other words, it's better able to pick up the emotional climate of a conversation. Since women's brains have a better connection between the two hemispheres than men's brains do, women are said to be more intuitive. Words often carry more emotional meaning for women than they do for men.

There are four lobes in each hemisphere: the frontal lobe, the parietal (middle) lobe, the temporal (side) lobe, and the occipital lobe. Each has specific talents. For example, when you appreciate a specific object, such as a chair you sat on at your friend's house, the thoughts and feelings you have about the chair are dispersed throughout your brain. You remember the elegant shape of the chair through your right parietal lobe. You remember the words your friend used to describe his trip to Costa Rica through your left temporal lobe, and you process the tone of his voice through your right temporal lobe. You remember looking back at the chair as you were leaving the room and noticing its deep cinnamon color through your occipital lobe.

Women have a greater density of neurons in the temporal lobe, which specializes in language. This verbal advantage begins to appear during the first two years of life, when little girls develop the ability to talk about six months earlier than little boys do. When developing verbal strategies, women activate the left hippocampus (a part of the brain related to memory) more than men do. Men generally have greater visual and spatial skills, because they show greater activity in the right hippocampus than women do.

The most recent addition to our evolutionary development is the frontal lobe, which makes up about 20 percent of the human brain. In comparison, the frontal lobe of a cat occupies about 3.5 percent of its brain. The frontal lobe is the last part of the brain to mature in humans; its development is not complete until sometime in the third decade of life.

At the forefront of the frontal lobe, the *prefrontal cortex* (PFC) gives us many of our most complex cognitive, behavioral, and emotional capacities. The PFC enables you to develop and act on a moral system, because it allows you to set aside your needs and reflect on the needs of others. The PFC is part of a system that provides you with the capacity for empathy. If your PFC is damaged, you are likely to engage in antisocial and impulsive behaviors or not engage in any purposeful behavior at all.

One of the principal parts of the PFC is the *dorsolateral prefrontal cortex* (DLPFC). *Dorsal* means "fin" or "top," and *lateral* means "side." The other significant prefrontal area is called the *orbital frontal cortex* (OFC), because it lies just behind the orbs of the eyes.

The DLPFC is very involved in higher-order thinking, attention, and short-term memory (which is also called working memory because it processes what you are working on at any one time). You can usually hold something you're working on in your mind for twenty to thirty seconds. The DLPFC is the last part of the brain to fully develop, and it is also the earliest to falter during the later years of life. This is what's behind the phenomenon of walking purposely into a room and then forgetting what you intended to do there. The DLPFC is involved with complex problem solving, so it maintains rich connections with the hippocampus, which helps you to remember things for later.

The OFC, in contrast, appears to have a closer relationship with the parts of the brain that process emotions, such as those generated by your amygdala. The OFC develops earlier in life and is closely associated with what is called the social brain. Without your OFC, you would be like the classic case of Phineas Gage. In an accident at work, a steel rod pierced Gage's brain and skewered his OFC but left everything else in his brain intact. Gage retained his cognitive abilities but lost much of his ability to inhibit impulses. He had previously been a supervisor who was widely respected, but now he became unstable (in stark contrast to his previous emotional reserve), erratic, rude, and hard to get along with. Gage was eventually reduced to working in a circus freak show, and he died penniless in San Francisco twenty years after the injury. His skull is on display at Harvard Medical School.

Highly influenced by bonding, the OFC thrives on close relationships. If those relationships are trusting and supportive, the OFC becomes more capable of regulating your emotions. In contrast to the DLPFC, the OFC does not falter much in old age. Older adults remember faces as well as younger adults do.

Finally, there are differences between the left and the right prefrontal cortex. The right PFC helps to develop foresight and to get the gist of what's happening in a given situation. It helps you to make plans, stay on course toward your overall goal, and understand metaphor. If someone says, "Michael Phelps is a fish," it's your right PFC that enables you to understand what this person is really saying about the Olympic swimmer. Your left PFC, in contrast, helps you to focus on the details of individual events, like how many points were scored in the second half of a football game.

Neurons and Their Messengers

Within all these lobes, hemispheres, and modules are a hundred billion neurons waiting to be used. They are highly social; if they weren't used by working with neighboring neurons, they would die. Each neuron is capable of maintaining connections with about ten thousand other neurons. These connections change as you learn things, such as a new tennis swing, a new language, or the layout of a new supermarket.

Neurons function partly on chemistry and partly on the electrical firing of impulses in an on-and-off manner. Neurons communicate with one another by sending chemical messengers called *neurotrans-mitters* across a gap called a *synapse*. This is how one neuron gets another neuron to fire. More than sixty types of neurotransmitters exist in the brain. Some make you excited, and some calm you down. There are many different shapes and sizes of synapses, and the shape and size of a synapse changes as you learn something new.

Two neurotransmitters account for about 80 percent of the signaling in the brain: glutamate, which is excitatory and stirs activity, and gamma-aminobutyric acid (GABA), which is inhibitory and quiets down activity. Glutamate is the workhorse in the brain. When it delivers a signal between two neurons that previously had no connection, it primes the pump for later activation. The more times this connection is activated, the stronger the wiring is between these neurons. GABA, in contrast, helps to calm you down when you need to be calm. It is the target of drugs like Valium and Ativan, which used to be prescribed as a panacea for anxiety. You need optimum GABA activity to keep your anxiety down, but you don't need those drugs, as I'll explain in chapter 6.

Although glutamate and GABA are the principal neurotransmitters, there are scores of others that play important roles in the brain. They account for only a fraction of the activity between the neurons, but they have a powerful influence on those neurons. They are widely researched, and many drugs have been designed to affect them.

The three most researched neurotransmitters are serotonin, norepinephrine, and dopamine, and they are sometimes called *neuromodulators* because they alter the sensitivity of receptors, make a neuron more efficient, or instruct a neuron to make more glutamate. They can also help to lower the "noise" in the brain by working to override other signals that are coming into the synapse. Sometimes, however, they intensify those other signals. These three neurotransmitters can either act directly, like glutamate and GABA, or fine-tune the flow of information that is being processed in the synapses.

Serotonin has attracted much publicity because of the widespread use of drugs like Prozac. Serotonin plays a role in emotional tone and in many different emotional responses. Low serotonin levels are correlated with anxiety, depression, and even obsessive-compulsive disorder (OCD).

Serotonin is like a traffic cop, because it helps to keep brain activity under control. It's common to hear people who take drugs like Prozac say, "Things don't bother me the way they used to." However, there is also a downside: these drugs generally provide such an even keel that people say, "I know that the beauty of that sunset would've had a bigger effect on me in the past, but now I'm sort of numb to things like that."

Norepinephrine activates attention. It amplifies the signals that influence perception, arousal, and motivation. Like serotonin, norepinephrine has been associated with mood and depression. It has been targeted by antidepressants such as Ludiomil and Vesta.

Dopamine sharpens and focuses attention. It has also been associated with reward, movement, and learning, and it is one of the principal neurotransmitters that code pleasure. When registering pleasure, dopamine activates an area called the *nucleus accumbens*, sometimes referred to as the pleasure center. Activation of the nucleus accumbens has been associated with drug abuse, gambling, and other types of addictive behaviors. When this area is frequently activated, it becomes hard to stop doing the things that activate it.

Drugs that activate dopamine, like Ritalin, are used to help people with attention-deficit/hyperactivity disorder (ADHD). People (usually children and adolescents) who are given Ritalin or similar drugs not only pay attention better but also report feeling calmer.

Cells That Fire Together Wire Together

In the last twenty years, there has been an overwhelming amount of evidence that the synapses are not hardwired but are changing all the time. This is what is meant by synaptic plasticity, or *neuroplasticity*. The synapses between the neurons are plastic.

Neuroplasticity is what makes memory possible. I will devote an entire chapter to how you can improve your memory; for now, the point is that the brain changes its synapses when you remember something new. The brain would not be able to record anything new if it were hardwired. Remembering something new is, therefore, rewiring the brain. By making connections between ideas or images, you also make connections between the neurons that encode those ideas and images.

Neuroplasticity illustrates the phrase "Use it or lose it." When you use the synaptic connections that represent a skill, you strengthen them, and when you let the skill lie dormant, you weaken those connections. It's similar to the way that your muscles will weaken if you stop exercising.

"Cells that fire together wire together" aptly describes the way your brain reorganizes when you have new experiences. The more you do something in a particular way, use words with a specific accent, or remember something about your past, the more the neurons that fire together to make this happen will strengthen their connections. The more the neurons fire together, the more likely it is that they will fire together in the future.

Just as "Cells that fire together wire together" has become a sort of mantra in neuroscience, so too has an opposite phrase been coined: "Neurons that fire apart wire apart." This means that neurons that are out of sync will fail to link. It is the neural explanation for forgetting.

In other words, the more you do something, the more likely it is that you will do it again in the future. That's why baseball players go to batting practice, golfers go to driving ranges, and piano players practice for hours on end. The same goes for thinking. The more you think about your Aunt Matilda, the more she will pop into your mind again and again. Repetition rewires the brain and breeds habits.

When neurons fire together often, they begin to fire together at a quicker rate. This leads to increased efficiency, because there is more precision in the number of neurons that are required to do a particular skill. For example, when you learned to ride a bicycle, you used more muscles and neurons at first as you wobbled; then, once you learned to ride efficiently, less muscular effort and fewer neurons were required, and your ride was much smoother and faster.

The neurons that were required to fire with their partners had teamed up and wired together.

As you become more talented at a specific skill, a greater amount of space in your brain is devoted to making that possible. Alvaro Pascual-Leone of Harvard Medical School used transcranial magnetic stimulation (TMS) to measure specific areas of the cortex. He studied blind people who read braille and found that the cortical maps for their reading fingers were larger than the cortical maps for their other fingers and also for the fingers of sighted readers. In other words, the sensitivity of their reading fingers required more space. Thus, cultivated movement enhances neuroplasticity, which creates extra space in the brain.

In another example of the power of neuroplasticity, musicians who play string instruments were examined to see if their brains had reorganized to accommodate more space. There was no difference between the string-instrument players and the nonmusicians in how much space was made available in the sensory motor strip (the area in the center of the brain that controls movement and physical sensation) for the fingers of the right hand (in right-handed players). However, the area of the brain devoted to the fingers of the left hand (in right-handed players) showed a dramatic difference. The fingers of the left hand must be nimble and dexterous in order to make all the fretting movements. The cortical space devoted to the fingers involved in fretting was significantly greater in these musicians than in nonmusicians. This difference was greatest if the musician had started playing the instrument before the age of twelve. In other words, although this use-dependent neuroplasticity occurs during adulthood, it is more dramatic the earlier and the longer that the person plays the instrument.

Not only does behavior change the structure of the brain through neuroplasticity; just thinking about or imagining particular behaviors can change brain structure as well. For example, researchers have shown that simply imagining a session of piano practice contributes to neuroplasticity in the area of the brain associated with the finger movements of playing the piano. Thus, mental practice alone contributes to the rewiring of the brain.

How Neuroplasticity Occurs

A process called *long-term potentiation* (LTP) occurs when the excitation between cells is prolonged. This strengthens the connections between the cells and makes them more apt to fire together in the future. Thus, LTP is relatively long-lasting.

LTP essentially strengthens the affinity between neurons by reconfiguring their electrochemical relationship. On the sending side of the synapse, the stores of glutamate (the excitatory neurotransmitter) are enhanced, and the receptor side is reconfigured to receive more. The voltage on the receptor side becomes stronger in its resting state, which attracts more glutamate. If the firing between these neurons continues, the genes within the neurons are turned on in order to construct more building blocks for the infrastructure and enhance the relationship.

One of the most important players in both neuroplasticity and neurogenesis is something called *brain-derived neurotrophic factor* (BDNF). This belongs to a family of proteins that enhance brain cells. BDNF has been shown to help build, grow, and maintain the infrastructure of cell circuitry. It is one of the hottest areas of research in neuroscience today, and more than a thousand articles have been written about its amazing fertilizer-like functions. It has even been called "Miracle Grow" by many, because when it's applied to cells, it causes them to grow. A vivid illustration of BDNF's super-fertilizing effect occurs when researchers sprinkle BDNF onto neurons in a petri dish. Those neurons sprouted new branches much as they do in the brain during learning and development.

BDNF does its magic in variety of ways. It works within the cell to activate the genes that increase the production of proteins, serotonin, and even more BDNF. It binds to the receptors at the synapse, triggering a flow of ions that increases the voltage, which in turn strengthens the connectivity between the neurons. In general, BDNF prevents cells from dying and enhances their growth and vitality. BDNF is activated indirectly by glutamate and increases the production of internal antioxidants and protective proteins. It stimulates LTP, which is fundamental to neuroplasticity.

LTP and BDNF go hand in hand. Researchers who work with the brains of various animals have shown that stimulating LTP by learning increases the BDNF levels. When researchers deprived the brains of BDNF, the brains also lost their capacity for LTP.

Use strengthens connections, and nonuse weakens them. Old connections that are not strengthened by relationships will fade.

Just as the brain needs the LTP mechanisms that strengthen the connections between neurons so that you can remember, it also needs those that will help it to forget. A process known as long-term depression (LTD) helps you to unlearn bad habits. (Note: LTD has nothing to do with the emotional state called depression.) LTD helps you to weaken the connections between the neurons that support an old habit. The weakening of old connections gives you more available neurons to use for the new connections that you establish with LTP.

To understand this principle, consider that the age at which you learn a language affects whether you speak with an accent. If you learn a new language while in your twenties, it's highly probable that you will speak that new language with an accent from your first language. If you learn a new language at age nine, however, you probably won't have an accent tinged by your first language. When you learn a new language as an adult, the neurons that have always connected to make specific sounds tend to continue to fire together even when you try to make different but related sounds.

The more you talk to people who don't share your accent, the greater is the chance that your accent will fade. For example, both my parents grew up in the Greater Boston area. A few years after I was born, my family moved west. My parents gradually lost their Boston accents as they spoke with people who had moved west from all over the country or who had grown up there.

When you develop new ideas or insights, change in your brain occurs much more quickly than when you learn a new language or lose an accent. Certain parts of the brain are very talented at putting information together quickly so that you can make decisions without mulling things over for hours or even days.

The discovery of *spindle cells* (or *spindle neurons*) has focused attention on people's ability to make effective snap decisions. Spindle neurons are found in great numbers in the part of the brain called the *cingulate cortex*. These neurons are able to connect divergent information quickly and efficiently in ways that have not been seen in other species. Spindle cells provide a unique interface between your thoughts and your emotions. As such, they aid your ability to maintain sustained attention and self-control. They provide you with the flexibility to make quick but complex problem-solving decisions in emotionally stirring situations.

Spindle cells can't do their magic, however, if they have little to work with. In other words, you have to lay the rewiring groundwork in your brain by learning new information and forming new talents. Snap judgments and insights are made by integrating information from neural nets that you have already formed.

Snap Judgments

The spindle cell is a class of neurons that responds extremely quickly. It is found to be more abundant in the human brain than in that of any other species. The human brain has a thousand times more spindle cells than our closest ape relatives possess. Many theorists regard this as one of the reasons we can make snap judgments. These cells are so named because they look like spindles, with a large bulb at one end and a long, thick extension. Because they are about four times larger than other neurons and have such long and thick dimensions, they are believed to make high-velocity transmission possible. Hence the *snap* in *snap judgment*.

The location of spindle cells and their connection of the regions of the social brain illustrate their importance in social relatedness, emotion, and therapy. Spindle cells have rich synaptic receptors for dopamine, serotonin, and vasopressin, which play a role in mood and thus in our emotional experiences and bonding. They form connections between the cingulate cortex and the OFC.

The front portion of the cingulate cortex contains many spindle cells that connect diverse parts of the brain and are involved in bonding and social communication.

Let's say you are on your way to New Orleans for vacation when you hear a radio report that Hurricane Katrina is about to hit the city. Your spindle cells kick into action, and you immediately reroute to Houston. Once you are in Houston, you hear that hundreds of Katrina evacuees are being sent to the Astrodome, so you decide to spend part of your vacation volunteering in a soup kitchen there. These were all snap decisions that were made in complex and emotionally charged circumstances. Years later you may view that vacation as one of your most rewarding and memorable.

Every time you remember that story, certain synaptic connections are strengthened and certain ones are weakened, based on the details that you remember. As you discuss the events that led you to Houston, the story becomes modified, and so does your brain. Your friends may talk about the government's poor response, and other synaptic connections are made with those memories. You are essentially rewiring your brain every time you review the story in your mind.

Deep within the brain are two structures that are involved in memory. One is the *amygdala*, named after the Latin word for "almond," *amygdalon*, because of its shape. The amygdala is triggered by intense emotional states like fear, and it assigns emotional intensity to the incoming information. The amygdala can be triggered by a quick glance from a very attractive person or by your boss glaring at you. It often serves as a sort of panic button.

The other memory structure is called the *hippocampus*, the Greek word for "seahorse," because of its shape. Researchers have recently discovered the birth of new neurons, or *neurogenesis*, in the hippocampus. Scientists had previously believed that neurogenesis was not possible. The discovery of new neurons in a part of the brain that lays down new memories highlights the importance of cultivating your memory skills to rewire your brain.

The hippocampus and the amygdala are involved in two different types of memory: explicit and implicit, respectively. Explicit memory is used when you try to remember what you had for dinner last night, when your next dental appointment is, or the name of a familiar-looking woman who's standing next to the water cooler. These are facts, dates, words: pieces of information. It is this type of memory that people often complain they are losing.

Implicit memory is often thought of as unconscious memory. It reacts to the emotional intensity of events and situations; when the situation is potentially dangerous, it activates the fear system in your body. This is often called the fight-or-flight response.

This alarm system is automatic; that is, it happens before you have time to think about it. Thousands of years ago, when our ancestors encountered a predatory animal like a lion, it was best to react immediately and not stand around thinking about the lion, admiring its beauty or wondering why it was bothering them instead of tracking down some tasty antelope. Thus, the fast track to the amygdala kept our ancestors alive.

A balance between your sympathetic nervous system (which activates you) and your parasympathetic nervous system (which calms you down) allows you flexibility. I'll describe this in detail in chapter 9. These systems, along with the circadian rhythm, nutrition, exercise, relaxation, and meditation, can help you to be calm and positive.

Let's change the Hurricane Katrina story and say that you didn't go to Houston. You might have been so filled with anxiety that you drove like mad straight north to escape the driving rain. At one point you pulled over because you couldn't see the road in front of you. A tree limb fell on your car, and you were filled with even more anxiety. Months later, during a rainstorm, you feel a surge of anxiety. You don't know why you feel this way, but your amygdala remembers quite well, because it triggers your hippocampus and cortex to remind you of the day you escaped Katrina.

The amygdala helped you by stirring enough fear in you to make you pull off the road, but it also made you oversensitive to rainstorms. The problem is that this fear system is activated even when you don't need to be fearful. In other words, sometimes it is turned on when it would be better to have it turned off. Chapter 2 describes

how you can tame your amygdala so that it doesn't become overactivated when you need to stay calm.

Your frontal lobes are sometimes called the executive brain or the
executive control center because they are important in orchestrating
the resources of the rest of your brain. The frontal lobes decide
what to do, how to stay positive, and how to appreciate the larger
picture of life. By being positive and active, you'll rewire your frontal
lobes.

The OFC and some other parts of the brain constitute what has
been called the social brain because this system of neurons thrives
on social interaction. When these neurons are activated effectively,
you experience fewer psychological problems and better mental
health. Chapter 7 is devoted to the many benefits of your social brain
networks.

The bonding experiences you have had with your parents
since the beginning of your life have affected your social brain. Your
later relationships then modify those neural connections. Positive
relationships enhance your sense of well-being, whereas negative
relationships leave you with the opposite feeling.

We know that neurochemicals such as oxytocin are involved in
childbirth and bonding, and that later in life they become activated
in intimate relationships. Higher oxytocin levels help to blunt pain
and make us feel comforted by other people. For this reason, oxytocin is referred as the "cuddling hormone."

The recent discovery of *mirror neurons* has shown that parts of your
brain are acutely sensitive to the movements and intentions of others.
Mirror neurons allow you to mirror another person, or to feel what
he or she feels without even thinking about it. For example, when a
friend yawns, have you ever found yourself yawning immediately
afterward? Mirror neurons are essentially the brain-based explanation
of empathy.

In the story of how you helped at the Houston Astrodome after
Hurricane Katrina, it was your mirror neurons that made you feel
empathy for the evacuees.

Mirror neurons give people the capacity to form relationships and
to thrive from them. People with autism have few mirror neurons

or dysfunctional ones. It has recently been proposed that the mirror neuron system is actively involved in your relationship with yourself as well as with others. For example, when you volunteered at the soup kitchen at the Astrodome, you felt good about yourself when people thanked you.

Some researchers have proposed that experiencing empathy and compassion through the mirror neuron system is equivalent to having compassion for yourself. Thus, "giving is receiving" is a brain-based truth. Insensitivity and selfishness are essentially bad for your brain and your mental health. In contrast, compassion and loving relationships are good for your brain and your mental health.

The mirror neuron system has also been identified as the part of the brain that is involved in mindfulness meditation and prayer. The calming and focused practice of mindfulness meditation or prayer wires the brain circuitry that promotes better health.

Many neuroscientists have recently explored the effects of meditation and prayer on the brain. Tibetan monks have been found to have rewired their brains from years of meditation practice. These monks were examined during certain types of meditation using functional magnetic resonance imaging (fMRI), positron emission tomography (PET), and other techniques. Thanks to these studies, we have a picture of what is occurring in the meditating brain. We know that the mindful brain can promote health and well-being. You, too, can benefit by rewiring your brain through mindfulness. I will explain how this is done in chapter 9.

FEED Your Brain

Now that you have a better idea of how the brain works, let's focus on a method of rewiring your brain that involves the following four steps:

- Focus
- Effort
- Effortlessness
- Determination

To help you remember these steps, use the acronym FEED, as in feeding your brain. Now let's examine each step in detail.

Focus

You need to pay attention to the situation, the new behavior, or the memory that you want to repeat or remember. Attention activates your frontal lobes, which ensure that other parts of the brain are also engaged. You may think of this step as the alert function. You can't rewire your brain without opening the gate or initiating the change. Focus gets the ball rolling.

Attention and the frontal lobes play important roles in neuroplasticity. Think of the PFC as the brain's brain: it helps to direct the resources to what is important. When you are on automatic pilot, such as when you are driving on a highway and talking to your friend in the passenger seat, your attention is directed to the conversation. The conversation is what you will remember, not the trees and the houses along the road. If, however, you talk about what you both notice on the highway, your attention has shifted and you will remember the physical details of the journey. If you talk about these details of the journey later, you'll strengthen those memories. If you don't discuss those details later—that is, direct your attention to them—the chances are that those memories will fade.

Thus, simply focusing attention doesn't ensure that your brain has been rewired. You focus on a hundred thousand experiences every day, and your brain can't possibly remember all the things you experienced. Focus allows you to pay attention to what's happening here and now, and this starts the process of neuroplasticity.

Effort

Effort shifts your attention from perception to action. Making a focused effort activates your brain to establish new synaptic connections. When you begin to make an effort, your brain uses a lot of glucose to learn something new. By observing PET scans, neuroscientists have amassed considerable information in the last two decades about what parts of the brain light up in the scan due to glucose metabolism when someone is thinking or feeling something.

When you're making an initial effort to do something, the area of your brain associated with that task shows up in the scan as being in use.

Effortlessness

After a new behavior, thought, or feeling has been established, it takes less energy to keep it going. It's like learning a new tennis swing or how to say hello in a new language. In the beginning, it takes focus, effort, and more energy in your brain, but after you make the swing or say hello enough times, it becomes effortless. Thus, to rewire your brain you'll have to stay with the new behavior long enough to make it become fairly automatic. In time, practice will make it effortless. Your brain won't have to work as hard once you reach this level.

The body and the brain follow natural laws, and the natural law that applies to the concept of effortlessness is called the Law of the Conservation of Energy. This means that the things that happen are usually things that happen easily. For example, all water flows downhill. The deeper the creek, the more water flows in it. The same is true for your brain: the more you use certain brain cells together, the more you will use them together in the future.

As PET scans illustrate, when a person becomes more proficient in a particular skill, the brain region associated with that skill labors less. This illustrates the fundamental principle of efficiency: what comes easily will be repeated because it's easy.

Once you have developed a pattern—the tennis swing or saying hello in French with the right amount of inflection—it will become easier to do the next time you try. What if you stop doing it, however? If you haven't played tennis in ten years, you won't swing as well immediately. If you go to France ten years after taking a class in French, you won't be as fluent as you were in the class (unless, of course, you have practiced in the meantime). You have to do the activity often to retain the ability. You'll certainly play tennis better than if you never played before, or your French will come back more quickly, but if you practice doing these things, your brain will remain wired to perform them effortlessly.

Determination

The final step in feeding your brain is staying in practice. Do the activity again and again. Being determined in this way need not be tiring and painful. If you practice the other three steps in feeding your brain, by the time you get to this one, it should come easily. That's because effortlessness precedes it. Thus, determination simply means that you stay in practice. By being determined, you'll complete the feeding process to rewire your brain.

Now that you know the four basic steps or principles, we'll look at how you can apply them in your daily life. In chapter 2, we'll discuss dealing with anxious feelings, needless worries, or just plain fear, and in chapter 3 we'll address how you can avoid feeling down in the dumps.

The story below illustrates how important it is to make a commitment to take an active role in rewiring your brain. This is not like simply learning a new trick; it requires the process we have described as feeding your brain.

Marlee Feeds Her Brain

Marlee came to see me, complaining that she was fed up with being moody and "always feeling out of sorts." She said that she tended to be irritable and easily stressed, and when she started to feel that way, it was hard to shake it.

"I want to be positive and enjoy my life like everyone else," she said, shaking her head woefully. "I heard that you know how to rewire people's brains. Please rewire mine."

"Are you willing to do the work that it will take to change your brain?" I asked.

"Why can't you do whatever it is that you do?" she insisted. "I'm tired of trying all these gimmicks that are supposed to work but never do."

"When you try something new, how long do you stay with it?" I probed.

"Long enough to know that it doesn't work," she stated matter-of-factly.

I gently prodded her for a clear answer of how long.

"A day or two is enough to know," she said, as if that confirmed her strong effort.

I explained that for neuroplasticity to work, especially for mood-related issues, she would have to stay with the new behavior until it became effortless to do it. "You must practice doing it until it becomes a new habit," I told her. "The key is that you need to get started. Usually, that means doing what you don't feel like doing and continue doing it until it becomes easy."

"You mean forcing myself to do something against my nature?" she asked incredulously. "Isn't that unnatural?"

"Actually, it's very natural," I answered. "That's how you learn new skills. When you study for a test you go over material repeatedly until it's not hard to remember it."

"I just crammed the night before and it worked just fine," Marlee informed me. "I passed the courses. That's all I cared about."

"Do you remember the subject matter now?" I asked. She shook her head no. I invited her to pick a habit that she wanted to break.

"My family would say it's my irritability," she admitted.

"Do you feel bad about it?" I wanted to know.

"When it happens, it seems as if they deserve what I say to them," she noted. "Only later does it become obvious that I was shooting my mouth off and they didn't deserve it."

"It's important to establish that it's *you* who really wants to change and not just that your family wants you to," I emphasized. Motivation is a very critical component of neuroplasticity. You can't change unless *you* really want to change. A passive effort just won't work. The activation of the PFC, the brain's brain, marshals all the resources.

"Yes. I'm sick of myself like this," she said solemnly. "I'm ready to do something."

"Let's start at the point at which you feel the impulse to say something," I instructed. "That's when we want to interrupt your impulse.

You say something before you allow yourself the time to think first and then do something else."

The first step for Marlee was to stop what she was doing and *focus* her attention on the moment before she reacted impulsively. A time-out step like this is used in anger management classes, yet here the task is to go further and focus on being an observer who is detached from the immediacy of the emotional reaction. This allows the PFC to gain better inhibitory control over the amygdala-driven emotional reactions. Marlee's PFC had to develop better adaptive strategies in order to draw attention to what she was angry about rather than the way she expressed her anger.

Next, Marlee needed to make an *effort* to do something different from her usual impulsive verbal comment. She had to act in a way that was different from her usual irritable manner in which she spoke first and thought later. She needed to learn to think first and speak later.

Marlee needed to repeat this effort enough times so that she eventually found it *effortless* to do so. She worked with focus and effort until it was effortless, feeding her brain for several weeks; then she came back in and said, "Well, I don't have to work on that anymore—I've got that down."

I told her that she needed to continue working with *determination* to solidify the new habit. Rather than become lazy and take a break, she had to continue to "work out" in order to "stay in shape." It is only by staying determined that she will be able to rewire her brain.

Test Yourself

Here is a quick quiz that will get to the heart of what's holding you back from rewiring your brain.

1. To rewire your brain, it's important to do what?
   a. Stay within your comfort zone
   b. Do what comes naturally to you
   c. Challenge yourself to change your behavior and then stay with it

    d. Wait until you feel motivated to change

2. What does the acronym FEED, a mnemonic device to help you remember the steps to rewire your brain, stand for?
    a. Feel good, Exhale, Excite, and Dictate
    b. Focus, Effort, Effortlessness, and Determination
    c. Fail, Engage, Encourage, and Describe
    d. Freedom, Effortlessness, Entertainment, and Doing little

3. If you're troubled by anxiety, it's best to do which of the following?
    a. Avoid what makes you anxious so that your amygdala will calm down
    b. Take some medication to numb your amygdala
    c. Expose yourself gradually to what makes you anxious
    d. Ask your family to shield you from stress

4. If you're down in the dumps, it's best to do which of the following?
    a. Hide out from family and friends until you feel up to seeing them
    b. Draw the drapes, stay inside, and rest
    c. Get out of the house, exercise, and engage in activities
    d. Self-medicate with alcohol and/or sweets to soothe your feelings

5. When you're trying to improve your memory, it's best to do which of the following?
    a. Rest your mind so that you will have enough energy to remember
    b. Multitask
    c. Rely on your friends to remember things for you
    d. Focus your attention, form associations, and review your memories

6. What should you do to improve your diet so that you can more easily rewire your brain?
    a. Eat large amounts of fried foods, sugar, and processed foods
    b. Eat three balanced meals per day and hydrate with water throughout the day

      c. Eat one good hardy meal and consume plenty of caffeine for energy

      d. Vary your food intake to meet your hunger pains

7. In old age, what is the best way to boost cognitive reserve and delay or prevent dementia?

      a. Minimize your mental strain by staying with a monotonous routine

      b. Vary your activities, learn new things, and stay socially connected

      c. Rest and stay away from any kind of stress

      d. Have a cocktail in the evening and ruminate about the past

8. Five habits that form the foundation for a healthy brain can be remembered as "planting SEEDS." What does this acronym stand for?

      a. Safety, Escape, Exit, Distance, and Soothingness

      b. Sensation, Entertainment, Ecstasy, Distraction, and Slipping away

      c. Stifle, End, Execute, Do, and Stonewall

      d. Social medicine, Exercise, Education, Diet, Sleep hygiene

9. To build a resilient brain, you should do which of the following?

      a. Cultivate optimism, inoculate yourself with manageable stress, and challenge yourself

      b. Make pessimism your default mode so that you will never be surprised

      c. Avoid stress at all costs

      d. Save your energy for times of need

10. A mindful brain does which of the following?

      a. Shuts down, checks out, and is otherwise mindless

      b. Is in the here and now, savoring every moment and sensation

      c. Looks for constant distraction from the stress and strain of the moment

      d. Is holier than thou

I will explain in detail what you need to know to answer these questions in the remaining chapters of this book.

2

Taming Your Amygdala

J ane came to see me for help with her fear of public speaking.
She had been asked by her employer to give a presentation on a
new product line that her department had developed. She told me
that she was chosen to make the presentation because she was one
of the principal designers of the project. However, the thought of
standing in front of fifty people made her fear that she would "make
a fool" of herself.

I agreed to help her succeed and offered to go one step further:
to help her become proficient at public speaking. She first said that
she thought I was joking. Then she became curious.

Jane had experienced frightening public speaking episodes in the
past. One time in particular had made an indelible impression on
her mind. It occurred moments after she was asked to report on her
college class project. She remembers standing in front of her peers
and freezing like a deer in the headlights. After a few terrifying
moments she rushed out of the classroom.

I told her that public speaking is one of the most common fears
that people report in surveys. Although she had the full-blown stress

response associated with this fear, she could learn to modify it and eventually turn it off.

I suggested that we work together to rewire her brain so that her fears about public speaking could be neutralized. Her frontal lobes could be trained to have better veto power over her amygdala. Then she would be better able to present her thoughts and feelings about the new product.

To begin to rewire her brain, Jane first needed to shift her *focus* to an enjoyable aspect of her subject matter, and it had to be something she wanted to share with others. This shift in focus engaged her frontal lobes, which helped her to distance herself from the overwhelming anxiety about standing up in front of people. The engagement of the frontal lobes helped to boost the neuroplasticity that was necessary for rewiring her brain.

When I told her about the importance of focusing and the other elements of FEED, she said, "All I can focus on is all those people watching me trip over my words!"

I explained that she could choose to focus on a constructive part of speaking in front of people. She could shift her focus from the speaking performance to the subject matter. This was simply the first step in activating her frontal lobes to calm down her amygdala, which was overreacting with fear.

Since Jane was a principal designer of the new product, there was an opportunity to tap into her enthusiasm for it. She had to make a concerted *effort* to fuse positive emotions into the task ahead of her. By describing her product to various individuals before her presentation, she could tap into this reservoir of enthusiasm. This effort brought her left frontal lobe into a greater role.

I asked Jane to explain the project to me. As she did, her face lit up and her voice became more animated. I pointed this out to her. At first she was surprised. Then she said, "Well, you're just one person, not a crowd of strangers!"

"True," I replied, "but you sure got me interested, not just by the details of the project but by how you described it. The people you'll be talking to already have an interest in the subject."

I asked her to make a strong effort to practice with her family and her friends at least five times before she returned for another appointment. When she returned, she told me that each practice presentation had been more useful.

I reminded Jane that those people weren't computer engineers like her upcoming audience. She apparently managed to generate interest in people who might not be interested in the subject matter at all. She also became more at ease with the experience of talking about the subject each time she spoke to a new person or a small group of people.

On the day before her presentation, Jane experienced a surge of anticipatory anxiety as she imagined herself in front of all those strangers. She shifted her focus back to the subject matter of her talk and managed to kindle neuronal networks that represented excitement in telling others about it. By combining her positive feelings about the project with the practice of presenting the information to friends and family, she linked up the neurons that were associated with talking about the project.

Jane managed to get through the first part of her talk by again making a concerted effort to stay focused on her enthusiasm for the project; she also confronted her anxiety instead of running from it. I had taught her that this effort was critical because exposure to the anxiety-provoking experience while staying focused on the subject matter allowed her to break through a barrier. She, like many people, had simply avoided public speaking. Consequently, the barrier had become bigger for her. Now she was able to get through the barrier. During the last part of her presentation, she was on a roll. It wasn't that speaking in front of large groups was becoming effortless—that came later. However, she had a taste of how much easier public speaking was than she had thought it would be. Her left frontal lobe was taming her amygdala.

After the presentation, Jane congratulated herself for having challenged her old fears. She was amazed that she had gotten through the experience with a boost in confidence instead of what she feared: humiliation. She even had the further reward of receiving compliments from some of the audience about her command of the subject matter.

When we discussed her success, I suggested to her that she continue to practice speaking. Her initial response was that she had "gotten through it, so why would I want to risk all that I gained by putting myself out there again?" I told her that in order to rewire her brain so that public speaking would no longer incite fear and would remain *effortless*, she had to be *determined* to repeat her efforts.

With this in mind, Jane accepted the opportunity to speak about her project again. During that presentation, a computer engineer in the audience asked a question that she had never considered. Instead of clamming up and becoming defensive, she thanked him for the good question and told him that she would get back to him. She was actually excited to get back to him later with the answer. His question helped her team to make important changes to the project. Thus, talking to the audience about the project served as a means by which to gather useful information.

Jane had to remain determined to stay with her gains in public speaking and to follow through on other opportunities to speak in front of people. It wasn't long before her supervisor asked her to speak at another meeting. Despite all her gains, she told me that she had "done my bit" and wanted to decline. I reminded her that this was another opportunity to share her enthusiasm for the project and hear useful ideas from the audience.

Other opportunities to speak would come later, and they were just what she needed to get to the feeling of effortlessness when speaking in front of people. By developing the determination to stay with the practice of public speaking, Jane tore down her wall of anxiety that she had associated with public speaking. She rewired her brain so successfully that she was even sought out for public speaking events to express her enthusiasm for her project.

You might not choose to become a public speaker, but I'm sure that there are other things that you might not have tried because you feel uneasy about them. There might also be bad habits that you want to break and good habits that you want to develop. You can rewire your brain to succeed at your goals.

Jane's story represents some key points about how to tame your amygdala. Her effort to feed her brain with the challenge of public speaking illustrates the following key points about dealing with stress and anxiety:

- Excessive anxiety often results from false alarms.
- Moderate anxiety is actually useful for neuroplasticity.
- You can tap into your parasympathetic nervous system and calm yourself down.
- Avoiding avoidance and maximizing exposure reduces anxiety in the long run.

Stress and False Alarms

Anxiety has a lot to do with fear. Jane feared embarrassing herself and drawing social ridicule. If you feel too much fear, an alarm is triggered, and you are overwhelmed with anxiety symptoms such as shortness of breath, rapid heartbeat, and worrying. When the alarm stops and it becomes apparent that there was really nothing to fear, you are able to say in retrospect that it was a false alarm. Dealing effectively with anxiety requires you to turn off a false alarm or keep it from turning on.

People who come to my anxiety class often say that once they get a clear picture of what's going in their brains, they feel more hopeful that their anxiety can be mastered. The unreasonable mystery of what was happening to them is simply swept away. You, too, can manage your anxiety level by understanding how it is triggered in your brain.

Let's start at the center of fear: the amygdala. Ideally, your amygdala and your OFC maintain a harmonious relationship with each other. For many people, this healthy relationship is based on warm and nurturing relationships early in life and is maintained throughout life. In my anxiety class, I explain the importance of taming the amygdala.

In addition to setting the emotional tone of any experience, the amygdala can also serve as a panic button, becoming activated for false alarms as well as genuine ones. This is possible because of the reciprocal relationship between the amygdala and the OFC. When the amygdala is overactive, it can overpower the OFC. Nevertheless, the OFC can tame the amygdala. I use the word *tame* rather than *shut down*, because you need the amygdala. It contributes to emotional responsiveness in general, not just fear. You don't want to shut it down; rather, you want it to work for you.

There are two principal ways to activate your amygdala: the slow track or the fast track. The slow track goes through the cortex. This means that you can think about things before you become fearful. This is both good and bad: good because you can remind yourself that there is nothing to fear; bad if you develop irrational fears.

The fast track to activate your amygdala can trigger your sympathetic nervous system into action and can potentially cause anxiety and/or panic. Your amygdala can sound the alarm before your cortex knows what's happening. This means that you can *feel* anxious before you even think about something that makes you anxious. Within a fraction of a second, the amygdala can use norepinephrine to spark electrical impulses throughout your sympathetic nervous system to activate your adrenal glands. These glands will dump epinephrine (adrenaline) into your bloodstream, which jolts your system to increase your breathing, your heart rate, and your blood pressure. This is called the fight-or-flight response.

A full-blown fight-or-flight response is very effective in the wild. All mammals have this lifesaving capacity. It starts with freezing. When you're driving on a country road at night and you see a deer standing in the road staring at your rapidly approaching car, the deer is not stupid. It's merely doing what animals have done for millions of years to keep themselves safe. When they hear the approaching sounds of a potential predator, they freeze so that they have time to see the predator before the predator sees them. Since many predators look for movement, freezing is a good way of instantly becoming invisible. Once the animal sees where the predator is located, it can continue with the rest of the fight-or-flight response. The deer is actually preparing for action when it freezes. Although it might seem to us that the deer is doing nothing, its body is actually bracing to fight or to flee.

Just as with the deer, the rush of adrenaline that you experience pre-pares your body to get moving by increasing your heart rate and your breathing so that you can send more oxygen to your muscles. Adrenaline binds to your muscle spindles, intensifying the resting tension so that your muscles can burst into action. The blood vessels in your skin constrict to limit any potential bleeding if you are wounded, and your digestive system shuts down to conserve energy. Saliva stops flowing (so your mouth becomes dry), and the muscles in your bladder relax so as not to waste glucose.

The shorthand sequence goes like this: The amygdala signals the hypothalamus, which is responsible for many metabolic processes and involved in the autonomic nervous system. This signals the pituitary gland, which signals the adrenal glands to release adrenaline and later cortisol. This chain is called the *hypothalamus-pituitary-adrenal* (HPA) *axis*.

Neurochemically, norepinephrine, along with a substance called the *corticotropin-releasing factor* (CRF), is sent from the amygdala to the hypothalamus, which signals the pituitary gland. The pituitary gland then sends a slow message through your bloodstream to your adrenal glands, telling them to secrete cortisol, a stress hormone that can keep you charged up a little longer than adrenaline does, to deal with the stress. On a short-term basis, cortisol facilitates dopamine, which keeps you alert and activated. However, cortisol can be corrosive to the brain and the body if it stays activated too long. With excessive and prolonged cortisol, the levels of dopamine become depleted, and this makes you feel awful.

On a short-term basis, however, cortisol is actually very useful. If you encounter stress that requires a prolonged response beyond a quick flight or a fight, your body needs a way to manufacture fuel (glucose). Epinephrine (adrenaline) immediately converts glycogen and fatty acids, but when the stress is longer-lasting, cortisol takes over. It works through the bloodstream, so its effects are slower than adrenaline's.

Cortisol works more systemically than adrenaline does. It triggers the liver to make more glucose available in the bloodstream while it also blocks insulin receptors in nonessential organs and tissues so that you get all the glucose (fuel) that you need to deal with the threat. Cortisol's work is a long-term strategy of insulin resistance, which serves to provide the brain with a sustained level of glucose. However, you don't always have a lot of glucose floating around, so cortisol works to stockpile energy. It converts protein into glycogen and begins to store fat. If the stress is chronic, the increased body fat is stored in the abdomen. If you have a growing bulge in your midsection, it may be due to cortisol working to store energy. Unfortunately, that's not the way you want it to be stored. It's better to burn off such stored energy by exercise.

One of the many problems associated with chronic stress and high levels of cortisol is that parts of the brain bear the brunt—especially the hippocampus. The hippocampus has many cortisol receptors; under normal circumstances, this helps to trigger the shutting-off of cortisol, much like a thermostat, so that it can turn down the production of cortisol. However, when cortisol production is excessive and prolonged, the hippocampus receptors themselves shut down. The hippocampus then begins to atrophy, and with it your memory capacity.

Unfortunately, the reverse happens for the amygdala. Instead of enduring atrophy, it is hypersensitized. The amygdala actually becomes more sensitized by an increase in cortisol. From an evolutionary perspective this makes sense, because if our early ancestors were stressed by something like dangerous predators, they needed to be hyperalert and not think about anything else.

Because the amygdala can become hypersensitive, chronic stress can make you more jumpy and anxious. This is why a war veteran with posttraumatic stress disorder (PTSD) will hit the floor and cover his head when he hears the loud blast of fireworks. Before he has a chance to think about it, the blast reminds him of an improvised explosive device (IED) exploding or a gunshot. His amygdala triggers the fight-or-flight response—a false alarm.

When you experience severe trauma or excessive chronic stress, the once-cooperative partnership between your hippocampus and your amygdala becomes skewed in favor of the amygdala. This is because the hippocampus is assaulted by excess cortisol and glutamate when the amygdala is pumped up. Cortisol and glutamate act to excite the amygdala, and the more it is excited, the more easily it is triggered.

Since your hippocampus provides the context for your memories, your ability to put stressful events into perspective becomes impaired. The amygdala, in contrast, is a generalist. When it gets excited, it doesn't care about the context. Any loud noise sets off the fight-or-flight response.

Just as excessive and prolonged cortisol can be destructive to the hippocampus, so can a surplus of the excitatory neurotransmitter glutamate. Cortisol initially encourages LTP by increasing glutamate transmission in the hippocampus. This too makes evolutionary sense, because when our ancestors were stressed by something, such as a particularly dangerous area near a lion's den, they needed to remember it. However, in our modern world, this tendency locks us into rigid or fixated patterns. You can't forget what stressed you, and more glutamate helps you to remember.

Too much of a good thing can cause bad things to happen. Like excess cortisol, excess glutamate damages the hippocampus by allowing electron-snatching calcium ions into cells, which creates free radicals. If you don't have enough antioxidants in your system, free radicals can career around and punch holes in your cell walls, rupturing the cells and potentially killing them. Dendrites, the branches of a cell that reach out to other neurons to be potentially receptive to gather information, begin to wither back into the cell body. Thoughts and emotions become more rigid and simple. Your decisions will be rigid and will probably be destructive instead of constructive.

Fortunately, there are ways to shut down false alarms before they become destructive. One way to do it is supported by the pioneering research of Joseph LeDoux of New York University. LeDoux has shown that one area of the amygdala, the central nucleus, is particularly involved in the snowballing effect of fear and anxiety. The central nucleus links nonthreatening stimuli with presumably threatening stimuli. This is why you can associate a bridge with death or talking to a stranger with humiliation.

However, there is another part of the amygdala that can circumvent the central nucleus. It is called the *basal nucleus stria terminalis* (BNST) and is an action pathway. By taking action, you can activate the BNST and circumvent the central nucleus and its inappropriate linking of nonthreatening stimuli with legitimate stimuli.

By taking action, you also activate the left frontal lobe, which can decrease the overreactivity of the amygdala. The right frontal lobe is often overactivated in people with anxiety disorders. The left frontal lobe is also more action-oriented, whereas the right frontal lobe is more passive and withdrawal-oriented. Furthermore, the left frontal lobe promotes positive emotions, whereas the right frontal lobe promotes more negative emotions.

Thus, you have within you the capacity to turn off the fight-or-flight response and the false alarms. The left PFC and the hippocampus work together to tame the amygdala and shut down the HPA axis. Taking action and doing something constructive can shut down the feeling of being overwhelmed, which is generated by the overreactivity of the right frontal lobe.

Moderating Anxiety

The brain is a high-energy consumer of glucose, which is its fuel. Although the brain accounts for merely 3 percent of a person's body weight, it consumes 20 percent of the available fuel. Your brain can't store fuel, however, so it has to "pay as it goes." Since your brain is incredibly adaptive, it economizes its fuel resources. Thus, during a period of high stress, it shifts away from the analysis of the nuances of a situation to a singular and fixed focus on the stressful situation at hand. You don't sit back and speculate about the meaning of life when you are stressed. Instead, you devote all your energy to trying to figure out what action to take. Sometimes, however, this shift from the higher-thinking parts of the brain to the automatic and reflexive parts of the brain can lead you to do something too quickly, without thinking.

This is what happens when you are overwhelmed with anxiety. In an extreme situation, such as when you are having a panic attack, you might rush off to an emergency room for treatment for a heart attack—not because you are actually having one, but because you think you are having one.

Stress is a fact of life; it's not something that you can or should totally avoid. Rather, it should be managed and used to accomplish your goals. If you try to escape all stress, when you encounter a mild stressor or even the threat of stress, you will feel extremely stressed. Some stress and anxiety actually serve as useful motivators. Without a little anxiety, you wouldn't get to work on time, complete projects efficiently, or drive within the speed limit.

Mild stress is therefore useful, and it can be regulated, as Jane discovered. The brain needs a little stress in order to remember important events and situations; your job is to learn how to regulate the stress. A little stress helps to code memories. No stress means no activation, which means that you're bored and inattentive, which in turn means that you won't remember what you are experiencing. Too much stress, however, narrows your focus and is not helpful for learning.

Jane rewired her brain by making use of a moderate degree of anxiety. She had already experienced feeling overwhelmed with too much anxiety, and she had done what she could to avoid public speaking. That avoidant behavior, ironically, simply increased her anxiety.

Neuroscientific research has shown that a moderate degree of anxiety is optimal for neuroplasticity. Too much or too little anxiety is not useful in this regard. Thus, rather than shy away from anxiety, you should confront it and make it useful. Consider the following skiing analogy: Leaning back on your skis increases your chance of falling, but if you lean forward just a little, you'll have more control of your skis—even when you are skiing down a very steep slope.

Think of it this way: Being bored, overconfident, and lazy about studying for an exam prepares you to fail. Being panicked about it also serves you poorly. The balance between too much and too little anxiety is what's best for learning and memory. This balance is referred to as "the inverted U" (technically, it's called the Yerkes-Dobson curve). The inverted U means that moderate activation (i.e., stress or anxiety) keeps your brain alert, generating the correct neurochemistry to allow your brain to thrive and promote neuroplasticity and neurogenesis.

The efficient way to deal with stress is to strive toward a moderate path. When there is a moderate degree of stress, cortisol, CRF, and norepinephrine bind to the cell receptors that boost the excitatory neurotransmitter glutamate. When the glutamate activity in the hippocampus is moderately increased, there is a corresponding increase in the flow of information and in the associated dynamics at the synapse that is critical for neuroplasticity. The more often a message is sent along the same pathway, the more easily it will fire the same signals and use less glutamate—making the cells fire together so that they can wire together.

The main point here is that you shouldn't try to run away from stress and anxiety; you should learn to manage it. By managing it, you'll promote a healthy, thriving brain that generates neuroplasticity.

Activating Your Parasympathetic Nervous System

The autonomic nervous system has two parts: the sympathetic nervous system and the parasympathetic nervous system. The sympathetic nervous system excites you, and the parasympathetic nervous system relaxes you. In extreme situations, the sympathetic nervous system triggers the HPA axis and the fight-or-flight response.

Just as there is a balance between the sympathetic and parasympathetic nervous systems, there is a counterbalance to the fight-or-flight response. Dubbed the *relaxation response* by Harvard professor Herbert Benson, it is your body's parasympathetic nervous system in action. It helps to lower your heart rate, lower your metabolism, and slow your breathing rate.

Fight-or-Flight Response	**Relaxation Response**
↑Heart rate	↓Heart rate
↑Blood pressure	↓Blood pressure

↑Metabolism   ↓Metabolism
↑Muscle tension   ↓Muscle tension
↑Breathing rate   ↓Breathing rate
↑Mental arousal   ↓Mental arousal

The principle of taking action that I described earlier activates the BNST and the left PFC. This effort paves the way for the parasympathetic nervous system to calm you down later.

The quick shift from the sympathetic to the parasympathetic nervous system through the actions of the PFC and the hippocampus might not occur as quickly if you suffer from PTSD. The amygdala is highly sensitized to the context of the trauma you endured. Earlier we cited the example of a war veteran who is startled by fireworks. Yet even war veterans with PTSD can tame their amygdalas, as I have described in my book (with Dr. Victoria Beckner) *Conquering Posttraumatic Stress Disorder*.

Different breathing patterns promote different emotional states. Your breathing rate speeds up when you are experiencing anxiety. The muscles in your abdomen tighten up and your chest cavity becomes constricted when you breathe too fast.

If you tend to breathe very quickly, you may be like some people who come to my anxiety class: They have a tendency to talk very fast, and they don't give themselves a chance to breathe. As they go from one sentence to another, they stir up anxiety in themselves. The neutral topic that they began talking about is lost because of their fast breathing and their anxiety. The increase in their anxiety stimulates memories and reaction patterns that are connected to the same neural networks that promote anxious thinking. Soon the new topic becomes laced with more anxiety and worries.

Most people breathe nine to sixteen breaths per minute at rest. Panic attacks often involve as many as twenty-seven breaths per minute. When your breathing is accelerating, you can experience many of the symptoms associated with a panic attack, including numbness, tingling, dry mouth, and light-headedness.

Since the cardiovascular system includes both the respiratory system and the circulatory system, rapid breathing will make your heart rate speed up and can make you more anxious. If you slow your breathing down, your heart rate will slow down and you will become more relaxed.

To learn to relax, you'll have to make an effort to develop some new habits, such as the way you breathe. Since one of the most common symptoms of panic is shortness of breath, you'll have to learn to breathe differently. Actual physiological changes occur in your brain and body during hyperventilation, or breathing too fast.

When you hyperventilate, you inhale too much oxygen, which decreases the carbon dioxide level in your bloodstream. Carbon dioxide helps to maintain the critical acid base (the pH level) in your blood. When you lower your pH level, your nerve cells become more excitable, and you may feel anxious. If you associate the feelings with uncontrollable anxiety, this can even spur a panic attack.

The excessive dissipation of carbon dioxide leads to a condition called *hypocapnic alkalosis*, which makes your blood more alkaline and less acidic. Soon you'll have a vascular constriction, which results in less blood reaching your tissues. Oxygen binds tightly to hemoglobin, which results in less oxygen being released to the tissues and the extremities. The paradox is that even though you inhaled too much oxygen, less is available to your tissues.

Hypocapnic alkalosis leads to dizziness, light-headedness, cerebral vasoconstriction (which leads to feelings of unreality), and peripheral vasoconstriction (which leads to tingling in your extremities). If you're prone to panic attacks, you tend to overrespond to these physiological sensations and to breathe even more quickly.

Challenging the Paradox

A paradox occurs when you avoid what you fear, because your fear then grows. This is counterintuitive, because when you avoid what you fear for a short time, your fear does decrease. Over a longer period, however, avoidance allows the anxiety to flourish. For example, let's say that you are anxious about going to a dinner party because you fear talking to strangers. For a brief time, avoiding the evening enables your anxiety to lessen. However, if you avoid the next dinner party invitation, and then the next and the next, you have created a problem. Because of your avoidance of those dinner parties, you have made your anxiety about talking to strangers worse than it was at the start.

You have to try to work against avoidance, even though it seems to make you feel better. I call this *challenging the paradox*. Challenging the paradox involves doing away with avoidance and replacing it with exposure. Exposure means facing what makes you feel anxious. By exposing yourself to anxiety-provoking situations, you become habituated to them, and your anxiety will eventually diminish.

Our earlier example of a war veteran with PTSD can illustrate this point. When the soldier comes back to civilian life, he avoids situations that make him anxious. Ironically, as he avoids those situations, his anxiety gets worse. His therapy involves exposing himself to situations that make him anxious so he can tame his amygdala. Its hypersensitivity dulls with each time he hears fireworks and nothing bad happens. Soon he begins to see the explosion of colors instead of exploding buildings. He slowly begins to reassociate the sounds of the loud booms with entertainment. The taming process can go on even without his cortex (i.e., his thinking process) being involved. When he includes the thinking process by saying to himself, "Wow, those are spectacular fireworks. There's nothing to get panicked about!" the taming occurs more quickly.

The following types of avoidance contribute to anxiety:

- Escape behavior
- Avoidant behavior
- Procrastination
- Safety behavior

Escape behavior consists of the things you do in the heat of the moment in an anxiety-provoking situation. You essentially escape the situation to avoid feeling anxious. Suppose you are in a room with a crowd of people and you begin to feel anxious. Fleeing the room to avoid feeling anxious is an escape behavior. Your anxiety increases over time, however, because your tolerance of it decreases.

If you escape instead of allowing yourself to adjust to even a little anxiety, you'll eventually feel extremely sensitive to the slightest hint of anxiety. This is called *anxiety sensitivity.*

Avoidant behavior includes the things you do to stay away from anxiety-provoking experiences. Let's say that a friend invites you to meet her at the home of one of her other friends. You decide that going to the other friend's home would make you anxious, so you don't go. That's an avoidant behavior. Consequently, your long-term anxiety will increase, because when you avoid situations that make you anxious, you never allow yourself to learn that those situations are really tolerable.

Procrastination means that you put off things because you think (erroneously) that it's easier on your stress level. For example, you put off going to the friend's home, waiting until the very last moment to finally go. When you wait and wait until the last possible moment, you build up anxiety in all that time. You're subtly teaching yourself that the situation *was* worth putting off until the last moment, because when you finally arrived, you were indeed nervous and tense. Holding yourself back from an anxiety-provoking situation builds up more anxiety than you experienced initially.

Safety behavior involves doing or carrying things to distract yourself or give yourself a sense of safety. Suppose you go the friend's home and begin to feel anxious. To prevent yourself from becoming more anxious, you begin to fiddle with your watchband to draw your focus away. That's a safety behavior. Safety behavior allows you to hang in there and not escape, but eventually the behavior becomes a nervous habit, and by engaging in it you're telling yourself that you're too nervous to simply face whatever is causing your anxiety.

All these forms of avoidance are ineffective methods of dealing with anxiety because they keep you from habituating to that which makes you anxious. Avoidance makes it next to impossible to learn to overcome the anxiety.

Because avoidance results in a temporary reduction of fear, it serves as a powerful short-term reinforcer. It is therefore difficult to resist. The more you avoid what makes you anxious, the more elaborate the forms of avoidance can become. If avoidance is taken to the extreme, you can even become agoraphobic, afraid to leave your home. Once you begin avoiding, it's difficult to stop.

Avoidance is difficult to avoid for the following reasons:

- It works to reduce fear for a short amount of time.
- The more you engage in avoidance, the harder it is to resist engaging in it in the future because it becomes a habit.
- There is a superficial logic to avoidance, such as, "Why wouldn't I avoid something that makes me anxious?"
- You get a secondary gain from it, like extra care, because people around you are sympathetic.

By engaging in avoidance you stir up the "worry circuit" in the brain. The worry circuit stirs up the amygdala, which increases your sense of fear, and the overactivity of the amygdala preoccupies the OFC, which tries to figure out why you feel anxious. The extreme version of the worry circuit occurs with people who suffer from OCD, a condition in which the worries become obsessive.

Another way that you might try to avoid anxiety, but that actually increases it, is to try to rigidly control it. An obsession with being in control can lead to avoidance. By trying to control every experience in order to avoid anxiety, you put yourself in a mode of always trying to anticipate the future so that you can steer yourself away from the *possibility* of anxiety. Here's where your avoidance can become rather elaborate. When you anticipate what *might* happen, you brace yourself for anxiety that you might never have experienced.

The more you retreat, the more you will have to retreat. First you are vigilant only about what you *know* will be anxiety-provoking, but soon you will be vigilant about what *might* be anxiety-provoking. You limit yourself to activities and situations that you are certain will not be anxiety-provoking. When you encounter a little anxiety in a situation that you thought would be anxiety-free, you begin to avoid *that* situation in the future. Soon the range of your activities shrinks dramatically. As your world shrinks, the things that trigger anxiety increase. If you take it to the extreme and become agoraphobic, you won't want to leave your house because you will have grown to fear everything outside it.

In short, avoiding what makes you anxious leads you to restrict your activities, which makes your anxiety generalize, which then prompts more avoidance, which in turn promotes more general-ized anxiety, which stirs up even more avoidance. As you can see, it becomes a vicious cycle.

The key to taming your amygdala is to break this vicious cycle. You must make sure that you expose yourself to what you were fearful of in the past. By keeping your behavioral options open to anxiety-provoking experiences, you allow yourself to be flexible and resilient in changing situations. By exposing yourself to what made you anxious in the past, you can learn to recondition yourself and habituate to the situation.

When you apply detached attention to your worries, a paradox occurs: the worry circuit calms down. This has been found to hap-pen in people who have OCD. Thus, if you are prone to worry excessively, instead of engaging in the details of what worries you, simply observe. This technique is used in mindfulness meditation, which I will explain in chapter 9.

Activating the Frontal Lobe and Changing Your Narrative

The frontal lobe—and particularly its foremost section, the PFC—decides, through its powers of attention and emotional regulatory skills, what is important and what is not. The hippocampus provides the context for any memories that are associated with the situation. When you're walking through a park one evening and you notice through the corner of your eye a large hunched figure, you imme-diately brace yourself for a mugger. Your fight-or-flight response kicks into gear. That's your sympathetic nervous system in action. Then your PFC directs your attention to the figure. Your hippo-campus helps to remind you of the context of the figure and the shrubs along the path. As you look closer, you see that the figure is just a shrub. Your PFC tells your amygdala to calm down, and your

HPA axis—which leads to the release of stress hormones—is shut down.

The emotional tone and perspective with which you describe each experience can potentially rewire your brain. The more you describe your ongoing experiences in a particular way, the stronger the neural circuits that represent those thoughts will become. Your narratives can be positive or negative. For example, if you find yourself constantly assuming, "This is hard," "I wonder whether I'm going to survive," or "It looks like this is going to turn out badly," it's time to restructure the way you think.

Your ongoing narrative is organized by three general levels of thought: automatic thoughts, assumptions, and core beliefs (Arden, 2009). On the surface are your automatic thoughts. These are like short tapes that momentarily flash through your mind. They are a form of self-talk that you use throughout the day. You produce a variety of automatic thoughts, some consciously and some unconsciously. For example, as you walk into a roomful of strangers you might say, "I don't like this," or "Oh no! People I'll have to get to know." Both of these automatic thoughts can contribute to increased anxiety. In contrast, you could say, "Oh great. New people to meet. This should be interesting." Your automatic thoughts can be rewired in your brain to represent more adaptive self-talk.

Your assumptions, which are positioned midway between your automatic thoughts and your core beliefs, act as a kind of translator between the two. They aren't as fundamental as core beliefs, yet they aren't as superficial as automatic thoughts. Like your automatic thoughts, your assumptions can be rewired by reflecting reality instead of your worries. Assumptions are one of the prime targets of cognitive-behavioral therapy, which aims to restructure a person's thoughts to reflect adaptable and constructive thinking problems. For example, in the roomful of strangers you might say, "I'm not good with strangers," or you could say, "I may be a little shy, but I find meeting new people exciting."

Your assumptions can serve as theories that help you to cope with your core beliefs. Core beliefs are broad generalizations about yourself and how the world works. When these beliefs are associated with anxiety, they paint you into a corner psychologically, so that whatever you do, you're faced with an insurmountable challenge—one that will always fail.

Negative core beliefs can contribute to anxiety. For example, you might have a core belief that you are a deeply damaged person or that you don't have what it takes to make use of any kind of help. Negative core beliefs keep you away from any hope or expectation of relief from anxiety. They set you up to fail because you leave yourself no hope. For example, you could believe that "I'm incapable of forming new relationships," or you could cultivate a core belief such as "I'm a good person, and when people get to know me they agree."

Restructuring your core beliefs is a more ambitious challenge than adjusting your automatic thoughts and your assumptions. However, if you work on them simultaneously with feeding your brain to reformat your core beliefs, the two more shallow levels can be harmonized to work effectively.

3

Shifting Left

Megan came to see me after a prolonged period of feeling sad. Although she denied having many of the symptoms associated with full-blown depression, she said, "When things don't go right, I crawl into my shell, and it's hard to crawl out again." She described the shell as a "dark and gloomy place."

She said that her husband asked her to see a psychologist because "he was tired of my pessimistic attitude and what he described as my endless negative comments."

"Is his description correct?" I asked.

"Sort of. Hearing him say that put me in a blue period," Megan replied. "He was right, but when he said that he was tired of propping my mood up all the time, I got pretty down about myself."

"What do you do when you're feeling frustrated with yourself?" I inquired.

She gave me an ironic smile. "I guess I really punish him with more of the same. It's not that I plan it. I just can't seem to stop it."

"You get more passive and feel more blue?" I asked.

"Yup," Megan said, as if she knew that there was a twisted logic to this pattern that I would understand. She explained that she had learned from her parents that "when they heard any sort of criticism or something went wrong, they'd get quiet until somebody pulled them out of it."

"Can we say that your passivity in response to anything going wrong makes things worse?" I inquired.

She reflected for a moment. "Well, honestly, until my husband said that he was tired of it, I didn't know I was doing it."

We talked at length about how passivity increases depression. I described how the brain processes passivity and simultaneously spurs depression. The left frontal lobe promotes positive feelings and taking action, and the right frontal lobe promotes passivity and negative emotion.

"So, he was, in effect, functioning as your left frontal lobe," I observed, and I explained to her how the two frontal lobes process emotions differently.

"Yeah, I guess I was all on the right side, and he balanced me out with all of his optimism with, as you say, his left. But he said that he's tired of doing all the work while I drag my feet and complain," Megan admitted.

"Are you tired of it?" I asked. "If you're not motivated to change your behavior, whatever we work on together will be just going through the motions. From another perspective, being angry enough with your situation might be a positive thing. It may give you the fuel to take action. From a brain-based perspective, to be able to rewire your brain so that you can curtail this bad habit, you'll need your left frontal lobe to be fully activated—taking action."

"From what you're saying," Megan concluded, "I ought to thank him for saying that he'll stop doing things for me. It's time to make some changes."

This agreement was only the first step. The idea of making the changes sounded good, but actually making the changes took some work. It was just too easy for her to fall back into her old habit of being passive and thinking negatively.

Megan came to understand that her tendency to be passive represented how underactive her left frontal lobe had become. She needed to kick-start it by taking action, however small a step it seemed, to get her left frontal lobe engaged.

I also taught her to use the FEED method. By labeling her emotions and her passive behavior, she could activate her left frontal lobe. I explained that this link occurs because her left frontal lobe is involved in expressing language.

When Megan found herself becoming passive and sinking into negative emotions, she would say to herself, "Whoops, those negative thoughts mean that my left frontal lobe is going to sleep again. I need to do something to give it a wake-up call."

The tendency to revert to her old habits occurred several times when something went wrong. It was too easy to shift into a pessimistic attitude and make the situation worse. By using the FEED method to shift her pessimism to optimism, she was able to rewire an attitude and not cultivate a negative mood to spoil the day.

Megan learned that the emotional state she was in at any given time shaded her perceptions, thoughts, and memories. That is, the mood she was in would color all her experiences. This is because all the cells that fire together to create the mood also fire with other neurons to create thoughts and memories.

The more that you are in a particular mood, the more prone you'll be to be in that mood. Think of it as a gravitational pull or an attractor state. The attractor pulls in your thoughts, feelings, and memories, and motivates your behavior.

This tendency can occur spontaneously and can spiral out of control if you don't make an effort to pull yourself out of it. Let's say that you're rushing to your aunt's house for a dinner that you don't want to attend. You're driving through rush-hour traffic when you suddenly notice that the gas gauge reads almost empty. Now you're really feeling rushed and sulky. As you pull into a gas station, you notice how many cars are lined up at the pumps. To make matters worse, some of the people who are pumping gas are taking their time, washing their windshields, and even leaving their cars to go to the restroom.

You're already in a bad mood, and now you imagine your aunt getting upset with you for being late, so your bad mood deepens. The more you think about your aunt's disappointment, the worse you feel. There are so many things that you would rather be doing at the moment, and waiting for people to move on so that you can get to the gas pump is not one of them. These feelings intensify the firing of the neural networks that support the bad mood.

The woman who has been pumping gas in front of you is finished, but she leaves her car at the pump and rushes into the station to buy some snacks. You angrily pull up to a different pump. Why didn't she pull into a parking space after she finished pumping her gas? Didn't she realize that there were people waiting behind her?

As you are finally pumping your gas, she walks back to her car, carrying an iced drink, and hands it to her child, who is sitting in the backseat. She left her car at the pump for a drink! You glance at the child, see that he has no hair, and realize that he must be undergoing chemotherapy for cancer. In a flash, your spindle cells kick in with the insight of how you have been in a pathetic self-perpetuating bad mood. What did you have to feel sorry about, compared to this woman? Your mirror neurons reflect a deep sense of empathy for her and her child.

The child spills the drink all over the seat and begins to cry. His mother tries to comfort him as she wipes up the mess. You rush into the store to buy the child another drink. When you return and hand it to the boy, he responds with a sad smile.

As you finish pumping your gas, you reflect on how these two people helped you to snap out of your sulky bad mood. You decide to go to your aunt's house with a renewed sense of compassion and selflessness.

This little vignette illustrates how easy it is to drift into a bad mood. Once the neural networks begin firing together, they recruit other neurons to keep the bad mood going. As you feed the bad mood with sulky thoughts, it becomes deeper and harder to shake. These bad moods can go on for hours or days at a time. Some people are plagued by them for months or even years at a time.

If you have a tendency to be in a particular mood more often than not, we can say that this mood forms a chronic foundation for your experiences in life. It's the background emotional current, the default mode, or the center of gravity in your life. Most of your experiences are based on it and revolve around it.

Let's say that during the past few months you have been sad because of the death of your mother. The emotional tone that is created by this sadness recruits related memories and feelings that resonate with it. You may even tell yourself, "I'm going to stay with these sad feelings, because it's a way to honor her."

Yet if you cultivate the sadness, perhaps even thinking that you are releasing it, you're keeping those neurons firing together and thus cultivating a chronic foundation of sadness. More often than not you will feel sadness and will think, remember, and behave in ways that cultivate that emotional foundation.

The longer you stay in a low emotional state, the greater is the probability that those neurons will fire together when you are sad and will therefore wire together. As a result, this will become the chronic foundation of your emotional experience. Sadness and the thoughts and feelings that revolve around that sadness become perpetuated.

I am not saying that you should suppress your feelings of grief. Sadness is a normal and natural reaction to losing someone close to you. The point is that you need a balance. You have to move on with your life in addition to acknowledging the feelings of sadness.

If you have a chronic emotional foundation that is sad, depressed, or angry, it might seem like a scratched record. The needle on the turntable gets stuck in the scratch, and the same lyrics play over and over. This is the origin of the phrase "sounds like a broken record." You have to get up and bump the needle over a few grooves to make the song stop repeating itself. You need to find ways to "bump the needle" if your emotional foundation is sad, angry, or depressed.

There are a number of ways to rewire your brain to promote positive moods. They include the following:

- Priming positive moods
- Light chemistry
- Constructing narratives
- Taking action

- Aerobic boosting
- Wiring positive thinking
- Social medicine

Priming Positive Moods

You can start to rewire your brain by priming a positive mood through acting as though you are in a good mood when you're not. Let's say that you've been sad recently and have been pulling back from your friends. Maybe you've said to yourself, "I don't want to put on a happy face."

You should force yourself to call a friend and go out to lunch when you don't feel like it. Once you are at lunch, even just smiling can activate parts of your brain associated with positive emotions.

Researcher Kelly Lambert has drawn attention to the effort-driven reward circuit in the brain as being particularly critical for lifting depression. This circuit involves three principal areas: the nucleus acumbens, the striatum, and the PFC. The nucleus accumbens is a peanut-sized structure that is involved in emotion and memory. It evolved to keep us engaged in behaviors that are critical for our survival, such as eating and sex. Because it is a pleasure center, it is also involved in addictive behaviors.

The striatum is involved in movement, and because of its rich connections with the accumbens and the PFC, it serves as an interface between our emotions and our actions.

The PFC, as we have noted, is involved in problem solving, planning, and decision making.

The accumbens-striatal-PFC network connects movement, emotion, and thinking. Thus, the effort-driven reward circuit links what you do or don't do with rewards or the absence of rewards. When, for example, you lose a sense of pleasure, the accumbens is deactivated. When you are sluggish in your movements, the striatum is deactivated. If you have poor concentration, the PFC is deactivated.

Without knowing what brain systems are involved, cognitive-behavioral therapists have encouraged depressed people to increase their activity level and have found that these people become less depressed. Behavioral activation, as this is called, appears to trigger the same effort-driven rewards circuit that involves the accumbens, the striatum, and the PFC.

The following correlations have been made between hemispheric asymmetry and depression:

- Evidence from neurology indicates that a left-side stroke has a *catastrophic* effect and causes the person to become very depressed, whereas a right-side stroke has a laissez-faire effect and causes much less depression.
- The relative inhibition of the left PFC and the relative activation of the right PFC are associated with depression (O'Doherty, Kringelback, Rolls, Hornak, and Andrews, 2001).
- The left PFC is associated with positive emotions and is action-oriented.
- The right PFC is associated with negative emotions and is passive-oriented.
- Language, making interpretive sense of events, and generating positive and optimistic emotions are all products of robust left hemispheric functioning.
- Instead of putting details into context, depressed patients are overwhelmed by a global negative perspective. The right hemisphere favors global thinking.
- Behavioral activation (the left PFC) is one of the principal therapies for depression.

Thus, making an effort to put yourself out there helps you lift depression. In fact, "putting on a happy face" is actually helpful. Here's how it works: There are neural pathways that link the facial muscles, the cranial nerves, the subcortical areas, and the cortex. Information flows down from the brain to the face and also back up again. For example, if you contract the muscles on the right side of your face, that activates your left hemisphere, which creates the likelihood of a positive emotional bias. In contrast, if you contract the muscles on the left side of your face, that activates your right hemisphere, which creates the likelihood of a negative bias.

Mona Lisa

The connection of the right facial muscles to the left hemisphere and the left facial muscles to the right hemisphere is called *contralateral functioning*.

Think of *Mona Lisa*. The right side of her face is smiling, but the left side of her face indicates a neutral or negative emotion. This difference can be seen more clearly if you paste together two left sides of her face and two right sides of her face.

Since the left hemisphere processes more positive emotions and the right hemisphere processes more negative emotions, those emotions are reflected in each side of the face.

Thus, when you force a smile or a frown, you're triggering the feelings associated with happiness or sadness. By smiling or frowning you send messages to your subcortical and cortical areas that resonate with happy or sad feelings. So put on a happy face—it helps you to feel better!

In addition to being linked to sad feelings, the right hemisphere is also generally more passive. The left hemisphere, in addition to processing positive emotions, is associated with action. Taking action helps people to feel less depressed, whereas inaction or passivity creates sad feelings. People who are depressed under-activate their left frontal lobes. If you are prone to feeling down more than up, activating your left frontal lobe by doing something constructive will help you to shift out of the chronic low emotional foundation.

The left field of vision corresponds to the right hemisphere, and the right field of vision corresponds to the left hemisphere. In other words, when you look to the left, you're activating your right hemisphere, and when you look to the right, you're activating your left hemisphere.

Sometimes you need a dose of detachment to move yourself beyond negative thoughts and emotions. In other words, you need to learn how to take things less seriously. Humor promotes neuroplasticity, and it is a wonderful treatment for what ails you. If you are sad, humor serves as a brief nudge from one mood state to another.

Avoid tear-jerker dramas, because they promote a tearful mood. Try watching comedies to help you detach from negative thoughts and feelings. Comedies allow you to lift out of the sad state you were in and move into another, happier state. In this sense, humor is a soothing method of detachment, especially if the humor is not degrading to another person.

Humor Chemistry

Humor is a boost to your biochemistry. It helps to lower the levels of the stress hormone cortisol while it increases immunoglobulin, natural killer (NK) cells, and plasma cytokine gamma interferon levels. Immunoglobulin consists of the antibodies that help the immune system to fight infections; it serves as one of the body's primary defense mechanisms. NK cells seek out and destroy abnormal cells; they are a key mechanism for what is called *immunosurveillance*. Plasma cytokine gamma interferon orchestrates or regulates anticellular activities and turns on specific parts of the immune system.

If you are able to develop a sense of humor about yourself, you'll find that incredibly liberating. It ensures that you don't take your current situation and yourself too seriously. Laughing at yourself allows you to see yourself as part of a greater whole. By not taking yourself too seriously, you can let things slide off you and not "sweat the small stuff." I'll describe how humor boosts your body and brain in greater detail in chapter 7. For now, just be aware that by developing a sense of humor, you'll cultivate positive thoughts and feelings.

Maximize the time that you spend in the emotional state that you want to be in so that it comes naturally to you. You want it to be your default mood. Do everything that you can do to promote the thoughts, perspective, and behaviors that kindle a positive mood.

Light Chemistry

Many depressed people keep the drapes drawn because they don't want to let the outside world in. This is a bad strategy, because it cuts them off from natural light and changes the biochemistry of the brain. Low levels of light have been associated with depression.

The brain picks up signals from the retina of whether it is dark or light outside and sends that information to the pineal gland. If it is dark, the pineal gland will secrete the sleeping hormone melatonin, which is sedating. If it is light outside, the pineal gland won't secrete melatonin. Melatonin is very similar in chemical structure to serotonin. When there is an overabundance of melatonin, it competes with serotonin, and the serotonin level decreases. Low serotonin is correlated with depression.

Low light is the operative mechanism in people who are suffering from seasonal affective disorder (SAD). People with SAD often find themselves becoming more depressed during the winter, when there are fewer hours of daylight. A disproportionate number of people in the northwestern United States and in northern Europe suffer from SAD because of the overcast skies and shorter days in the winter. Therefore, if you're depressed, you should maximize your exposure to natural sunlight.

One of the treatments for SAD is to sit under a full-spectrum light. Sunlight is better, of course, but if you live in an area with low levels of light in the winter and you suffer from SAD, check into getting a full-spectrum light.

To take advantage of the benefit of light chemistry, maximize the natural light that you receive during the daytime so that you will help your brain chemistry promote good feelings. The emphasis is on natural light because you need a full spectrum of light. By the way, you'll also need to provide yourself with a dose of vitamin D, which is important for your immune system.

Aerobic Boosting

Exercise has numerous positive side effects. It boosts your mood in a variety of ways. For example, exercise enhances oxygenation of the blood. When blood is transported to your brain, you feel alert and calm. Exercise also lowers the acidity in your body, which increases your energy level.

Your muscles are endowed with a rich blood supply. Just as exercise promotes better blood flow to the muscles and results in an energized feeling, so, too, does stretching. By stretching your muscles, you force or pump the used and deoxygenated blood back to your lungs for refueling. This blood flow is complemented by the replenishment of reoxygenated blood in your muscles. Stretching promotes refreshed and invigorated muscles and the release of tension.

Exercising forces an increased output of norepinephrine, which revs up the heart rate. This increased output of norepinephrine also occurs in the brain. A higher level of norepinphrine can boost your mood. Some antidepressant medications increase the transmission of norepinephrine.

Study after study has shown that exercise is an antidepressant. It does not have to be confined to a specific method, such as running. You can get an aerobic boost by climbing the stairs, raking the leaves, or taking a brisk walk.

Research has shown that exercise is one of the easiest ways to promote neuroplasticity and neurogenesis. I'll describe how that occurs in chapter 8. For now, just remember that when you combine exercise with changing the way you think, you powerfully boost your mood.

Constructing Narratives

As I have explained, the two hemispheres function differently. Your right hemisphere is more holistic and more emotional. Your left hemisphere, though more linear, is also the interpreter of your experiences. Interpreting or labeling helps you to make sense of your experiences. Psychologists call this a narrative.

Think of yourself as the narrator of your life. For example, perhaps you are facing a challenge because your old neighbors moved out and new neighbors have moved in. You considered your old neighbors to be irreplaceable. The new neighbors, meanwhile, have a completely different lifestyle. You can construct a positive narrative that describes how you are now being given an opportunity to get to know people whom you have never been exposed to before. Although it was sad to see your old neighbors go, your new neighbors present a new interpersonal adventure. You'll rise to the occasion to embark on this new adventure.

Your left hemisphere utilizes language and puts your narratives in a linguistic form. Since your left hemisphere is more positive, if you maximize its ability to put a positive spin on your narratives, you cause your brain to rewire with a positive perspective.

You modify your memories each time you remember them. Your left hemisphere can activate and change those memories with a positive spin. It also helps you to cultivate a positive narrative about what you will remember.

Neither hemisphere is good or bad. Your two hemispheres must work like equal partners. Your right hemisphere is important for the subjective essence and for autobiographical memory. It sees the whole picture, but it needs the input from your left hemisphere, which provides details and a positive spin.

The Power of Belief

Belief and specific types of thinking patterns can have a powerful effect on your mood. In recent years, research has illustrated how changing your thinking patterns can affect your mood. Brain-imaging studies have shown different patterns of brain activity with different types of treatment for depression. Cognitive-behavioral therapy (CBT) activated the hippocampus, whereas Paxil lowered the activity of the hippocampus. CBT appears to turn down the over-activity of the OFC, which is involved in endless ruminations. CBT cuts through the negativistic thinking and replaces it with realistic thoughts that quiet down the useless activity in the frontal lobes.

The new positive and realistic thoughts are coded into memory through the hippocampus, but this does not necessarily occur with Paxil. Also, after a person stops taking Paxil, there is a rebound of depression. In contrast, when CBT is stopped, what the person learned is remembered. In addition, a significant number of people do not respond to antidepressants. When these medications do work, they must be taken on a long-term basis. Both the placebo effect and antidepressant medications activate the same areas of the brain, the cortex.

The controversial power of belief has been addressed in psychiatry by comparing the effects of placebos to medication. For example, Irving Kirsch of the University of Connecticut reported that between 65 and 80 percent of responses to antidepressant medication can be duplicated by placebos.

Researchers at the University of Toronto addressed the phenomenon of response to placebos by taking a look at brain physiology. They showed that depressed patients who believed that they were taking a powerful antidepressant medication, but were actually taking a placebo, nevertheless experienced changes in their symptoms that were related to changes in brain glucose metabolism.

At least some of the benefits of taking medication are due simply to believing that it will work. The placebo effect highlights the power of belief, and the effect is not limited by mood.

A recent *Scientific American Mind* article reviewed the variety of studies that measured the placebo effect in medicine (Nieme, 2009). Many different medical conditions have been treated with placebos. Some of these studies are shown in the table below.

Placebo Medicine

Disease	Average percentage of patients for whom a placebo therapy worked	Number of studies
Cancer	2%–7% (tumors reduced in size)	10
Crohn's disease	19%	32
Duodenal ulcer	Healing in 36.2%–44.2%	79
Irritable bowel syndrome	40%	45
Multiple sclerosis	11%–50% (less after two to three years)	6

If physical conditions respond to a placebo, how much more would psychological conditions respond, because the placebo effect is psychological? Thus, what you believe has a powerful effect on what you experience—even physically.

Wiring Positive Thinking

There is a two-way street between your moods and your thoughts. This is why CBT is very effective in treating depression. The goal of CBT is to "correct" your dysfunctional thoughts so that you can change how you're feeling. In CBT you repair your cognitive distortions. If you are depressed, you probably get bogged down by cognitive traps, or beliefs that promote negative moods. These cognitive traps are distortions of reality. There are many cognitive distortions, too many to list extensively. Here are some common ones:

- **Polarized thinking:** black and white, all or nothing, good or bad, wonderful or rotten
- **Overgeneralization:** taking one unfortunate incident that occurred at work and jumping to conclusions about your entire life
- **Personalization:** interpreting every glance or comment made by someone as a negative reflection on you
- **Mind reading:** negatively assuming that you know what other people are thinking
- **Shoulds and should nots:** making rigid and inflexible rules that provide little flexibility to adapt to today's complex social environment
- **Catastrophizing:** perceiving any event as a major catastrophe or a sign of one on the way ("Oh, no, a red light! I might as well not even go.")
- **Emotional reasoning:** basing opinions on how you feel
- **Pessimism:** seeing a negative outcome for most events

If any of the above cognitive distortions apply to you, you will need to restructure them so that you don't paint yourself into a depressing corner. By using what CBT therapists call *cognitive restructuring*, you can train yourself to change the way you think.

By considering possibilities instead of limitations on a regular basis, you'll rewire your brain. When you focus on possibilities, you recruit new connections between your neurons instead of using the well-worn connections that reinforce negative emotions.

There are several methods of thinking that can help you to resist negative thinking and moods and rewire your brain. These include the following:

- **Thinking in shades of gray:** This perspective counters black-and-white thinking. By considering all possibilities between the two extremes, you allow yourself to adjust to a reality between extremes.
- **Context checking:** Here you adjust your opinions and perceptions to the context of the situation rather than just going with a preset opinion.
- **Optimism:** You consider every situation as an opportunity.
- **Detaching:** You disconnect yourself from repetitive negative beliefs.
- **Externalizing problems:** When something unfortunate happens, consider it a problem rather than a reflection of your worth.

The key to making these methods work is to practice them often and consistently. By applying the FEED method to each of these thinking methods, you can rewire your brain.

Megan, whom you met at the beginning of this chapter, learned to shift from a pessimistic frame to an optimistic one. Optimism is one of the most important aspects of emotional intelligence. By developing, cultivating, and keeping an optimistic perspective, you can weather most storms of misfortune. Optimism provides you with durability and resiliency. I'll have more to say about optimism throughout the book because it is so fundamental to your mental health.

Social Connecting

You are a social creature, whether or not you think you are, and your mood can be lifted by support from other people. Mirror neurons help you to feel and convey empathy. Unfortunately, when you're down in the dumps, you may feel like withdrawing from people. Don't forget that withdrawing from people overactivates your right prefrontal cortex, and you need the action-oriented left prefrontal cortex to be activated. Making an effort to develop positive emotions depends on positive relationships. From your first few breaths, your brain craved positive bonding experiences with your parents, and later this was repeated with others. Your OFC became wired to the type of bonding experiences that you had, and it prepared you to try to repeat the same type of emotional relationship with others.

When your connection with people is positive, your OFC is relieved. When your relationships are negative, your OFC goes through withdrawals. Some neuroscientists, such as Jaak Panskepp from the University of Indiana, has noted that the OFC is rich in natural opiates. Positive feelings of closeness with another person help these natural opiates to activate your OFC. Separation from an intimate partner and the subsequent feelings of withdrawal may be the result of those opiate receptors losing excitation.

The neurotransmitter dopamine is activated when you are attracted to another person; this leads to feelings of pleasure. Then the neuro-hormone oxytocin is activated simply by cuddling with your partner. Thus, it is biochemically and neuronally comforting to have close relationships. Positive relationships lead to positive emotions. We can, therefore, call positive relationships *social medicine*. Because social medicine is so important, chapter 7 is devoted to its benefits.

When you are feeling down, you should maximize your dose of social medicine to make yourself feel better. You may say that you don't feel like being around other people when you feel down, but just as you take your medicine when you're ill, you should take a healthy dose of social medicine, because it will help you to feel better.

Brenda's Bumps

Life was going along fairly well for Brenda. After graduating from college, she managed to get a good job as a registered nurse in a community hospital. She married a bright and funny man named Brett. Soon they had a son, and her sisters told her that she seemed to have an ideal life compared to them. Brenda was the most attractive of the three sisters. When she was growing up, she always had a boyfriend and was pursued by other boys. Her sisters, in contrast, went through much adolescent angst in response to rejections and shifting friendships during their high school years.

Nevertheless, Brenda was the most pessimistic and least durable of the three sisters. She complained often, and her sulky moods seemed to control the social climate no matter whom she was with at the time. Her two sisters dealt with various challenges through their lives—difficult marriages, health problems—but they seemed to be optimistic that things would get better as long as they tried to make them improve.

Brenda had few if any major challenges in her life. Everything seemed to go rather smoothly, which is what she had learned to expect as she grew up. Her first major "bump" came at work. She had worked for seven years in a credential office, where the stress was low, but she complained that it was high. She worked under a supervisor who gave her stellar performance evaluations. Then she was transferred to the intensive care unit, and her world suddenly turned upside down. For the first time in her life, she encountered real stress. She encountered a charge nurse who Brenda thought was the most controlling and critical person that she had ever met.

Brenda was given a performance evaluation that pointed to areas where she needed to improve; these were areas in which she thought she had been doing quite well. She perceived these criticisms as harassment, so she met with the nurses' union and explored how to file a grievance. The union representative told her that although he would help her to file the papers for the grievance, the hospital was gearing up for a National Commission on Quality Association (NCQA) review because the administration had been told that it was out of compliance. The NCQA review had everybody under the microscope, and top performance was critical.

Brenda responded, "Are they looking for a scapegoat? Because if they are, I won't put up with it!"

"No, actually. You aren't the only one who received this kind of evaluation," said the union representative.

"Well, it feels like it," she said, and walked out of the office feeling bruised and uncertain if she should file the grievance papers.

By the time Brenda returned home that night, she had decided that quitting was her best option. She would ask her husband to work overtime until she found a new job. Her husband looked glum when she walked in the door. "So you've heard, huh?" she asked.

"Yeah, they said that the layoff will occur immediately," he said.

"How dare they!" she exclaimed. "I didn't even file the grievance. I was just thinking about it."

Brett starred at her, trying to connect her response to what he had said.

Then it hit her like an earthquake. He wasn't talking about her, he was talking about himself. She couldn't quit now.

It was hard for Brenda to comprehend that Brett was feeling dejected, because she was so upset about her own job situation. Now she felt trapped. Her plans of quitting suddenly were impossible in light of Brett's layoff. Instead of feeling empathy for him, she felt a confusing sort of anger.

Going back to work the next morning was hard. Since Brenda had decided to quit and then found out that she couldn't, she felt hopelessly trapped. She began to feel depressed. The more she thought about the conflict, the stronger her feelings of hopelessness and depression became.

She dragged herself through the next work week as if she were on slow-motion autopilot. Her ability to care for her patients began to suffer. By the end of the week, her friend Molly had to remind her to go back in and check a patient's blood pressure. It was Brenda's responsibility to stay on top of such routine tasks, but the combination of the self-pity she was cultivating and the resentment she felt for management was dampening her ability to function. Her ability to think clearly was colored by her new mood and her sense of meaninglessness about her work.

Soon Brenda found herself resenting the patients because they somehow represented the hospital management that she had come to resent. She was relieved to be off for a weekend. Unfortunately, she didn't use the weekend to refuel herself. Instead, the weekend served to drag her down even further. First she turned down an opportunity to go to a dinner party on Saturday night. Then she told her husband to take their son to the park so that she could be alone. She closed the drapes, sat on the couch, and stewed about her situation. Her food intake dropped, and she added a few glasses of wine at night to "get my mind off things."

The weekend only kindled the neurons that cultivated depression. Her shift to passivity led to greater activity in her right frontal lobe. By the next week she was even more depressed.

Brenda slogged through another week with the same depressive pattern brewing. Molly approached her with the concern that Brenda's patient care was suffering. Instead of using this as a wakeup call, Brenda responded by feeling worse about herself.

At that point she realized that she needed to do something to break out of this downward spiral. Brenda came to me a few days later, suffering from a mild depression. She said that she needed a "quick fix" and wanted an antidepressant medication. I offered instead to help her adapt to the situation at work and to boost her mood at the same time. Antidepressant medications usually take as long as a month to begin to work.

"What about Valium?" she asked.

"You're a nurse," I replied. "You probably know that it's very addictive and that one of the side effects is actually depression. You could change your brain chemistry immediately by cutting out the wine and forcing yourself to eat three balanced meals per day. Also, maximize natural light and walk for at least a half hour per day."

I explained that she needed to eat because her body makes neurotransmitters from specific amino acids that she consumes in her food. Also, her neurotransmitters GABA and serotonin were being decreased because of the wine she was drinking. (I'll explain these factors in greater detail in chapter 6.) The bottom line for Brenda was that she needed better neurochemistry, not worse.

I explained that when her depressive pattern began, her brain fired circuits that perpetuated her depression. Brenda needed to take action to break out of the passive mode that overactivated her right frontal lobe and to shift instead to doing something to activate her left frontal lobe. She therefore had to do some things that she didn't feel like doing to get out of the emotional rut she had cultivated.

It was evident from her history that she was used to having things go easily for her, despite her complaining about whatever was going on at the time. As a result, Brenda had not developed the emotional intelligence to deal with the kinds of challenges that she now faced. She needed to rewire her brain so that she could be more durable for the bumpy road of life, because she had wired her brain to deal only with a smooth road. Consequently, when she hit one of the few bumps in her life, she experienced it as catastrophic.

One of the cognitive distortions we confronted immediately was that Brenda had come to expect things to be too easy. Her passivity mode had developed because things had come so easily for her. She didn't need to make an effort, because things usually turned out well without her making any effort. In fact, she even went into nursing because it was "easy to find a job."

It was evident that Brenda was a warm and compassionate person. I knew that we needed to tap these emotional skills to rewire her brain to deal with this challenge and subsequent challenges in her life. Her compassion represented the cognitive and emotional bridge we could use to establish a connection between the patients and the hospital's effort to pass the accreditation review.

I asked her to describe the patients that she was currently treating in the intensive care unit. She told me about an old man with congestive heart failure whose family lived out of state and had called only once to check on him. There was a man with multiple injuries from an auto accident. There was also a mother of a five-year-old who was being treated for complications from surgery for ovarian cancer.

As Brenda continued to tell me about other people, I could see a stream of warmth and compassion rekindling in her. After she described the mother, her eyes welled up and she gazed to the left, apparently reflecting on the sadness that the woman and her family were going through. Then she looked at the chair in which she was sitting, apparently having an epiphany that in comparison to that woman, her "trauma" was petty. She glanced back at me with a flash of guilt and then reconstituted herself.

I asked her to reconnect with those patients before our next session and report back to me on their progress in treatment and how they were doing emotionally.

"What's that got to do with why I came to see you?" Brenda asked.

"You need to remind yourself why you are working there," I replied. "Then we can connect that with how you can cope with the administrative changes."

What I didn't tell her yet was that her homework assignment would serve multiple functions. It would help her to detach from her exaggerated sense of hurt that fueled her negative reaction to her supervisor's evaluation, and it would enable her to refocus on the hospital's mission to care for people. She needed to rekindle motivation that would activate her left frontal lobe instead of her overactive and passive right frontal lobe.

When Brenda returned for the next session, there was more color in her face. The angry sullenness was gone, and her voice had a soft and warm quality. After hearing about her patients, I asked how the rest of her colleagues were doing as they tried to prepare for the reaccreditation and care for their patients at the same time. Here I was implicitly asking her to develop a greater context for her perspective.

"It's been hard," she said. "They're all stressed out."

"And your supervisor?" I asked.

"Especially her. She looks very run down," she noted sadly. Then Brenda reverted to her old victim mode. "But she didn't have to treat me that way."

I acknowledged that her supervisor wasn't perfect. This seemed to free her up to recognize that her supervisor was under tremendous pressure from the administration to get everyone in line. Brenda's supervisor had quite a challenge on her hands. This discussion helped Brenda to move from black-and-white thinking to a perspective with shades of gray. As we discussed what the hospital was going through, she was able to externalize her problem.

Initially, Brenda was able to change by first *focusing* on the need to shift to other moods. However, focusing alone didn't make it happen. She needed to make an effort to change her behavior until it became *effortless* to be in a new mood. Because she didn't want to make the effort, because her chronic low emotional foundation demotivated her, the extra effort was critical. Thus, she had to do things that she didn't feel like doing.

Next I helped Brenda learn to *focus* on how and when she began to drift into a sulky reactive mode and to make an *effort* to shift into action. By tapping into her mirror neuron system, she was able to stay with the empathy that she had for her patients and let that serve as the central motivating force. Consequently, she restructured her effort to support the accreditation process so that she and her colleagues could be free to treat the patients as they deserved to be treated.

I explained that a moderate degree of anxiety is useful to make neuroplastic changes. Brenda's negative evaluation spiked her anxiety enough to stimulate the necessary changes for her to get out of the passive (right frontal lobe) mode and shift to an active (left frontal lobe) mode. These changes helped to prepare her for the bumps that will inevitably come later in her life.

Taking Action

Brenda learned to channel her anger about her situation into taking action to change it. When you can do something about what angers you, the situation can potentially change. Recent research suggests that anger stirs motivation and activates the left frontal lobe. This shift to the left frontal lobe helps you rebalance the activation of your two frontal lobes; in turn, you feel more positive about your situation in life. Rather than feeling helpless about your situation, doing something constructive puts you into an action mode.

If you are down in the dumps or just plain depressed, become active. Taking action gets you going and makes you feel better.

I often say to people who are down in the dumps that the best prescription for depression is action. In contrast, passivity indirectly promotes feeling bad. You generally won't see the connection between your passivity and feeling bad. Being passive might even seem to be a good way to make yourself feel better, because you're "conserving energy."

Nevertheless, being passive doesn't pay off. Even if you can get someone else to do things for you, there are major negative emotional consequences. Passive-aggressive people tend to be more pessimistic than active, optimistic people are. They drift into a pessimistic mode because they sit back and let other people do for them what they can do for themselves, yet it's never enough!

When you feed your brain so that you can get out of an emotionally depressed period, first *focus* on the mood that you would rather be having. This focused attention will help you to be aware of the difference between the more positive mood state you want to be in and the negative one that you would like to abandon.

Next you must make an *effort* to do things that will move your mood to a more positive one—from passivity to action, from your right frontal lobe to your left frontal lobe. You must make a rigorous effort to do what you don't really want to do—for instance, going to the movies with your friends even though you'd rather stay home alone because you are in a bad mood.

You should make an effort to prime positive moods, take action, and construct positive narratives. By wiring positive thinking and ensuring that you're reconnected socially, you can make the new mood last.

The need to focus comes into play again when you drift back into your old mood. Be alert so that you notice each time you begin to drift back into a passive and negative mood. You'll have to make a concerted effort to do many of the things I've described. Eventually your efforts will change the default mood of your brain into a positive one. Soon you will begin to feel at ease with your new, more positive mood, and it will become *effortless* for you to remain in that mood. As you begin to feel good about yourself and enjoy the positive feelings, note that you have indeed rewired your brain.

You may begin to enjoy things so much that you sit back and passively wait for the next series of good things to happen to you. If you sit back too long, you'll run the risk of reverting back to the old pattern. This could happen quickly if an event or a crisis arises that makes you upset. This is when you need to be *determined* to stay with your new strategy to ensure that the previous three steps of feeding your brain are practiced.

If you stay determined when an unfortunate incident occurs, you can weather the storm despite the complications of fierce winds. This resiliency depends on a sense of optimism that the plan will work. You need to remind yourself that the previous steps helped you to feel good before. Now you must stay in practice to make sure that this new emotional foundation is your default emotional mode.

Being in a positive mood is not only more pleasurable, it's also more practical. If your moods are positive, you'll be more prone to think about possibilities and potentialities and to view your challenges in life as vitalizing.

4

Cultivating Memory

Sylvia was a fifty-five-year-old mother of three who came to see me with complaints that her memory had been failing in the last few years. She insisted that she was "too busy" to have memory problems. Then she looked at me, horrified, and said, "I just saw a TV show on attention deficit disorder. Maybe I've come down with it?"

Sylvia was indeed quite busy, but she didn't have attention deficit disorder. She had teenage daughters and was holding a job as a sales representative for a furniture wholesaler, so she was always on the go. During the first fifteen minutes that she was sitting in my office, she received two text messages from her daughters. Despite the fact that we were meeting for the first time, she felt compelled to pick up her cell phone and read the messages. Each time, she turned to me afterward and asked, "Now, what were we talking about?"

Sylvia told me that she barely had time in the morning to make coffee before her daughters needed something from her and she had to get them out the door to school. I asked her if she had time for breakfast. She laughed and responded, "You're kidding, right?"

As she described the rest of her day, it quickly became evident that her typical day was disorganized and required much crisis management. Sylvia was perpetually putting out fires that she had unknowingly set because she rarely followed through on things that she had begun earlier. That part of it did sound like attention deficit disorder, but there was more to her story than that. She told me that she had recently lost a few accounts for new orders with furniture stores because of her failure to remember to close the deals. Her supervisor put her on probation after the last time. That's what prompted her to come in to see me.

As for her hunch that she had "come down" with attention deficit disorder, I explained that people don't develop that condition like the flu. In fact, it was clearly evident that up until three years ago, and even well back into college and high school, Sylvia did not suffer from the symptoms of attention deficit disorder. In fact, she had been a very attentive and focused student who earned good grades. Her problem had developed recently, and it had a lot to do with her lifestyle.

Our first task was to change her practice of not eating breakfast. The next task was to minimize the scatter in her life. I told her that it was no wonder she wasn't remembering anything, since she rarely focused attention on anything long enough to code it into her memory.

We began to structure Sylvia's day so that she was present with whatever she was doing at any given time. The text messaging and the calls on her cell phone were scheduled to a specific time of the day. She learned to *focus* attention on each task until it was completed. With better DLPFC activation, her working memory (which used to be called short-term memory) began to function well so that she could code information into her long-term memory.

Sylvia had to get over the simplistic notion that her memory was something to be either lost or found. Rather, her memory represented a range of skills that she could enhance. She learned the distinctions among the various memory systems so that what she expected of herself would be reasonable.

As soon as her diet had improved and she had made a concerted *effort* to structure her day so that she was better able to focus on one task to completion, her stress level dropped. Sylvia said, "I can't believe that I'm not on edge all the time. It feels strange!" She was gaining confidence in herself as she stopped spinning her wheels and actually accomplished tasks. The fires that she had perpetually put out in the past seemed to die down or never ignite at all.

"It's like I'm getting my brain back again," she said during one of our sessions. Sylvia described how her working memory had improved to such a degree that it seemed easier and at times even *effortless* to remember things. At the end of the day, she remembered all the important plans that she needed to carry over to the next day.

Then, just as we began to work on enhancing her memory skills, one of her daughters broke her arm. This abruptly halted her progress. She reverted to her old habits, saying, "What do you expect from me? I'm a single working mom." When I reminded her that she could take better care of her daughters if she got back to the program, she nodded knowingly and resumed where we left off. To develop durable memory skills, she had to be *determined* to stick to her effort, even when she had to care for her daughters.

As Sylvia learned to organize her time, she noticed that her memories, too, were contingent on organization. That organization was used to develop memories based on associations. She learned to organize what she wanted to remember by linking each item, image, or piece of information into a coherent series of associations. Since she learned that her brain worked best to construct memories based on associations, she was more willing to make the effort to form the associations.

I taught her a series of mnemonic devices that served as memory tricks to form associations. These became fun games, about which she said, "Who would ever have thought I'd be rewiring my brain by playing memory games?"

Perhaps you're like Sylvia and the 90 percent of people who would like to improve their memory. A Roper survey found that nine out of ten people complain that they have faulty memories. A majority of the people who were surveyed reported that they have gone into a room and forgotten why they went there. Could most of us be experiencing declining memories?

As Sylvia discovered, memory is not a thing to be lost or found. Memory skills can be cultivated or left to atrophy. In today's society, cell phones, BlackBerrys, instant messaging, and mass media bombardment combine to erode our attention and our memory skills. To improve your memory skills, you have to resist having your attention fragmented. You can still use your BlackBerry, but you'll have to be present, focused, and organized.

There's a lot you can do to improve your memory, but there are also limitations. The following are some ways to improve your memory:

- Improve your attention skills.
- Learn how to use the different types of memory.
- Use associations such as mnemonic devices.

The following are some of the limitations:

- Being able to pay attention to several things at once and remembering all with great accuracy. This is why you can forget to look for the correct road signs while you're driving if you're talking on your cell phone at the same time. Fortunately, many states are making it illegal to use a cell phone while driving.
- Expecting to improve your memory without effort. Memory is not something you have or don't have, like an inheritance. Your memory must be exercised to be enhanced.
- Assuming that you will remember everything you've ever experienced. Memories are not frozen in time like indelible snapshots. They are constantly revised as you recall them, or they fade away if they are not used again.

Attention: The Gateway to Memory

Attention is critical for redirecting the resources in your brain and promoting neuroplasticity. Attention also serves as the gateway to memory. You might forget all the details of what a friend told you during a conversation at a party if you were only half listening to what she said. You will probably forget what little you do remember during the next conversation. If you place emotional importance on the next conversation, you will listen more attentively and remember it later.

Paying attention is a function of your frontal lobes. They tell the rest of your brain what is important and what should be remembered. To promote neuroplasticity and improve your memory requires that you engage your frontal lobes. The gateway to memory has to be open to remember, and your frontal lobes open the gate.

Your PFC, and specifically the DLPFC, is responsible for maintaining working memory. Your working memory is called *working* because the short-term memories it holds relate to what your mind is working on at the moment. Your daily life involves going from one experience to another, using your working memory to navigate, and your working memory holds on to these experiences for up to thirty seconds. Generally, you're able to weave a sense of continuity from one experience to the next. Thus, for instance, you're able to remember that you're on your way to your aunt's house. Without your working memory, you'd forget to turn onto the correct street when you saw the street sign.

Since your DLPFC is also a sort of executive control center, it plays a major role in determining what you pay attention to and what you remember. If something occurs that you want to remember— such as being told that the stock that you just bought will plummet soon because the company is about to declare bankruptcy— various neurotransmitters (especially norepinephrine and dopamine) help to elevate your attention and your anxiety. The synaptic activation of the dopaminergic systems heightens your attention, and your DLPFC says, "Remember this conversation." The feedback between the DLPFC and your hippocampus paves the way for the formation of a long-term memory. You'll remember the stock tip (and the person who gave it to you) for some time to come.

Working memory is therefore the route to long-term memory. If working memory is impaired, long-term memory will experience a famine of new information. If the road to long-term memory through working memory is blocked, the "supplies" (memories) can't get through. If, for example, you spend your time at a party checking

your e-mail on your BlackBerry and engaging in superficial conversations, your attention will be fragmented and your working memory
compromised. The road is closed.

Working memory can be disrupted in a number of ways. Since
attention and concentration are so closely tied to working memory,
any distraction, such as getting a text message on your cell phone,
can hamper working memory. If you're distracted by an e-mail about
a colleague abruptly leaving the company for a new job, you will
probably forget what you were holding in your working memory
because your attention shifted to that other provocative piece of
information.

The initial demands of a good memory are as follows:

- Attention is the key. The door is locked without it. Your PFC
  must be engaged so that you can pay attention to remember.
- The more important a piece of information is to you, the stronger the memory will be in long-term storage.

When I use psychological tests that measure working memory,
I'm also measuring someone's ability to pay attention. If I give a person tests that measure various other types of memory and find that
he or she is deficient, I must try to rule out working memory as the
cause. The bottom line is that if you don't pay attention, you won't
be able to move a short-term memory into long-term memory.

The Types of Memory

Working memory and long-term memory differ in many ways. The
main distinguishing factor is the length of time that a memory is
stored, but another major difference is storage capacity: there is a
limit to how much you can store in your working memory, whereas
your long-term memory is not bound by such constraints.

Long-term memory is an archive, yet that archive is in a constant state of being restocked. Long-term memories are not stored
in fixed areas of the brain; rather, storage seems to be a product
of dynamic activity in and throughout many different areas of the

brain. However, memories are biased to particular neural structures, as I will soon describe. Whether an experience, a piece of information, or an emotional impression becomes encoded in long-term memory depends on complex dynamics among the various neural systems.

Your capacities to learn and to remember are highly overlapping functions. As your relationships with people deepen, your memories are shared in either implicit enactments or explicit discussions. If you recall something about your past—events, information, images, or content—it's called *declarative memory*. The recall of language-based information is called *semantic memory*. Overlapping memories about your past are referred to as *episodic memory*. These types of explicit memory are distinguishable as follows: If you remember getting a paper cut, that's episodic memory. If you remember the facts about how you got the paper cut, that's declarative memory. If you remember the words you used when telling someone about the paper cut, that's semantic memory.

If the episodic memories involve strong emotions, they are referred to as *emotional memory*. Habitual styles of moving, such as riding a bicycle or writing your name, are called *procedural memory*.

Although all these memory subsystems are considered forms of long-term memory, they can be regrouped as two large subsystems, *explicit* and *implicit* memory. This distinction is important for your understanding of how to cultivate your memory skills. Explicit memory involves facts and declared experiences. Implicit memory involves procedural skills and emotional memory. The components of the two kinds of memory are shown below.

Explicit Memory	Implicit Memory
• Declarative	• Procedural
• Semantic	• Emotional
• Episodic	

Some implicit memories, such as emotional memory, are acquired rapidly, such as being traumatized by assault, whereas procedural memories, such as the learned ability to play the cello, are acquired only with painstaking repetition.

The hippocampus, which is largely responsible for encoding explicit memories, generates thoughts from previous learning and information. If you didn't have that ability, then every day would be a new day—literally. That might, for a moment, sound good, but it is not. For example, Henry Molaise, one of the most famous patients in the history of neurology and neuropsychology (he is called "HM" in the research literature), taught us a lot about the hippocampus and explicit memory.

Henry lost the ability to consolidate new explicit memories after he had brain surgery as a young adult. He had been hit by a car when he was nine years old and had begun having medically intractable seizures, so a neurosurgeon removed Henry's right and left hippocampus in 1953 to try to control the seizures, before the role of the hippocampus was well understood. After this surgery, Henry's seizures got better but he could not remember people. If he was introduced to a stranger and chatted amiably with him, and the visitor then left the room for a few minutes and came back, Henry would not remember having ever seen the person before.

Henry remained capable of remembering events from long ago and of forming procedural memories, however. For instance, he could walk around the block and remember how to get home—not explicitly, but in a procedural way. He could be taught a certain movement and, when asked to make that movement again later, could do so with greater facility than when he first learned it, but he would have no recollection of having ever performed the task before.

Through the many evaluations performed by neuropsychologist Brenda Milner, neuroscience discovered that the hippocampus is centrally involved in the laying down and retrieval of memories of past experiences. The hippocampus is necessary for consolidating an explicit memory about a situation that arises in our current life, but not for recalling the events associated with an old autobiographical memory.

The health of the hippocampus plays a central role in aging. Later in life there is a gradual atrophy of the hippocampus.

Many Alzheimer's patients lose declarative memory while, like Henry, retaining parts of their procedural memory. They continue to perform procedural memories out of habit while having an increased difficulty remembering recent facts about their lives.

Emotionally significant events are more likely to be remembered in the long run not only because they hold more personally meaningful themes but also because they are associated with higher levels of arousal. Emotional events stir a physiological reaction, including an increase in the level of blood glucose, which promotes the process of memory consolidation.

Emotional events resonate in your mind, creating neuroplastic change and enhancing memory consolidation. If you want to remember something, become emotionally involved in it. You're more likely to remember emotionally significant events not only because they hold more personally meaningful themes but because they are associated with higher levels of arousal.

The emotional memory's neural networks can often be associated with the experience of fear. As I noted in chapter 2, classically conditioned fear responses to auditory and visual stimuli are mediated by the subcortical pathways that connect the thalamus (the central switchboard of the brain) to the amygdala. In other words, as researcher Joseph LeDoux of New York University has noted, "This circuit bypasses the cortex and thus constitutes a subcortical mechanism of emotional learning."

Despite the importance of the amygdala in emotional learning, it appears to play no significant role in most declarative memory processes. The cortex, in contrast, is unnecessary for the acquisition of conditioned fear, but it is essential for the extinction of conditioned fear. In other words, fear can be conditioned without your awareness but cannot be eliminated without it. The cortex is also critically important in taming the amygdala to conquer anxiety.

The power of emotional conditioning varies, based on your state at the time. If the norepinephrine level is high, conditioning occurs more rapidly, and the conditioned response not only is learned more quickly but also lasts longer.

Like most animals, you can learn tasks that require the activation of your amygdala but not of your hippocampus. On the other hand, you can't learn tasks that require the hippocampus but not the amygdala.

The amygdala activates generalized attention and mobilizes the entire brain-body system through its interactions with the HPA axis. You are able to store episodic memories even when emotional arousal is not a component of an incident. When your brain is working well, the amygdala sets up the emotional state that is optimal for memory. Later, when you are once again in that emotional state, you are more likely to remember explicit material that is congruent with that state.

You typically have few explicit memories of the first three or five years of your life. Sigmund Freud inaccurately referred to this phenomenon as *infantile amnesia*. However, you haven't forgotten or repressed these memories; rather, the memories are not conscious, and they are available to your consciousness only as an emotional reaction. The implicit memory system develops before the capacity to code explicit memories.

Implicit memory is the basis for many emotional predispositions and cognitive habits. A preference for using withdrawal to deal with conflict, for example, may become refined with cognitive development and experience, but its implicit function (maintaining limited connections to other people) is likely to remain the same unless you work hard to make neuroplastic change in your social brain system. Hence, in situations in which fear conditioning and procedural learning occur simultaneously (possibly outside your awareness, but prior to the maturation of episodic learning), you may have acquired habits and conditioned responses as a child, outside your awareness.

Many of the habitual emotional responses and behavioral patterns that you consider an integral part of your identity are implicit memories. Because they are habitual, they are not easily changed without consistent effort, such as following the FEED method. Implicit memories are not readily available through insight, and insight typically doesn't change them. Because much of what you experience and respond to is based on implicit memories, unconscious processes play an important role in all your relationships.

The fact that you are able to read this book automatically and relatively effortlessly (unless you're distracted) indicates that you have procedural memory. Because of procedural memory, you could even read a page or two without any of the content entering your consciousness; this is a result of procedural memory, which you acquired for reading when you first struggled with understanding letters and words.

Procedural memory contrasts with declarative and episodic memory in some important respects. Whereas declarative and episodic memory allow you to remember *events,* procedural memory allows you to recall how to repeat specific *processes,* including skills and habits: reading, gargling, typing, riding a bicycle, and so on. In procedural learning, no content is necessarily involved. Instead, you remember *how to do* things. With enough practice, procedural memory allows you to perform different actions or processes automatically and unconsciously. Procedural learning is also essential for the development of the aspect of personality referred to as *character:* the remarkable behavioral, emotional, and cognitive consistency that one acquires over time.

Procedural memory becomes neuroplasticity ingrained in your long-term memory by following three steps:

1. **Acquiring a memory:** Sometimes this is called coding a memory. This occurs, for instance, as you learn the basics of riding a bike.
2. **Storing a memory:** At this stage you file the memory away for later use as you work at learning to ride.
3. **Retrieving a memory:** At this point you recall the memory the next time you hop onto the bike.

Now that we understand the difference between implicit and explicit memory, let's look at explicit memory in greater detail. Because it is of paramount importance, I have devoted the entire following section to it.

Associations and Mnemonic Tricks

Cultivating memory skills and cultivating neuroplasticity go hand in hand. This is because forming memories requires neuroplasticity. Each new memory represents a neuroplastic change in your brain.

Essentially, these memories are the result of forming and strengthening synaptic connections.

One of the interesting facets of long-term memory is that once you begin to describe an event from earlier in your life, you may be surprised by how much you remember. As you begin to describe the event, you're reminded of other circumstances that surround the event. You unleash a whole chain of associations and rekindle a much wider spectrum of memories. This is because memory involves establishing synaptic connections among large groups of neurons. These connections represent associations with images, ideas, and feelings that you had when you coded the memories as well as every time you recall those memories. The synaptic connections and associations are two aspects of the same process.

Since memory represents associations, you can cultivate your memory skills by using mnemonic devices, which enhance memory through association construction. Mnemonic devices that grab your attention and make remembering fun are the most effective. If your mnemonic device is stale and boring, you'll want to forget it. Let it stand out by making it silly, funny, absurd, or even titillating.

Memory aids such as mnemonic devices provide you with ways to trick yourself into remembering. Many mnemonic devices have been used throughout history, and I recommend the following four, which are particularly useful and easy to learn:

1. Pegs
2. Loci
3. Story links
4. Link

Pegs do just what the name says: they peg a word to another word that is easier to remember. They are hooks that you can use to capture the word you are trying to remember. When you think of the peg word, you'll think of the word you want to remember. For instance, in "One, two, buckle my shoe; three, four, open the door," *two* is attached to *shoe* and *four* is attached to *door*.

Pegging can also involve associating a letter or a number with a word that you want to remember. The acronym FEED is a peg. You could, instead, associate each letter of the alphabet with a number. You can remember a string of numbers by remembering their corresponding letters arranged as a word.

Twenty-six hundred years ago, Mnemosyne, the Greek goddess of memory, was said to know everything: the past, the present, and the future. Storytellers called bards learned how to remember long poems and epic tales by relying on Mnemosyne. Actually, however, they used the mnemonic technique called loci.

Loci (LO-sigh) is the plural of *locus*, which is Latin for "place" or "location." Sometimes the loci system is referred to as the topical system. *Topo* means "location" in Greek.

When you're using loci, you're coding your memories with specific locations. If you want to be able to remember the contents of a speech you have to give, you can associate each point with a specific location in the room. Then when you're giving the talk, you can look at each location and be reminded of what you want to say.

The Roman philosopher and statesman Cicero once told how the loci method was used by the poet Simonides while he chanted a lyrical poem at a large banquet in honor of the host, Scopos. When Simonides included a passage with praise for the gods Castor and Pollux, Scopos became angry and refused to pay Simonides the full fee, telling him that he could obtain the balance from the gods. During the argument Simonides was summoned by a messenger who said that two young men were waiting outside and wanted to talk to him immediately. When Simonides went outside to meet the men, they were nowhere to be seen. In the meantime the building caught on fire and collapsed, killing all the occupants inside.

As the cleanup and rescue effort got under way, no one was able to identify the bodies of the victims—except Simonides. He identified each person by where he or she had been sitting at the time he was summoned outside.

The loci system has two main steps:

1. Commit to memory several locations of a place in the order that you want to remember them. The place can be your living room or a room in which you must give a presentation.

2. Associate something you want to remember with each location.

By taking these two simple steps, you can recall what you're trying to remember by looking at the location, walking by it, or simply picturing it in your mind.

Let's say that you want to memorize a presentation. While you are rehearsing your lines, walk around the room and make a specific association to each object in the room or each part of the room. At the lectern, remember the first part of your speech. Then go to the laptop, the projector, the first row, the back row, and so on, remembering a different part of your presentation at each location.

As you practice, walk around the room and time your presentation to match each location with each part. Next, stand in one spot and look at each location as you go through the presentation again, matching each part with each location. Finally, leave the room physically but reenter it mentally, going through your presentation and making the same matches.

By the time you actually begin speaking, you'll be able to glance at areas in the room and make the presentation by using each location as a cue.

The third mnemonic technique is story links. Throughout history people have gathered around storytellers, read novels, and enjoyed movies. Stories are an essential part of the fabric of our culture. You use stories as a way to learn, teach, and pass the time. You can also link stories to information you want to remember.

By teaching yourself a story, you can link it to information you hope to remember later. Then when you tell yourself the story, you'll be reminded of the information you wanted to remember. You develop a story that reminds you of a list of words or a group of concepts that you have to remember. The story should weave together the items in the order that you want to remember them. Those items connect with one another as the story unfolds.

The fourth mnemonic system is called link. It requires a little more time to construct. To use this technique you develop a list or group of words or concepts that you need to remember. One particularly powerful way to use the link technique is to link a visual image with something you want to remember. The visual association route has been found to be effective because people tend to remember unusual visual images quite well. That is why advertisers craft ads so that the positively proactive images of their products stick in your mind. For example, many companies try to link an attractive person with their product. You can use the same brain circuits to link what you want to remember with a provocative visual image. Let's say that as you are about to lie down to go to sleep, you want to remember to call for a service appointment for your car in the morning because the engine light went on as you were driving home. Tell yourself that when you see the light on the coffee maker go on in the morning, you will link it with the engine light in your car.

There are some commonalities and dissimilarities among the four mnemonic techniques. When you don't have a lot of time and you need to develop a quick way to remember something important, it is wise to use a peg. One of the advantages of the peg over the story link is that you can pick out individual items from a list. The story-link system, in contrast, relies on a sequence.

Like the loci system, which is dependent on prememorized locations, the peg system also uses prememorized word or number links. With a peg, the information is connected to nouns or verbs (such as FEED).

Whatever mnemonic system you use, make sure that it's flexible and that it meets the demands of what you're trying to remember. Practice using mnemonic devices so that you'll be versatile in their use.

Eduardo's Tables

Eduardo came to see me because he wanted to improve his memory performance at work. He was a waiter in a very high-end Nob Hill restaurant in San Francisco. He believed that his tips could be as high as his colleagues' if he could just remember "a little something about each customer" whom he served. He explained, "As it is now, I'm barely getting by remembering what table to bring the dishes to."

After ruling out many contributors to poor memory such as diet, substance abuse, and poor sleep habits, we explored what mnemonic system would be the most appropriate for his use in the restaurant. We settled on the loci system because he had a set arrangement of tables and chairs on which to build a system. Since Eduardo was an avid traveler, we agreed that he could assign a certain continent to each table. (More than one table could be given the same continent.) He not only entertained himself by paying attention to who sat in a particular continent but also whether or not they ordered dishes that were from that continent. He remembered these congruities or incongruities when he served them their respective dishes. By making each evening a fun game of geography, Eduardo transformed the loci mnemonic system into a great way to increase his tips and enjoy his customers. They, of course, never knew of his imaginary travels and associations.

How to Improve Your Memory

There are many things you can do to improve your memory. No one thing alone will give you the memory skills that you want and deserve. Thus I offer nine simple ways to improve your memory.

1. Consume a Balanced Diet

Just as you wouldn't expect to run your car on an empty gas tank, so, too, you should not expect to run your brain with no fuel. You want your brain to run at its optimal level.

By eating three balanced meals a day, you give your brain what it needs: fuel, the right building blocks to function at its potential. It's the most basic foundation you can provide to allow your brain to remember.

A balanced meal includes a complex carbohydrate, a fruit or a vegetable, and a protein. By eating three balanced meals a day, you're giving your brain the combination of amino acids it needs to manufacture a spectrum of neurotransmitters, the basis of your brain chemistry.

Each neurotransmitter allows you to think and feel in ways that make you feel good about your life and make you capable of memory. The neurotransmitter acetylcholine, for example, is critically important for your brain's ability to process memory.

2. Get Enough Sleep

You need a calm and alert mind to be able to use your memory skills to their full potential. The basic way to tune yourself up to be ready to remember is to get enough sleep.

If you don't get enough sleep, you won't be able to maintain enough attention to code what you want into your memory. Attention is the gateway to memory. If your ability to pay attention is compromised, the gate won't be open. Keep the gate open, relax, and get enough sleep.

3. Exercise Your Memory

Your body is the result of millions of years of evolution. You need regular exercise to keep your body running properly. Your distant ancestors didn't sit around all day in chairs or on a couch.

By exercising, you allow your body and your brain to keep all your organ systems operating at their optimum. By exercising, you rev up your cardiovascular system, your metabolism, and the flow of nutrients to your brain. Exercise also helps you sleep at night and minimizes the stress you build up during the day. Doing all this will help you to maintain a clear head and remember what you experience.

4. Take Supplements (but Keep It Simple)

Vitamins, minerals, and herbal supplements help your brain to achieve the biochemistry it needs to remember well.

Supplements, however, should *never* be thought of as an alternative to a balanced diet. Make sure that you always eat three balanced meals a day. If you take supplements, consider them just that: supplements.

We have become a very pill-oriented society, so don't buy into the notion that you should take every supplement that has been reported to boost memory. If you take too many supplements and combine them with the medications you take to treat various illnesses, you run the risk of creating problems, including memory problems.

If you take supplements, operate on the maxim that less is more. Stick to the basics:

- Vitamin C
- Vitamin E
- Calcium and magnesium
- Omega-3 fatty acid
- Multivitamin with all the essential Bs

5. Stimulate Your Mind

If you want to improve your memory, you'll have to exercise your mind. A lazy mind produces lazy memory skills.

Whatever your age, make sure that you're always challenging yourself. Not only does your brain respond by stimulating more connections between your neurons (through dendritic branching), you'll also keep yourself alert and engaged with the world around you.

If you watch television excessively, your mind will turn off. (Even watching educational programs is still a mentally passive activity.) If you spend an inordinate amount of time ruminating about the trivial mishaps of the day, you'll not only make yourself and those around you miserable, your memory skills will also suffer because you're preoccupied with irrelevant sidetracks.

Think of intellectual exercise as a way to keep your memory skills sharp. Engage yourself in the following:

- Read nonfiction books.
- Take classes.
- Travel.
- Engage in stimulating conversation and debate.

6. Develop Your Attention Span

Attention is critical to your memory. Pay attention in order to remember. If you don't pay attention, you won't be able to move short-term memories into your long-term memory. Whatever you can do to improve your attention, do it. Practice focusing on an activity for longer and longer periods. Don't multitask or jump quickly from one thing to another. Allow yourself to become immersed in an activity you enjoy, and concentrate fully and deeply on it. Structure some routine activities so that you have an opportunity to pay attention to each step that you take to complete the task. Even if this slows you down, consider it an important exercise. Not only will you be working to increase your attention span, but you will also probably find that you do a much more complete and quality job with your tasks.

7. Stay Organized

By keeping yourself organized, you'll be better able to code into memory whatever you hope to remember. Staying organized doesn't mean being rigid. It means being able to differentiate your experiences and code them into relevant associations.

If your life is disorganized, your memory will be, too. By being disorganized, you won't know how to retrieve your memories; even worse, you won't have any to retrieve.

Get organized so you can remember to remember.

8. Associate, Pair, and Connect

Your brain has multiple systems that provide multiple means of coding memories. If you use several of these systems to code information, that will make the memory richer and more easily remembered. The more ways you can remember something, the better chance you'll have of remembering it.

If, for example, you want to be able to remember a car, you'll be far more successful at recalling it later if you take note of its name, its shape, and its color as well as its smell, the sound of its engine, and how it feels to drive it.

9. Use Mnemonic Devices

Use the four mnemonic devices described earlier: pegs, loci, story links, and link.

5

Fueling Your Brain

Sonya came to see me because she suffered from lethargy as well as periods of anxiety, depression, insomnia, and short-term memory problems. After detailing those complaints, she asked that I "fix" her brain.

Hearing that her primary concern was lethargy and the secondary concerns of anxiety and depression, I asked her about her diet.

She said, "I start my day with a tall skinny latte for that little boost."

"And what about breakfast?" I asked.

"Oh no," she replied. "I'm trying to lose weight."

"Then what and when do you first eat something?" I inquired.

"An energy bar and another latte will do me until dinner," Sonya said with a smile. Then she shrugged her shoulders. "But I can't seem to shed the pounds. Maybe it's because I sneak a few candy bars. You know, another little boost," she added, as if I would understand her special needs.

Since weight was such a concern to her, I told her that skipping breakfast actually made it harder to lose weight, because her body was being fooled into storing fat cells while it was trying to store energy. More important, she was depriving her brain of nutrients that are critical for a healthy level of biochemistry for the rest of the day.

With that information in mind, she asked, "How 'bout if I eat energy bars for breakfast?"

"That's not what I mean by breakfast." I noted that simple carbohydrates should be avoided and that sugar was the most destructive type.

"But what about my energy problem?" Sonya asked in an exasperated tone.

"You're *causing* your energy problem by your diet," I informed her. "Once you start eating three or four balanced small meals per day, your energy will be on the rise. That's, of course, if you cut out the sugar and moderate your caffeine intake."

This was not good news to Sonya. Despite everything that I explained, it all seemed counterintuitive. "Why should I cut out the things that boost my energy?" she wanted to know.

"Because you're perpetually crashing from those boosts," I explained. "What goes up must come down. But the problem is that you go further down from where you started."

Like Sonya, you might not know that your diet has a major effect on the biochemistry of your brain. A bad diet can have a major impact on the brain's ability to function properly, making you less apt to think clearly, pay attention, and cultivate neuroplasticity. The bottom line is that the food you eat is fuel for your brain that can enable you to rewire your brain or hinder you from doing so.

In recent years, a field of study called nutritional neuroscience has emerged that sheds light on how particular types of foods affect brain chemistry. Some foods enhance your brain's ability to thrive, whereas others bog it down, making it not only difficult to rewire your brain but adding to the risk factors for dementia.

To illustrate how your diet affects your brain, I'll start this chapter by describing how one simple meal can affect the way you think. Then I'll describe how your brain chemistry develops and how you can ensure that it has what it needs to keep you from being anxious or depressed. Finally, I'll describe how to enhance the structure of your brain so that you can lower your risk for dementia and enhance your ability to rewire your brain.

"But I don't have an appetite in the morning," Sonya protested. "The thought of food makes me sick to my stomach."

"You've developed a bad habit, and your gastrointestinal tract has adjusted," I told her. "Don't worry, it can be retrained."

She shook her head. "How 'bout we talk about my other problems, like memory, and give this food thing a rest?"

"Since your brain is doing the memory work, you need to give it fuel," I said. "I'll give you a great example. One of the neurotransmitters you need to process memory is called acetylcholine. Your body needs an amino acid called choline in order to manufacture acetylcholine. One source of choline is eggs. How about eating an egg, a piece of whole-wheat toast, and a glass of juice for breakfast? Then I'll teach you how to deal with stress and give you some memory-improvement techniques."

Sonya still was not convinced. It seemed to me that she was having difficulty accepting the need for change as well as making the effort to change. It was so much easier to wake up and go from zero to sixty with her boost, only to crash down to less than zero, rather than doing anything to change her lifestyle. My job was to help her understand that her life could be so much richer and healthier.

"Would you like to have more energy and to sustain it throughout the day without crashing?" I asked.

"Of course," she said immediately.

"Great. But to get that energy you'll need to make the following changes." I suggested that she avoid drinking coffee on an empty stomach and instead eat a nutritious breakfast. Lunch, too, had to be balanced. I asked her to cut out simple carbohydrates from her diet altogether. She was to take a multivitamin, an omega-3 pill, and a vitamin E tablet daily. Throughout the day she was to stay hydrated, keeping a bottle of water as her constant companion.

"How 'bout I try one at a time?" she asked sheepishly.

"To make the new diet work, you'll need to do it all together," I said, then I presented her a challenge I thought she would accept. "Want to prove me wrong?"

She nodded, grinning widely.

For the next week she made all the changes that I requested. When she came back for the next session, she looked more relaxed and focused. "Okay, I feel a little better," she admitted reluctantly.

"A little?" I repeated.

"Well, more than a little," she said, not pleased to admit it. "Can we get started with my problem now?"

"Sure."

We started working together on this foundation. Sonya learned the FEED technique and various memory-improvement techniques. Had she not begun to eat breakfast, our efforts would have been built like a house of cards on shifting sand.

Breaking a Fast

I am constantly astounded by the number of people like Sonya who come to see me, wanting help to deal with stress, anxiety, and/or depression, and then respond to my questions about diet by saying, "I'm just not a breakfast person" or "I don't have time for breakfast." Yet they do have time to check their e-mail or make an extra phone call in the morning before heading off to work.

When they fail to "break a fast" with a nutritious breakfast, it costs their brain dearly. They don't know that if they had eaten breakfast, they would be far more able to think clearly, remember important information, keep their energy high, and maintain balanced moods. In some ways, breakfast is the most important meal of the day. It is the meal that ends the longest amount of time without eating— hence the term *break-fast*. Think of breakfast as the fuel for the day. I often say, "Would you run your car on an empty tank of gas?" Just before your car runs out of gas, it runs unevenly, then splutters to a stop. The same goes for your brain. The symptoms are low energy, decreased short-term memory, anxiety, and mild depression.

Breakfast is the foundation meal for your brain, so that it can pay adequate attention, remember what you experience, and learn. For example, in a study measuring these cognitive skills, schoolchildren were given a glucose drink, a breakfast cereal, or no breakfast at all on difficult days. Their attention and memory were measured at intervals of 30, 90, 150, and 210 minutes later. Those who drank the glucose drink or ate no breakfast showed poorer attention and memory than those children who ate the breakfast cereal.

There are a number of cognitive benefits to eating breakfast and a number of costs to your thinking ability if you don't eat breakfast. Here is a brief summary of what has been shown to occur with either eating or not eating breakfast:

Skipping Breakfast	Eating Breakfast
↓Problem-solving ability	↑Problem-solving ability
↓Short-term memory	↑Arithmetic skills
↓Attention and episodic memory	↑Vigilant attention

Mood and energy are two other critically important factors to keep in mind when considering the importance of eating breakfast. The emotional and energy-related symptoms of not eating breakfast include the following:

- Difficulty concentrating
- Low energy
- Increased stress reactivity
- Mood swings
- Increased anxiety and depression

If stress is what you're concerned about, consider this: skipping breakfast is associated with high cortisol levels, whereas eating a nutritious breakfast cereal is associated with lower cortisol levels and lower susceptibility to colds and upper respiratory tract infections.

In a study involving hundreds of inner-city elementary school students in Baltimore and Philadelphia, it was found that those who ate breakfast had 40 percent higher math grades and were less apt to be absent from school or tardy. Those who did not eat breakfast were twice as likely to be depressed, four times as likely to suffer from anxiety, and 30 percent more likely to be hyperactive.

To achieve optimum brain performance throughout the day, you'll need to consume a smart balance of foods at each meal. For example, an optimum breakfast is an egg (protein), whole-grain toast (carbohydrate), and juice (fruit). As I pointed out to Sonya, the egg provides not only protein but also the amino acid choline, the precursor of acetylcholine, the neurotransmitter that is critical for memory. I'll describe the role of amino acids and how they help to develop neurotransmitters later in this chapter. The point here is that a balance of foods helps you to start the day with the biochemistry you need to thrive so that you don't drag yourself through the day.

For lunch, eat a meal that is higher in protein than in carbohydrates. This will contribute to less of a tired feeling in the afternoon. If you eat a high-carbohydrate lunch, you'll dampen your ability to focus and pay attention, a phenomenon known all too well to seminar leaders who speak to audiences right after lunch. Your dinner can be the reverse: higher in carbohydrates than in protein. Then you'll be sedated and mellowed out in the evening before you go to sleep.

Generally, when your stomach is full, a hormone called *gastrin* is secreted by the lower part of your stomach. Gastrin acts as a neurotransmitter on the vagus nerve, which enables the belly to communicate with the brain. Another hormone, called cholecystokinin (CCK), acts on your appetite. CCK is released after food moves into the small intestine. Like gastrin, it appears to act on the vagus nerve. Two neurotransmitters, norepinephrine and serotonin, are also very active in the digestive system. When activated, they signal the feeling of satiety. In fact, more serotonin is potentially active in your gut than in your brain.

Finally, consider that the older you get, the more protein you'll need in your diet. Also as you age, you'll be less tolerant of sugar in your blood and will have trouble absorbing vitamins when you consume them. Let's take a closer look at the role of sugar.

Sugar Factors

The brain uses glucose as fuel, but when it gets too much of it at one time, this can create a number of problems. It is no accident that many of your organs—including the pancreas, the liver, the thyroid, the adrenal glands, the pituitary gland, and the brain—are enlisted in controlling the amount of glucose in your blood. When your blood sugar drops too low, your brain (specifically, the hypothalamus) signals your pituitary gland and your thyroid gland to alert your liver to process more sugar from body fat.

Too little blood sugar results in hypoglycemia, and too much sugar results in hyperglycemia. Either way, your ability to think clearly and maintain balanced emotions becomes compromised. When your blood sugar rises after eating, your pancreas secretes insulin to help move sugar out into your cells. If your blood sugar drops below the normal level, your brain sends out a distress signal, which triggers the release of the hormone epinephrine (adrenaline) to signal your liver to make more glucose. As a result, you may feel nervous, dizzy and light-headed, fatigued, weak, or shaky, or you may have heart palpitations.

The symptoms of low blood sugar are particularly compromising if you tend toward hypoglycemia and consume coffee on an empty stomach. If you have diabetes, your system is all the more fragile, and you'll need to be scrupulous about managing your blood sugar. The symptoms I listed above, such as nervousness and fatigue, are more obvious than the ones that relate to your attention span, your short-term memory, and your mood stability.

After you consume an excessive amount of sugar, you'll trigger a boost in stress hormones that will last for as long as five hours. This occurs because excessive sugar makes your pancreas secrete more insulin than usual and takes too much sugar out of your system.

Anthony Cerami of Rockefeller University points out that a diet high in sugar contributes to accelerated aging. Sugar has an adverse effect on protein. It toughens up the molecules by creating pigments called *advanced glycosylated end products* (AGEs). A visual example of AGEs is what happens when you roast the skin of a chicken. Unfortunately, AGEs cause far more destructive results than simply toughening the skin. They act like a chemical glue that attaches molecules to one another, causing what has been referred to as a *cross-link*. Overcooked meat, for example, is cross-linked, which is why it is difficult to cut or chew. When your tissue has been cross-linked, many metabolic processes become impaired. For example, glycation (excess glucose) blocks protein from moving freely. As a result, the body's membranes become blocked, which slows down neural communication. This glycation causes inflammation.

Sugars are refined carbohydrates that can increase free radical inflammatory stress on the brain. A *free radical* is a molecule with a rogue electron that can rupture cell structure. After a series of reactions, AGEs lead to free radicals and inflammation. AGEs alter the structure and activities of proteins and also interfere with synaptic communication. Also, there is structural damage to the mitochondria, which are the energy factories in each cell that produce ATP (adenosine triphosphate)—the chemical energy fuel.

The negative effects of glycation are not immediate, but over time the neurons are damaged.

It is no wonder that high sugar consumption is associated with depression. Studies comparing the sugar consumption rates in countries such as Japan, Canada, and the United States find that Japan has lower consumption rates as well as lower rates of depression.

Because of the systemic ill effects of sugar, researchers were motivated to improve the methods of measuring its level in the body. The concept of glycemic load (GL) was developed at Harvard University in the late 1990s. The higher the GL of a food, the greater the expected rise in blood sugar and the greater the adverse insulin effects of the food. Long-term consumption of foods with a high GL leads to a greater risk of obesity, diabetes, and inflammation.

Researchers have shown that when people are given the amount of sugar in two soft drinks (75 grams of glucose), the free radical products of damaged fatty acids, called *isoprostanes*, rise by 34 percent in just ninety minutes after consumption.

Mild isoprostane elevation has been associated with Alzheimer's disease. Another blood marker of oxidative stress (free radical damage) and damage to fatty acids is called *malondialdehyde* (MDA). Researchers have shown a relationship between increased GL and MDA.

More than twenty-five years ago, researchers from the Massachusetts Institute of Technology (MIT) found a 25 percent difference between the IQ scores of children with high versus low consumption of refined carbohydrates (sugar and white flour) (Schauss, 1984). The differences in glucose result in significant costs to cognition and to the brain itself. Research at Britain's Swansea University found that dips in blood sugar are correlated with poor memory, poor attention, and aggressive behavior.

When researchers from Yale University gave twenty-five healthy children a drink containing the amount of glucose found in most soft drinks, the rebound in blood sugar boosted their adrenaline to more than five times their normal level for up to five hours. Most of these children found it difficult to concentrate and were anxious and irritable.

Similarly, researchers in Finland assessed the effects of sugar consumption on 404 children ages ten and eleven. They found that withdrawal, anxiety, depression, delinquency, and aggression were twice as frequent in those who consumed 30 percent more sucrose in the form of soft drinks, sugary snacks, and ice cream (Haapalahti, Mykkänen, Tikkanen, and Kokkonen, 2004).

The conclusions are clear: High sugar intake is bad for your brain and results in significant impairment of your ability to think clearly, maintain even moods, and behave effectively in a social situation. Keeping your blood sugar balanced and sustained is therefore critical for your brain to operate optimally.

The Amino Acid Cornucopia

The biochemistry of your brain is dependent on obtaining specific nutrients from your diet. Certain amino acids are the crucial building blocks for neurotransmitters, which your body makes by synthesizing these amino acids from the food that you eat. For example, L-glutamine is an amino acid found in foods such as almonds and peaches; when it is digested, your body synthesizes it into the neurotransmitter GABA, which helps you to stay calm. Tyrosine, which is manufactured by your body from the amino acid phenylamine, is a building block for the neurotransmitters epinephrine, norepinephrine, and dopamine. It is also an important building block of the thyroid hormone thyroxine.

Choline, which is found in egg yolks, serves as the raw material for the manufacture of the neurotransmitter acetylcholine. Richard Wurtman of MIT noted many years ago that inadequate choline causes the brain to cannibalize its own neural membrane to obtain enough choline to make acetylcholine. Because inadequate acetylcholine has been associated with memory problems and Alzheimer's disease, some researchers have tried to increase the body's choline level with various types of medications.

Many foods contain the essential amino acids. The table below shows some of the amino acid precursors, their associated neurotransmitters, and a few examples of the foods that contain them.

Amino acids can compete with one another for access to the brain. The brain's barrier allows only a certain amount of particular types of amino acids to pass through at any given time. For example, high-protein meals fail to increase the level of L-tryptophan in the brain because the other amino acids are more abundant in dietary proteins, and these have better access to the brain. This is why eating a high-protein meal in the evening may make it more difficult to sleep. To get a good night's sleep, eat a meal high in complex carbohydrates and relatively lower in protein so that you can get the amount of L-tryptophan you need to sleep well.

If you want good short-term memory and mental sharpness during the day, eat a breakfast or a lunch that is relatively high in protein. Consume foods that contain the amino acid that activates acetylcholine, norepinephrine, and dopamine.

Vitamins and Minerals

The foods that you eat must have a balanced spectrum of vitamins and minerals. Just like amino acids, vitamins and minerals have a direct effect on brain chemistry and the production and/or depletion of neurotransmitters.

Amino Acids and Some Foods That Contain Them

Amino Acid Precursor	Neurotransmitter	Effects	Foods
L-tryptophan	Serotonin	Improves sleep, calmness, and mood	Turkey Milk Whole wheat Pumpkin seeds Cottage cheese Almonds Soybeans
L-glutamine	GABA	Decreases tension and irritability; increases calmness	Eggs Peaches Grape juice Avocado Sunflower seeds Granola Peas
Tyrosine	Dopamine	Increases feelings of pleasure	Fish Oats Wheat Dairy products Chicken Soybeans
L-phenylalanine	Noreprinephrine Dopamine	Increases energy, feelings of pleasure, and memory	Peanuts Lima beans Sesame seeds Chicken Yogurt Milk Soybeans
Choline	Acetylcholine	Memory	Egg yolks

Many different vitamins and minerals are important for your brain. For example, vitamin B_1 (thiamine) turns glucose into fuel for the brain. Low B_1 makes you tired and inattentive. B_1 is particularly vulnerable to depletion by alcohol consumption. Even a glass of wine reduces the absorption of thiamine by your digestive system. Marinating meat in wine, soy sauce, or vinegar depletes 50 to 70 percent of its thiamine content (Winter and Winter, 2007). In addition to having a corrosive effect on thiamine, alcohol has been shown to reduce the levels of serotonin and dopamine.

Vitamin B_3 (niacin) is involved in as many as forty different biochemical reactions in the body and the brain. One of its principal effects is to participate in the process of increasing red blood cells, which carry oxygen to the brain. It also is involved in the pathways for ATP, which, as I mentioned earlier, is the cells' energy substance. In moderate doses B_3 lowers blood cholesterol, and in high doses it causes dilation of the blood vessels, increased blood flow to the brain, and decreased blood pressure.

Niacin can be manufactured from L-tryptophan, which, as I have noted, is a precursor to serotonin. The amount of L-tryptophan that is converted to niacin depends on your diet. Niacin and L-tryptophan should be balanced in your diet.

A severe deficiency of niacin causes a condition called pellagra, which leads to dementia, diarrhea, and dermatitis. The dermatitis symptoms include a condition of extremely red skin.

Here's a little factoid with which you can entertain people at a party: the term *redneck* has its origin in niacin-deficient white field-workers. Due to the deficiency, they developed a red "necklace" on the skin of their necks.

Good Sources of Niacin
- Chicken (white meat)
- Turkey (white meat)
- Chinook salmon
- Whole-wheat bread
- Peanuts
- Lentils

Conditions Caused by Niacin Deficiency
- Headaches
- Insomnia
- Anxiety

- Depression
- Psychosis
- Pellagra

Vitamin B_5 (pantothenic acid) is critical for your adrenal glands, which secrete epinephrine (adrenaline) to convert fat and glucose into energy. A deficiency can cause feelings of malaise and numbness in the feet. B_5 is required to make stress hormones and acetylcholine, which is critical for memory.

Vitamin B_6 (pyridoxine) acts as a partner for more than a hundred different enzymes. It plays a role in the synthesis of serotonin, epinephrine, norepinephrine, and GABA. Estrogen and cortisone deplete B_6. A word of caution: The B_6 content in vegetables is reduced from 57 to 77 percent by freezing them. Thus, if you depend primarily on frozen meals for much of your diet, you should shift to fresh foods.

Vitamin B_9 (folic acid) has received a lot of attention, especially in terms of its importance for pregnant women. A B_9 deficiency during pregnancy can contribute to birth defects such as spina bifida, a neural tube deficit. In general, folic acid is critical for the division and replacement of red blood cells, protein metabolism, and the utilization of glucose.

Vitamin B_{12} is involved in the metabolism of every cell in your body. It affects DNA synthesis and regulation as well as fatty acid synthesis and energy production. If you are a vegan, you should be sure to use supplements, because most sources of B_{12} are animal-based foods. You can find B_{12} in some fortified soy products and in clams, mussels, crab, salmon, eggs, and milk.

One way to keep the brain-damaging amino acid homocysteine in check is through adequate levels of B vitamins—especially folic acid, which breaks it down. Vitamins B_6 and B_{12} help to dispose of homocysteine. Another way to keep homocysteine in check is through the consumption of choline.

Another rarely mentioned B vitamin is B_7 (biotin). Biotin is involved in the metabolism of sugar and the formation of certain fatty acids. Although biotin deficiency is rare, the symptoms include insomnia, mild depression, anxiety, and oversensitivity to pain. Good sources of biotin are egg yolks, liver, peanuts, mushrooms, and cauliflower.

The following charts summarize a sample of B vitamin deficiencies and foods that are high in B vitamins.

Low B_1 Levels	Low B_2 Levels	Low B_6 Levels	Low B_{12} Levels	Low B_9 Levels
↓ Alertness	Trembling	Nervousness	Mental slowness	Memory problems
Fatigue	Sluggishness	Irritability	Confusion	Irritability
Emotional instability	Tension	Depression	Psychosis	Mental sluggishness
↓ Reaction time	Depression	Muscle weakness	Stammering	Depression
Sleep disturbance	Bloodshot eyes	Headache	Weak limbs	
Irritability	↑ Stress	Muscle tingling	Depression	
	Fatigue	Confusion		

High B_1 Foods	High B_2 Foods	High B_6 Foods	High B_{12} Foods	High B_9 Foods
Oatmeal	Liver	Wheat germ	Eggs	Carrots
Peanuts	Cheese	Cantaloupe	Liver	Dark leafy vegetables
Bran	Halibut	Beans	Milk	Cantaloupe
Wheat germ	Salmon	Beef	Beef	Whole wheat
Vegetables	Milk	Liver	Cheese	Apricots
Brewers yeast	Eggs	Whole grains	Kidneys	Carrots
Sunflower seeds	Brewers yeast		Sole	Orange juice
	Wild rice		Crab	

Vitamin C has received a great deal of attention because Linus Pauling regarded it as a cure-all. Common folklore regards it as a preventative for the common cold, but it is critical for many functions, including the prevention of scurvy. In the brain, vitamin C is necessary for the manufacture of norepinephrine (Subramanian, 1980). Vitamin C is one of the principal antioxidants and acts as a scavenger of free radicals.

Vitamin E, another significant antioxidant, has been reported to protect blood vessels and other tissues from oxidation. Vitamin E can reportedly slow down the progression of Alzheimer's disease (Sano, 1997) and lessen the severity of Parkinson's disease.

The brain is a highly efficient and adaptive organ, yet it can create processes that are self-destructive. Stress and bad dietary habits can, for example, produce free radicals, which steal electrons from other molecules and wreak havoc by damaging cells.

The cellular damage that results from free radicals, known as *oxidative stress*, can cause a decrease in energy level as well as cognitive and emotional problems. Oxidative stress and a lack of dietary antioxidants can have a cumulative effect as you age. According to one study, an increase in antioxidants, as measured by blood level, is associated with enhanced memory abilities in older adults.

Fortunately, you have an antioxidant defense system that can gobble up free radicals and even prevent their creation. Consuming antioxidant nutrients such as vitamin E is crucial to maintaining and operating this system.

Vitamin E works by nestling among the various fatty acids and cholesterol molecules. When free radical substances threaten or damage one of the fatty acids, vitamin E traps and neutralizes them before they trigger a chain reaction that damages the cells.

Good Sources of Vitamin E
- Almonds
- Walnuts
- Sweet potatoes
- Sunflower seeds
- Whole wheat
- Wheat germ

When you take omega-3 supplements or consume a lot of fish, vitamin E reverses a process in which fatty acids become rancid. This rancidity can be very damaging to cell membranes (Laganiere and Fernandez, 1987).

Minerals and Phytonutrients

Minerals, too, are important for the healthy functioning of the brain. There are two classes of minerals that are relevant to the brain: macronutrients and micronutrients. The brain contains more macronutrients than micronutrients. The macronutrients include calcium, magnesium, sodium, potassium, and chloride. The micronutrients are also called *trace elements* because they are found in tiny amounts in the brain and the body. They include iron, manganese, copper, iodine, zinc, fluoride, selenium, chromium, aluminum, boron, and nickel. These micronutrients can cause problems when they are found in large amounts in the brain. Aluminum, for instance, has been found in excessive amounts in the brains of people with Alzheimer's disease. Although the question of how aluminum gets into the brain is debatable, it is undebatable that the excessive presence of aluminum is destructive.

Calcium is the most abundant mineral in your brain and serves many functions, including the development of nerve tissue, the maintenance of a regular heartbeat, the formation of blood clots, the strength of bones and teeth, the production of iron, the maintenance of a steady metabolic rate, and the transmission of messages between your neurons. Calcium triggers the release of neurotransmitters and controls synaptic strength. After the neurotransmitters are released, the calcium enhances the strength of subsequent synaptic connections.

Good Sources of Calcium
- Dairy products
- Kidney beans
- Salmon

- Bok choy (Chinese cabbage)
- Almonds
- Broccoli

Magnesium is involved in as many as 350 enzymatic functions in your body. It plays a role in maintaining metabolism, aiding muscle contraction, and supporting liver and kidney functions. Magnesium is important in the conversion of blood sugar into energy and is needed by cells for the creation of genetic material. Magnesium also helps with the absorption of calcium, vitamin C, phosphorous, sodium, and potassium.

Magnesium, like calcium, is involved in the conduction of nerve impulses. A magnesium deficiency contributes to irritability, nervousness, and depression. Magnesium regulates a key receptor in the hippocampus that is important in learning and memory. A proper level of magnesium is essential for maintaining the capacity for neuroplasticity. Magnesium is the gatekeeper for a crucial receptor that receives the excitatory neurotransmitter glutamate. Magnesium helps this receptor to open up for meaningful input, which increases the efficacy of synaptic connections.

Good Sources of Magnesium

- Wheat and oat bran
- Brown rice
- Nuts
- Green vegetables

Iron is involved in the synthesis of serotonin, dopamine, and norepinephrine. It is a cofactor in many enzyme reactions that produce these neurotransmitters. Iron also plays an important role in the enzymes that convert dietary fatty acids into a form that is crucial for the brain.

Phytonutrients are substances that are found in the pigment of many plant foods. Phytonutrients have antioxidant abilities and include substances called *flavonoids* that are found in green tea, soy, apples, blueberries, elderberries, and cherries. This is why blueberries have received so much attention in the popular press.

Researchers have demonstrated that diets rich in blueberries are correlated with improved cognitive and motor functions.

The fruits with the highest oxygen radical absorbing capacity (ORAC)—that is, the capacity to absorb free radicals—are blueberries, blackberries, strawberries, raspberries, and plums, in that order. Plums have less than half the ORAC of blueberries and blackberries.

Nancy's Fat Problem

Nancy came to see me with complaints that she was tired all the time, felt easily stressed, and had memory problems. She thought that she had "some deep buried secrets that needed airing out."

When I asked her why she thought she suffered from a problem buried in the past, she answered, "Because I just feel bad, and there is nothing that should be bothering me. I should be happy. Everything is going great except how I feel."

My first task was to complete a mental-status evaluation to determine whether Nancy was suffering from depression. What became immediately clear, however, was that her diet was extremely poor. She started her day by picking up a fried breakfast burrito at the local fast-food drive-through. At her morning break she would eat a few doughnuts and drink some coffee. For lunch she had chicken nuggets. For an afternoon snack she would eat potato chips or cheese puffs. Her dinner consisted of fried chicken, french fries, fried mozzarella sticks, or some other fried foods.

Nancy had all the symptoms of essential fatty acid deficiency, including the following:

- Dandruff
- Dry skin
- Dry, unmanageable hair
- Brittle, easily frayed nails
- Excessive thirst

I pointed out that if she changed her diet, her energy level would probably increase and many of her symptoms would evaporate.

"What are you, some kind of fanatic?" she demanded. "I know a lot of people who eat the same things. Can't you help me and not get sidetracked?"

I told Nancy that we needed a solid foundation to work from and that her high trans-fatty acid consumption had to be addressed because it undermined her brain's capacity to think clearly and learn anything new through neuroplasticity.

"All right," she conceded, "I'll change my diet after I feel better."

"I don't think you're going to feel better until you make those changes," I informed her. "You need to eliminate all the fried foods."

We agreed that I would teach her some techniques to improve her memory after she added an omega-3 tablet and a vitamin E supplement each day. Cutting out the trans-fatty acids and adding the supplements would promote healthier cells and make neuro-plasticity possible.

After a month, Nancy started to have more energy and was able to think more clearly. Over the next few months, she was increasingly able to use the FEED technique to rewire her brain.

Getting the Right Fats

Nancy's dietary fat problem is actually very common. She didn't have to avoid consuming all fats, just the wrong kinds of fats. Nancy wasn't getting the right fats, like omega-3 essential fatty acids. These are so important that the next time someone calls you a fathead, you should say, "Thanks!" Your brain is actually composed of 60 percent fat. Therefore, you need the right fats to manufacture the cell membranes in your brain—and throughout the rest of your body. These fats are called *lipids* and are specifically a family of lipids that are called *fatty acids*. Fatty acids serve many critical functions, and if you don't get enough of the right fatty acids, your brain will not function optimally.

There are two fatty acids that are considered essential: *linoleic acid* (LA) and *alpha-linolenic acid* (ALA). Essential fatty acids cannot be made by the body; you must consume them in your diet. LA is an omega-6 fatty acid that is contained in vegetable oils, such as safflower, sunflower, corn, and sesame oil. ALA is found in walnuts, flaxseed, and green leafy vegetables. You need to eat both LA and ALA; one cannot produce the other.

A single neuron can make an average of ten thousand synaptic connections with other neurons. Neuroplasticity is dependent on changing your thoughts and your behavior and on the health of your synapses, and the health of your synapses depends on getting the right fats.

The synaptic membrane has a higher concentration of *docosahexaenoic acid* (DHA) than most tissues in your body. DHA is an omega-3 fatty acid found in salmon, mackerel, sardines, herring, anchovies, and bluefish. If you have deficiencies in DHA, the integrity of your synaptic membranes will be impaired; at best, your neurons will not function well, and at worst, they will die.

DHA is critical in keeping cell membranes soft and flexible. Saturated fats, in contrast, make cell membranes rigid. This difference has profound consequences. DHA is important for holding receptors (cells that receive stimuli) in place. Soft and flexible membranes are capable of alternating the shapes of the receptors, which is essential in order for the neurotransmitters to lock into place. If the receptor is made of rigid or hard fat, however, the receptor is immobilized— unable to wiggle or expand to let the neurotransmitter lock into place. Consequently, the interaction between neurons is short-circuited or interrupted. This means that your brain has trouble transmitting information between neurons and developing neuroplasticity.

Researchers at the National Institutes of Health have found a positive relationship between the omega-3 fatty acid DHA and the level of serotonin. The higher the DHA, the higher the serotonin (Hibbelin, 1998). When the fat composition of cell membranes changes, this alters the actions of critical enzymes. For example, essential fatty acids are involved in the conversion of L-tryptophan to serotonin and the control of its breakdown. The body uses DHA to manufacture more synapses with more nerve endings, which in turn produce more serotonin. This makes DHA important in maintaining a stable and positive mood. DHA also plays a role in preventing cognitive decline, especially Alzheimer's disease.

Eicosapentaeonoic acid (EPA), one of the active ingredients in omega-3 fatty acids, has been associated with support for the activities of neurotransmitters such as serotonin and dopamine, and it therefore helps with mood regulation. EPA is found throughout your body, but, unlike DHA, it is not found in the brain in significant amounts. It is found in the same foods that are a source of DHA, but in higher amounts. It plays a role in helping the flow of blood in your brain, influencing inflammation, blood clotting, blood vessel activity, and blood supply.

Another way that essential fatty acids help the brain is to facilitate what is called the *second-messenger system*. This system is activated when a neurotransmitter successfully penetrates the fatty membrane of a cell and sends signals into the nucleus of the cell, where they turn genes on or off. These genes then send chemicals to the outside of the cell, which creates more reactions.

Both EPA and DHA prevent excess *arachidonic acid* (AA), an omega-6 fatty acid, from accumulating in your tissues. Although AA is found throughout your body and brain, you can get too much of it through the fat in beef, pork, chicken, and turkey. AA is a precursor of many highly inflammatory conditions. For instance, high AA intake later in life increases the risk of developing dementia by more than 40 percent (Morris, 2006).

Prostaglandins

When fatty acids are triggered by viruses, bacteria, free radicals, or toxic chemicals, these fatty acids are released from the cell membrane and converted into compounds called *prostaglandins*, hormonelike substances that exert a variety of functions within your brain.

Specific prostaglandins are formed from dietary fatty acids through a series of steps. There are three prostaglandins (PGs) that you should know about:

1. **PGE1:** Formed from the dietary LA found in sunflower, corn, safflower, and sesame oils, PGE1 is important in the release of neurotransmitters. It possesses some anti-inflammatory

　　properties, reduces fluid accumulation, and enhances the immune system.

2. **PGE2:** Formed largely by the AA in animal fats, PGE2 is rarely found in plants. It is a highly inflammatory substance and causes swelling and increased sensitivity to pain. PGE2 can cause increased blood viscosity (which decreases blood flow), blood platelet clumping (which increases blood clotting), and spasms in the blood vessels. It can also cause an overactive immune system, which attacks the body and brain.

3. **PGE3:** Formed from the ALA found in flaxseed, walnuts, and pumpkin seeds, PGE3 is somewhat anti-inflammatory and immune-enhancing. It counters many of the effects of PGE2.

A dietary imbalance in fats alters brain activity and can cause multiple problems with the blood supply to the brain, including the following:

- Poor tone in the blood vessel walls
- Blood vessel spasms
- Increasing blood viscosity, causing the blood to be sludgelike and form clots

All the factors that impede the flow of blood to the brain interfere with the delivery of oxygen and nutrients to the brain cells. This decreases your clarity of thinking, dampens your mood, and slows down your behavioral responses.

An omega-6 fatty acid known as gamma-linolenic acid (GLA) is used in forming brain structure, even though it is not a brain fat itself. Nevertheless, GLA appears to help in neurological conditions when it is converted into PGE1, which can reduce the production of inflammatory conditions caused by excessive AA. Some people with multiple sclerosis who have been treated with GLA derived from primrose oil have been reported to have fewer symptoms.

High levels of isoprostanes, the free radical products of damaged fatty acids that were mentioned earlier in this chapter, are found in the cerebral spinal fluid, the plasma, and the urine of people with brain-related cognitive impairment, including Alzheimer's disease. The higher level of isoprostanes that is found in people with Alzheimer's disease implies that these substances are a possible predictor of the disease.

An increase in isoprostanes has also been found in the cerebrospinal fluid of children with traumatic brain injury. One study found that the level of isoprostanes was nine times higher one day after the injury than in people without brain injury.

Studies are increasingly showing that omega-3 fatty acids can lower the oxidative stress (the cellular damage that results from free radicals) and the inflammation that are associated with neurological and psychiatric conditions. Omega-3 has also been shown to promote the critical neural chemical BDNF, which, as you learned in chapter 1, plays an essential role in neuroplasticity and is a neuroprotective agent, a sort of Miracle Grow for brain cells. It is critical for memory and new learning, and a low level of BDNF has been associated with neurological and psychiatric conditions. Both inflammation and oxidative stress interfere with BDNF production.

Essential fatty acids balance the influences of cytokine activity. *Cytokines* are proteins, peptides (a derivative of amino acids), and glycoproteins (proteins with carbohydrates). When essential fatty acids are not balanced, cytokines can cause inflammation and turn your immune system against your own cells, attacking and killing them. An increase in cytokines has been associated with depression, anxiety, and cognitive problems.

The brain has both gray matter and white matter. The gray matter contains the neurons, whereas the white matter contains *glial cells*, which are more numerous than neurons and are regarded as support cells. Glial cells coat the nerve fibers, and this coating is called *myelin*. Along with its many other functions, myelin makes your neurons fire more efficiently. Myelin is made up of various fats, fatty acids, phospholipids (see below), and cholesterol. As much as 75 percent of myelin is fat.

Cholesterol makes up one-fourth of myelin and is essential for its development. Contrary to the oversimplified bad rap that cholesterol has received in popular culture, one type of cholesterol is actually good. High-density lipoprotein (HDL) is considered good cholesterol. Low-density lipoprotein (LDL) is considered bad cholesterol.

When myelin is inadequate or damaged, this impedes the nerve impulses. Damaged myelin is a factor in multiple sclerosis. This devastating neurological disease results in multiple impairments, including an inability to walk, memory problems, and depression.

Phospholipids

Phospholipids are another family of brain fats. They are actually both fat and mineral: *phospho* refers to the mineral phosphorus and *lipid* refers to fat molecules. Phospholipids are important in forming nerve membranes and protecting them from toxic injury and free radical attack.

The phospholipid *phosphatidylserine* (PS) is one of the structural molecules of the nerve cell membranes. PS is formed when the phospholipid complex combines with the amino acid serine. PS influences the fluidity of the nerve cell membranes and fosters the incorporation of membrane proteins that bind neurotransmitters in the brain. A good source of PS is soy.

Another phospholipid, *phosphatidylcholine* (PC), is an important part of the nerve cell membrane, because it manufactures acetylcholine. The common name for PC is lecithin. Lecithin is found in eggs and soy. It can also be bought in granulated form and sprinkled on your food, and vegans often use it as a substitute for eggs in recipes.

Lecithin has been reported to keep the level of the amino acid homocysteine in check. A high level of homocysteine has been associated with a number of degenerative diseases (Smith, 2006; Sehub, Jacques, Bostom, D'Agostino, Wilson, Belanger, et al., 1995). It contributes to the clotting of the blood vessel linings and the development of plaque in the arteries. It can also block the synthesis of neurotransmitters and trigger metabolic changes that injure the neurons.

Each type of neurotransmitter is released by the cell membrane, floats across the gap between the neurons (the synapse), and links with a receptor site like a key in a lock. The receptors are held in place by phospholipids and fatty acids. If the structures of the phospholipids and the fatty acids are damaged or are poorly formed (changed in shape), the receptor can't receive the neurotransmitter. It's partly for this reason that fatty acid supplements have been shown to improve the action of antidepressant medications.

Diet, Fats, and Depression

In the past century, the amounts of essential fatty acids consumed in the typical American diet have declined by more than 80 percent (Schmidt, 2007; Rudin, 1985). Moreover, the types of fats have changed for the worse, with an increase in animal fats, vegetable oils, and processed foods. The balance of fats has also changed dramatically: although there was once a balance between omega-6 and omega-3, that ratio has been skewed to 30:1. The vast reduction in omega-3 fatty acid consumption has occurred for the following reasons:

- The reduction of cereal germ (which contains essential fatty acids) by current milling practices
- Decreased fish consumption
- A 2,500 percent increase in trans-fatty acid consumption (which interferes with essential fatty acid synthesis)
- A 250 percent increase in sugar intake (which interferes with the enzymes of essential fatty acid synthesis)
- An increase in the consumption of LA oils (corn, sesame, safflower, sunflower)
- The hydrogenation of oils in commercial processing

Studies throughout the world have shown that there is a link between the levels of fatty acids and depression. For example, a study of 3,884 patients in Rotterdam, the Netherlands, found that the higher the ratio of omega-6 to omega-3, the higher the rate of depression. The researchers concluded that an adequate level of omega-3 is associated with positive moods.

In Melbourne, Australia, a similar correspondence was found between the ratio of omega-6 to omega-3 and the incidence of depression. As the omega-6 level was elevated over the omega-3 level, there was a corresponding increase in the symptoms of depression.

Similar results were found in a study in Belgium: people with depression had a higher ratio of omega-6 to omega-3. Supplementing one's diet with omega-3 has been a consistent recommendation in all these studies.

An elevated level of triglycerides (a group of lipids) has also been found to be associated with an increase in depression, whereas lowering the triglyceride level is associated with the alleviation of depression.

Nancy's old diet is unfortunately all too common, as she pointed out the first time I met her. The relatively recent increase in fried foods in the American diet has created multiple health problems, including obesity, cardiovascular problems, and compromised brain functions.

When an unsaturated fat is heated for a long time in a metal container, such as occurs with deep frying in fast-food restaurants, trans-fatty acids are formed. These are altered fats. In contrast to essential fatty acids, which are curved and flexible and thus help the nerve cell membranes to maintain their electrical properties, trans-fatty acids are straight, tend to be solid at body temperature, and act like saturated fat. This makes them more rigid and inflexible, which makes them interfere with the normal functional properties of the nerve cell membranes.

Researchers have shown that when trans-fatty acids are accompanied by a low level of omega-3 ALA, the absorption of trans-fatty acids by the brain doubles. Also, when the level of trans-fatty acids is high, omega-3 DHA is replaced by a poor substitute called *docosapentaenoic acid* (DPA) (Petersen and Opstvedt, 1992). This substitution occurs with excessive alcohol consumption, excessive omega-6 consumption, or insufficient essential fatty acids (especially DHA and ALA).

Common sources of trans-fatty acids are foods prepared with partially hydrogenated oils, such as the following:

- Cookies
- Doughnuts
- Potato chips
- Candy
- Mayonnaise
- Vegetable shortening
- Crackers
- Cake
- Deep-fried foods
- Cheese puffs
- Margarine
- Some salad dressings

Trans-fatty acids create major problems for the brain. They can do the following:

1. Be absorbed directly by the nerve membranes
2. Block the body's ability to make its own essential fatty acids that are so critical for the brain
3. Alter the synthesis of neurotransmitters such as dopamine
4. Negatively effect the brain's blood supply
5. Increase bad (LDL) cholesterol while decreasing good (HDL) cholesterol
6. Increase plaque in the blood vessels
7. Increase blood clots
8. Increase triglycerides, which cause the blood to be sluggish and reduces the amount of oxygen to the brain
9. Cause excess body fat, which can have a destructive effect on the brain

A twenty-four-year follow-up study in Sweden found that the larger the body mass index (BMI), the greater the risk of developing Alzheimer's disease. Researchers in Korea found that an increase in BMI has an inverse relationship to cognitive ability as measured by the Mini Mental Status Exam.

Belly fat appears to generate inflammation. In contrast to the old view that fat cells are dormant and inactive storage units, it appears that they release the same inflammatory chemicals (such as cytokines) that your body releases when you have an infection or have been traumatized with injuries. Cytokines are associated with inflammation and depression, and they lower the level of BDNF, the protector of nerve cells and the promoter of neuroplasticity.

A study of overweight adolescents showed that as body fat increased, so did the level of inflammatory chemicals, which are associated with cognitive deficits and depression.

A study of four thousand patients at Rush University Medical Center in Chicago examined the relationship among trans-fatty acids, saturated fats, copper, and cognitive decline. An increase in the level of copper in the body was found to be associated with cognitive decline, but only if the intake of trans-fatty acids and saturated fats was high.

Brain fats have to be nourished and protected. Since brain fats can be damaged by oxidative stress (free radical damage), they rely on a network of antioxidants for protection. Antioxidant nutrients and enzymes keep stray electrons from damaging the delicate unsaturated fatty acids of the cell membranes.

In Finland, approximately eighteen hundred people were assessed for depression. Those who consumed fish twice a week or more significantly reduced their depressive symptoms and suicidal thoughts.

A study in Japan of 256,118 people who consumed fish daily found them to have a lower suicide rate than people who consumed less fish (Tanskanen, Hibbeln, Hintikka, Haatainen, Honkalampi, and Vjinamaki, 2001). Among those who had attempted suicide, low levels of EPA were strongly correlated with impulsivity, guilt, and future suicide risk.

Healthy brain functioning depends on keeping brain chemistry at healthy levels and eating a balanced diet. A balanced diet can be the optimal foundation for your thoughts and emotions. Notice that I said *can be*, not *is*. That's because a healthy diet only lays the foundation. You can rewire your brain and build on this foundation by changing your behavior and your thoughts.

6

Healthy Habits: Exercise and Sleep

Tim came to see me for help with his insomnia. He said, "I hear that you help people get their brains back into sync. Mine is way out of sync." He had been experiencing increased stress at work and at home. His company was downsizing, which meant that he had to do the work of two people. He dared not complain, because the last thing he wanted to do was to draw attention to himself and be targeted in the next round of layoffs.

Even worse, his pay had been cut by 10 percent. This enraged his wife, because she had to go back to work so that they could pay the college tuitions for their two daughters. The added tension in the house spilled over into the evening when he tried to relax in order to go to sleep.

Tim looked both sleep-deprived and physically tense during our first session. I asked him how he was coping with all the stress at work.

"I can't keep myself focused and awake," he replied. "Five cups of coffee in the afternoon just doesn't cut it." He told me that he spent his evenings on the computer searching for jobs, just in case he was laid off.

Though in his mid-forties, Tim looked to be in his mid-fifties and carried quite an abdominal bulge. When I expressed concern about his health, he responded, with a sarcastic laugh, "That's the last of my worries. I need to get myself off this sinking ship. My health can wait."

When I suggested that improving his health might help him to get off the sinking ship, he almost jumped out of the chair and left my office.

Tim reflected on his options for a few moments, then shrugged his shoulders to indicate that he would make an effort. We started exploring ways that he could promote better sleep. The first thing he wanted was sleep medication. When I told him about all the side effects of these medications, which include difficulty concentrating the next day, he said, "I need sleep! What am I supposed to do? Drinking two glasses of wine doesn't seem to help."

When I asked if he woke up in the middle of the night only to find it difficult to get back to sleep, he looked at me, perplexed, and asked, "How did you know?"

"That's a hallmark symptom of drinking alcohol in the evening," I informed him.

"So what am I supposed to do?" he asked, exasperated.

"Let's start by stopping the things that make your insomnia worse." I told him that the coffee in the afternoon and the alcohol in the evening had to go. In addition, his computer use in the evening had to be curtailed.

"Get real!" he exclaimed, shaking his head.

I explained that his brain was picking up the light signals from the computer through his retina, and that these light signals were tricking his brain into functioning as if it were daytime rather than nighttime, suppressing the production of the sleeping hormone melatonin. He looked less perplexed and more curious.

Next I told him that he needed to promote a cooler body temperature during the night. One powerful way to do that, and burn off the extra cortisol that was circulating in his system, was to exercise three to six hours before he went to sleep.

"But I'm too exhausted at the end of the day!" he protested.

I explained that he would get an antianxiety benefit from the exercise as well as a boost of energy reserve for the next day. He would be far more energized and focused, and his stress tolerance would be greatly enhanced.

"What about rewiring my brain?" he asked, as if we had planned to simply put a bandage on his problems.

"Exercise and sleep not only get you back into a healthy cycle but also go a long way to set up the conditions for neuroplasticity and neurogenesis," I concluded.

In today's fast-paced society, we have developed habits like Tim's that make neurogenesis and neuroplasticity less possible. We exercise far less and consume far more calories than our ancestors did. Meanwhile, we have also increased our consumption of trans-fatty acids and saturated fats. In short, we are growing fatter, thus contributing to the sleep problems. This alarming trend—combined with the world of commuter traffic and multitasking with text messaging, constant cell phone calls, e-mails, and sensationalistic media bombardment—adds up to an increase in cortisol levels that is having a corrosive effect on the brain. The effects of insomnia and being out of shape are taking their toll.

Exercise and the Brain

Getting in shape always sounds good in theory, but engaging in regular exercise is too often relegated to something you do only when it's convenient. In this section I'll explain why it should be structured into your day as a must. There is no better way to jump-start neuroplasticity and neurogenesis.

Exercise provides an immediate treatment for the physical and emotional symptoms associated with stress. Exercise relaxes the resting tension of muscle spindles, and this breaks the stress-feedback loop to the brain. By breaking up this stress-feedback loop, you cue your brain that your body isn't stressed anymore, so it must be okay to relax.

Exercise was once thought to benefit health simply because it helped circulation and the heart. In recent years, researchers have not only confirmed that initial belief but have also shown that exercise pumps more oxygen through the brain, which increases the health of the small blood vessels called capillaries.

Exercise promotes lower blood pressure by increasing the efficiency of the cardiovascular system. As the heart rate increases a hormone called *atrial natriuretic peptide* (ANP) is produced by your heart. ANP tempers your body's stress response by putting the brakes on the HPA axis and its fight-or-flight response.

ANP does this by going through the blood-brain barrier and attaching to receptors in the hypothalamus to tone down the HPA axis activity. Meanwhile, other areas of your brain, including the amygdala, produce ANP. ANP works against the CRF, a term I introduced in chapter 2, which is part of the chain of neurochemical processes that induce the fight-or-flight response and panic. In this way ANP eliminates one of the main contributors to panic. It also stems the flow of epinephrine (adrenaline) and lowers the heart rate, defusing another trigger for panic symptoms. All this ANP activity helps you feel calmer.

Aerobic exercise can have an antianxiety effect. The physiological changes that occur by exercising can overpower the negative effects of the physiological contributors to anxiety. For example, in one study, the subjects were injected with CCK-4, a chemical that can induce a panic attack even in healthy adults with no history of panic. Thirty minutes of aerobic exercise prior to the injection of CCK-4 lowered the panic scores, whereas resting before the injection did not.

Exercise contributes to stress reduction by doing the following:

- Providing a distraction
- Reducing muscle tension
- Building brain resources (neuroplasticity and neurogenesis)
- Increasing GABA and serotonin
- Improving resilience and self-mastery
- Mobilizing feelings in order to take action

One study showed that a twelve-session aerobic exercise program reduced some of the symptoms of PTSD. This is significant, because the symptoms of PTSD are long-lasting and intermittent.

Exercise should be part of the overall strategy of preventing and treating general anxiety and PTSD. Exercise increases the levels of the specific neurotransmitters that promote antianxiety and anti-depressant effects. One of the ways it does this is by increasing the neurotransmitters GABA and serotonin. Simply moving your body triggers the release of GABA, your brain's primary inhibitory neu-rotransmitter. Antianxiety medications like Valium and Ativan target GABA receptors to calm you down, but those medications have ter-rible side effects, including depression, and they are very addictive. Once you remove the medication, the anxiety symptoms return—and at an increased level.

Serotonin, which has been associated with depression and anxi-ety when it is at a low level, is increased by exercise. An increase in serotonin level occurs when your body breaks down fatty acids to fuel your muscles. These fatty acids compete with the amino acid L-tryptophan (the precursor to serotonin) for a place on the transport proteins that increase fatty-acid concentration in the bloodstream. Once L-tryptophan pushes through the blood-brain barrier, it is synthesized into serotonin. Serotonin also gets a boost from BDNF, which also increases with exercise.

In *Spark: The Revolutionary New Science of Exercise and the Brain,* John Ratey points out that regular aerobic exercise calms the body so that it can prepare to deal with more stress. Aerobic exer-cise raises the threshold of physical reactions. It helps the brain by fortifying the infrastructure of the nerve cells by activating the genes that produce specific proteins that protect the cells from damage and disease.

Exercise also raises the stress threshold of neurons. Some people complain that exercise makes them tired; I respond by saying that's a good thing. In fact, you should want to get tired when you exer-cise, because then you know that you're gaining from it. You're pushing your body beyond its comfort level to strengthen it. Ratey points out that exercise promotes a stress-and-recovery process that strengthens the body and the brain. At the cellular level, this stress-and-recovery process occurs on three fronts:

- Oxidation
- Metabolism
- Excitation

Oxidative stress occurs in the cells during the conversion of glucose into energy that enables the cells to burn fuel. Waste by-products are produced when glucose is absorbed into the cells. The *mitochondria*, which are the energy factories of cells, turn the glucose into *adenosine triphosphate* (ATP), the principal type of fuel that a cell can burn. This conversion process produces free radicals, which I discussed in chapter 5. Normally, the cell produces protective enzymes as internal antioxidants that mop up the waste products.

Metabolic stress occurs when the cells can't produce enough ATP. It's as if they run out of gas. This happens because glucose can't get into the cell or because there is not enough glucose. Finally, *excitotoxic stress* (a condition destructive to neurons) occurs when there is not enough ATP to keep up with the increased energy demands of excessive glutamate activity.

Fortunately, exercise promotes repair mechanisms that deal with the different types of stress. These repair mechanisms promote recovery and strengthen the entire body, including the brain. This stress-and-recovery process goes beyond strengthening to actually rebuilding on multiple levels.

The names of the most powerful repair molecules look like a virtual alphabet soup, but what they do is profound. For example, exercise spurs into action the following brain-enhancing hormones:

- Insulin-like growth factor (IGF-1)
- Vascular endothelial growth factor (VEGF)
- Fibroblast growth factor (FGF-2)

IGF-1 is a hormone released by the muscles when there is a need for fueling the cells during a physical activity. It increases the production of receptors for insulin. Since glucose is the major energy source in the brain, IGF-1 works with insulin to deliver it to the brain cells and manage glucose levels. It teams up with BDNF, which increases in the brain during exercise, and together they activate neurons to produce more serotonin and glutamate. Although chronic stress increases cortisol and lowers IGF-1, exercise reverses that trend.

Getting fuel to the cells is critical, and exercise is a method by which to construct and enhance the blood vessels. VEGF comes to the rescue by building more capillaries in the body and the brain. VEGF increases the permeability of the blood-brain barrier, which allows substances vital to neurogenesis into the brain during exercise.

Finally, FGF-2 is critical for neurogenesis. It helps tissues to grow in the body, and while it is in the brain it aids in LTP (Ratey, 2008).

All together, these repair factors prevent the damaging effects of chronic stress, keep the stress hormone cortisol in check, and increase the regulatory neurotransmitters (serotonin, dopamine, and norepinephrine) that keep you calm, positive, and energized.

Exercise has also been shown to stimulate several genetic processes that enhance the health, longevity, and immunological functions of the brain. Exercise-stimulated transcription—the genetic process of constructing RNA from DNA—aids neuroplasticity, including the stimulation of BDNF, which enhances memory and promotes neurogenesis in the hippocampus.

When blood circulation increases during exercise, the BDNF that had gathered in reserve pools near the synapses is unleashed. During exercise, IGF-1, VEGF, and FGF-2 push through the blood-brain barrier, through the web of capillaries, and through the tightly packed cells that screen out intruders such as bacteria. These three hormones work with BDNF to increase the molecular processes that sharpen cognition and memory.

Stem cells can divide into neurons or glial cells through a process enhanced by exercise. However, exercise alone won't sustain the new neurons. Research has shown that exercise plus an enriched environment will allow you to keep the new neurons. In other words, you need mental exercise in addition to the physical exercise to maintain the new neurons. Perhaps this is why some professional athletes are bright and some are less than bright.

It has been shown that physical exercise, especially if it takes place in a new and stimulating environment, is an effective way to promote neurogenesis. Learning is critical because the development of new neurons takes place in the section of the hippocampus that is involved in new learning (memory). Thus, physical exercise and learning work together to stimulate neurogenesis. Exercise makes new stem cells, and learning prolongs their survival. The best exercise therefore combines a cardiovascular boost and learning a new skill.

Voluntary exercise seems to get the best results, because it is marked by the absence of stress and the inclusion of theta brain waves, which are present when you pay close attention to something. Theta waves are not present when you eat or drink or are functioning on automatic pilot. Voluntary exercise is not something you do mindlessly, out of habit; it is something you decide to do. Since your frontal lobe does the deciding, activating this part of your brain is a key part of neurogenesis. In other words, you can't learn something new unless you make an effort and you are paying attention.

In summary, there is abundant evidence that exercise can help you to learn, but the benefit occurs after exercising, not during. This is because during high-intensity exercise, the blood is directed away from the PFC to enable the body to deal with the physical challenge. Because the PFC is the brain's brain—the center of executive functions—it is necessary for learning. After you finish exercising, the blood shifts back to your frontal lobes, and with it you get an increased capacity for focus. Thus, as John Ratey suggests, don't study for the Law School Admission Test while you're on an elliptical machine at the gym. Wait to study until after your exercise session to get the full benefit.

How can exercise be included in a school curriculum to help the students boost their learning skills? One example has emerged just west of Chicago in the Naperville school system, which initiated an exercise program in its curriculum in an effort to boost academic performance and prosocial behaviors. When the eighth-grade class took the Trends in International Mathematics and Science Study (an international standards test that 230,000 students around the world also took), the class finished first on the science section and sixth on the math section (after Singapore, Korea, Taiwan, Hong Kong, and Japan). To put these gains into perspective, note that 50 percent of students in those Asian countries usually score in the top tier, whereas only 7 percent of U.S. students reach that mark. Thus, the Naperville students scored significantly above the norm for the United States.

Many factors account for these findings. One could be that only 6 percent of U.S. high schools offer physical education, or gym class. Another factor could be that American children spend an average of five hours a day in front of a computer, a TV, or a handheld screen.

The benefit of exercise on learning has garnered the attention of some state education departments. The California Department of Education has shown that students with higher fitness scores also have higher test scores, and it has also shown an overall positive influence on memory, concentration, and behavior in the classroom.

Exercise Medicine

Exercise is good medicine, and a lack of exercise is bad medicine. Evidence for the variety of health benefits of exercise has been accumulating for more than fifty years.

Exercise has been shown to lower inflammatory chemicals. For example, in an extensive study that examined the records of 13,748 people over the age of twenty, it was shown that exercise can lower the inflammation chemical C-reactive protein (CRP). The greater the amount of exercise, the lower the level of CRP. Only 8 percent of those who engaged in vigorous exercise had elevated CRP, whereas 21 percent of those who did not exercise had elevated CRP. This benefit can occur at all ages. When eight hundred men and women between the ages of seventy and seventy-nine were examined, both moderate and strenuous exercise were associated with lower levels of CRP.

Although a lack of exercise negatively affects stem cells in the brain and their differentiation into new neurons, so does excessive exercise. In contrast, both moderate and vigorous exercise support their development. The lesson here is that the extremes of no exercise or excessive exercise do not promote a healthy brain. Exercise moderately and vigorously.

Exercise and the Brain

Mechanism	Impact
Gene expression	↑ Neuroplasticity (Cotman and Berchtold, 2002).
BDNF	↑ Neuroplasticity (Adlard, Perreau, and Cotman, 2005)
IGF-1	↑ Neural protection (Carro, Trejo, Busiguina, and Torres-Aleman, 2001)
Nerve growth factor	↑ Neuroplasticity (Neeper, Gomez-Pinilla, Choi, and Cotman, 1996)
VEGF	↑ Neurogenesis (Fabel, Fabel, Tam, Kaufer, Baiker, Simmons, et al., 2003)
Hippocampus	↑ Available neurogenesis (Van Praag, Shubert, Zhao, and Gage, 2005)
LTP	↑ Connectivity (Farmer, Zhao, van Praag, Wodtke, Gage, and Christie, 2004)
Capillary growth	↑ Available oxygen and glucose (Swain, Harris, Wiener, Dutka, Morris, Theien, et al., 2003)

Even just *thinking* about exercise activates the same neuronal systems in your brain. The effects of mentally exercising were compared to the effects of actually exercising by observing cortical activity and subsequent physical performance. Mental practice not only creates changes in the brain but also improves physical performance.

The same parts of the brain are activated during mental practice and actual physical practice. This finding led the researchers to see if mental practicing improved subsequent actual physical performance. They found that five days of mental practice followed by two hours of physical practice improved performance as well as five days of physical practice did!

These findings support the long-held belief in sports psychology that visualizing and mentally rehearsing one's performance can improve that performance on the playing field. This is true regardless of the sport.

Although you may find that the faster you can imagine doing something, the faster you can actually do it, there are limitations to what is possible. This is because the mind and the brain are two aspects of the same process. For example, if you are right-handed, you'll be better at both imagining moving and actually moving your right hand than at imagining and moving your left hand.

This constraint occurs even if you have had a stroke and one side of your body is weaker. The side that was not affected is as quick in imagining moving as well as in actually moving. This is because you are using the same brain systems in imagining moving and actually moving.

Regulating Your Sleep

Sleep has been studied extensively for more than eighty years. Since the 1930s, researchers have been able to identify the types and the stages of sleep.

The first stage of sleep is actually a transition state between waking and sleeping. Here the brain waves are fast. If you wake up from this stage of sleep, you'll probably report that you were not really asleep.

The second stage of sleep is light, with theta brain waves. Many insomnia patients complain that they do not sleep, when in fact they are experiencing this stage of sleep. You spend half of the night in light sleep. During periods of stress, this stage increases relative to the next stage.

Stages 3 and 4 are considered deep sleep. In this phase you produce slow brain waves, or delta waves. Deep sleep gives your immune system a boost while allowing your bodily functions to slow down. If you are deprived of deep sleep, your immune system tends to be suppressed, and your body will ache. Stress increases the release of norepinephrine and epinephrine, which decrease the amount of slow-wave sleep. If you are sleep-deprived, the first stage of sleep to rebound is deep sleep, indicating its importance to your overall health.

A stage of sleep called rapid eye movement (REM) sleep is the stage at which people who are awakened report vivid dreams. REM sleep decreases as you age. In REM, most of your body functions are at an almost wakeful level of activation. Your metabolism goes up during REM sleep, and energizing neurotransmitters are active. REM sleep is also called *paradoxical sleep* for this reason. You may dream that you're running, and most of your organs will function as if you are doing exactly that.

Although you generally go through an REM period every ninety minutes, most REM sleep occurs later in the sleep cycle. It constitutes 25 percent of sleep time in healthy adults.

The Sleep Cycle, or Circadian Rhythm

Sleep is affected by daylight and darkness. Light comes in through the eyes, and the retina sends the information to the pineal gland, which is positioned in the middle of the brain. The pineal gland responds to light by suppressing the production of melatonin, convincing the brain that it is daytime and not the time to become sedated. When it's dark, the retina sends information to the pineal gland that it should produce melatonin to induce sedation. This cycle is called the *circadian rhythm*.

Since the amount of light you are exposed to during the day affects your sleep, you should maximize your exposure to bright light in the daytime in order to set your circadian rhythm to match the natural day-night cycle of the world around you. If you suffer from insomnia, don't use a computer in the late evening, because you're essentially looking at light. The light of a computer screen will trick your brain into adjusting to a daytime pattern. Since your circadian rhythm can become maladapted to the actual day-night cycle, you need soft light a few hours before going to sleep.

Your circadian rhythm is tied not only to the exposure to light but also to your body temperature. Ideally, when you go to sleep at night, your body temperature should be in the process of dropping. Just before you get out of bed in the morning, your body temperature is on the rise. As you get out of bed and expose yourself to light and move around, you promote a further rise in your body temperature.

If you have insomnia, you may have difficulty regulating your body temperature. Your body temperature may actually increase at night when it should be going down. This can occur if you fail to get any exercise in the daytime. By exercising during the day, you can promote a dip in your body temperature at night.

Sleep and the Brain

Sleep is critical for the maintenance of the brain. If you do not get an adequate amount of regular sleep, there are multiple deficits. For example, sleep has been shown to be crucial for certain genetic processes, protein synthesis, and myelin formation. Without myelin, the neurons do not fire efficiently. Sleep is also critical for the synthesis and transport of cholesterol, which forms a significant portion of myelin.

Sleep deprivation can lead to weight gain, even after just one week, because of an increase in the production of the hormone ghrelin, which promotes appetite and food intake. Simultaneously, there is a decline in the production of the hormone leptin, which curbs appetite. The increase in appetite associated with sleep loss tends to be for starchy, high-carbohydrate foods, sweets, and other high-calorie foods. Consumption of these foods by sleep-deprived people can be 33–45 percent greater than by people who are not sleep-deprived. This increase in appetite does not seem to be for fruits, vegetables, or high protein foods.

Sleep deprivation has been shown to compromise attention, new learning, and memory. The longer you endure sleep deprivation, the more compromised these essential functions become. One of the most revolutionary findings in neuroscience was the recent discovery that new neurons can grow in a certain area of the hippocampus. Studies have shown that sleep deprivation impairs the ability of these stem cells to grow and become new neurons.

Synaptic consolidation (strengthening of synaptic connections) is critical for the formation of memories. During sleep, unstable memory traces are reconfigured into more permanent ones for long-term storage (Frank, Issa, and Stryker, 2001). Thus, during sleep the experiences of the day are reactivated and consolidated.

The saying "Why don't you sleep on it?" actually reflects wisdom. Not only do you arise with a new vitality in the morning; your enlarged and fresh perspective is also based on having consolidated important memories from the previous day. It's from this extension of the neuroplastic process—begun during the day and extended through sleep—that you can arrive at new insights. In fact, throughout history there have been anecdotal stories of great insights being gained after a good night's sleep.

For example, this is how the Russian chemist Dmitry Mendeleyev conceived the idea of organizing the elements by atomic weight into the Periodic Table. German pharmacologist Otto Loewi, winner of the 1936 Nobel Prize in Physiology and Medicine, reported that he woke during the middle of the night with the insight of how neurons communicate through the chemical messengers we now call neurotransmitters.

Avoiding Insomnia

Some people try to improve their sleep by using techniques that actually exacerbate their sleep problems. Virtually everyone has had insomnia at least once in their lives, and for many it's an ongoing problem. Approximately half the population reports trouble sleeping once a week, and 15 percent have trouble sleeping two or more nights a week. Sleep problems are especially common among people who are experiencing anxiety or depression. If you're tense and preoccupied, it's difficult to unwind enough to fall asleep. Stress raises the levels of the activating neurotransmitters norepinephrine, epinephrine, and cortisol, which normally subside at night. If you experience stress, anxiety, or depression, you may keep yourself charged up and tense by thinking about what is waiting for you the next day.

Many factors contribute to insomnia, including aging, medical conditions, and drugs. As we age, the quality of our sleep deteriorates. There are also several lifestyle and environmental factors that contribute to insomnia, such as the following:

- Poor air quality in the bedroom
- High body temperature
- Caffeine
- Nicotine
- Alcohol
- Sugar
- Heavy meals before bedtime
- Hunger
- Exercise just before bedtime
- No exercise at all
- Daytime naps
- Computer use in the late evening
- Warm bedroom
- Sporadic and novel noise
- Light

Caffeine causes insomnia because it blocks the adenosine receptors in the brain. Adenosine is a sleep promoter, especially for slow-wave (deep) sleep.

Alcohol leads to a reduction in deep sleep and REM sleep. It can also contribute to awakening in the middle of the sleep cycle because the alcohol is wearing off. It has been estimated that 10 percent of all sleep problems are caused by alcohol. If you have sleep problems and you drink, you should stop drinking several hours before bedtime or not drink at all.

If you typically wake up very early in the morning and can't get back to sleep, you should expose yourself to bright light in the early morning. This will ensure that your pineal gland will not produce melatonin throughout the day and that your body temperature will be at its lowest when you sleep. If you wake up in the middle of the night and can't get back to sleep, you should expose yourself to bright light in the late morning. This will encourage a lower body temperature in the middle of the sleep cycle and promote staying asleep.

Medical Conditions Associated with Insomnia

- Fibromyalgia
- Huntington's disease
- Kidney disease
- Cancer
- Asthma
- Hypertension

- Hyperthyroidism
- Parkinson's disease
- Epilepsy

- Heart disease
- Bronchitis
- Arthritis

Some medications have been found to cause insomnia. Unfortunately, many physicians do not take the time to warn their patients that insomnia is a side effect of the medications they prescribe.

Some Medications That Contribute to Insomnia

- Decongestants
- Corticosteroids
- Diuretics
- Heart medications

- Parkinson's medications
- Asthma medications
- Appetite suppressants
- Kidney medications

Sleep Hygiene

There are several methods for improving sleep, including exercise, proper diet, light exposure during the day, and a cool bedroom. Researchers at Stanford University studied the effect of exercise on sleep in adults ages fifty-five to seventy-five and found that those who exercised for twenty to thirty minutes in the afternoon reduced the time that it took to go to sleep by one-half. Two meta-analyses have shown that exercise can increase overall sleep quality. These studies showed that exercise promotes not only an increase in sleep time but also an increase in slow-wave, deep sleep.

Exercising three to six hours before bedtime enhances sleep because it elevates the heart rate and the body temperature but also allows time to return to baseline before bedtime. Aerobic exercise has a calming and antidepressant effect that also promotes sleep.

Similarly, it's a good sleep-promoting practice to keep your body temperature cool at night. A cool bedroom promotes the deepest sleep. Warm bedrooms, in contrast, promote light sleep. Hot baths can be helpful as a winding-down activity. The body temperature is raised in the tub, but it drops sharply by bedtime.

Diet also has a major effect on your sleep. Foods rich in L-tryptophan (an amino acid that converts to serotonin) contribute to sedation, whereas protein-rich foods (such as fish) make you less sleepy. Protein increases the plasma-rich, large, neutral amino acids.

Simple carbohydrates (such as white bread) are not helpful for those who have sleep problems, but complex carbohydrates (such as whole-wheat bread) are helpful. This is because simple carbohydrates increase insulin, lead to a brief increase in L-tryptophan, and ultimately increase serotonin, but the conversion of L-tryptophan to serotonin is on a short-term basis only. Simple carbohydrates result in increased blood glucose and may awaken you during the sleep cycle. Complex carbohydrates, in contrast, trigger serotonin conversion on a long-term basis and create a slow and sustained rise in glucose.

Vitamin and mineral levels can also affect sleep. Deficiencies of B vitamins, calcium, and magnesium can inhibit sleep. Taking a calcium-magnesium tablet at night will promote relaxation and help with leg discomfort ("restless leg syndrome").

Since your brain is geared to pay attention to novelty, try to minimize nonrepetitive sounds. The television should be turned off well before bedtime, because it will periodically grab your attention and wake you up. White noise, in contrast (such as the noise of a fan), is monotonous and makes a good screen for other noises, such as a barking dog or a car alarm. Some people keep a fan on all night long just to provide white noise. Good-quality earplugs can also filter out noises.

Sedating Insomnia

The American Sleep Disorders Association lists the following symptoms of primary insomnia:

- A problem initiating and maintaining sleep
- Daytime fatigue associated with the sleep disturbance
- Significant distress in or impairment of one's social life or occupation
- Duration of more than one month
- Frequency of three or more nights a week
- A sleep latency, or time awake after sleep onset, longer than thirty minutes
- Waking more than thirty minutes before the desired time

- A total sleep time of six and a half hours or less
- A sleep efficiency lower than 85 percent

These indicators of primary insomnia are also associated with general anxiety and some forms of depression. Indeed, a significant number of people who are depressed and/or anxious seek treatment for insomnia. Ironically, excessive worry about the lack of sleep contributes to anxiety-related insomnia.

You may mistakenly believe that because insomnia is such a widespread problem, physicians are prepared to help. However, most physicians are not well-trained in sleep studies. In a congressionally funded study, the pioneering sleep researcher William Dement found that most medical students receive an average of just forty minutes of training in the study of sleep.

This void in training is reflected in the inadequate treatment of patients with insomnia. In millions of medical records that were surveyed, no reports of insomnia were found. Perhaps 95 percent of sleep problems are undiagnosed because physicians don't usually ask about the issue. When doctors do hear complaints from their patients about insomnia, they typically prescribe sleeping pills, despite the fact that most medical journals recommend a nondrug approach to insomnia.

People who are depressed often experience early-morning awakening, and this occurs during REM sleep. Too much REM sleep contributes to depression, and REM deprivation has been shown to alleviate depression. Sleep-deprived people generally recover about half of the REM they've lost, and REM rebound occurs only after regaining slow-wave (deep) sleep.

You probably feel worse when you awaken from a sleep-deprived night. You generally feel better as your body temperature rises, as you're exposed to light, and as you move around. The way you think about your sleep deprivation, however, will affect how you feel the rest of the day. If you think the loss of sleep is a major problem, your mood will be dampened and you'll continue to feel bad.

There have been numerous studies on the effects of sleep loss. Since most sleep research takes place at universities, we know much about the cost of sleep deprivation on college students. The students who were sleep-deprived but managed to have at least five hours of sleep a night suffered no significant drops in cognitive functioning. However, if they got less than five hours of sleep a night, their cognitive abilities dropped measurably.

More support for the five-hour hypothesis was raised by a prominent sleep researcher and avid sailboat racer who assessed the performance of around-the-world racers. He found that the sailors who slept less than five hours did poorly in the race because they made navigational mistakes. However, the racers who got more than five hours of sleep also did poorly, because they weren't awake enough to make the important navigational changes. The racers who had exactly five hours of sleep did better than either of the other two groups.

Many researchers now regard five hours of sleep as the minimum biological requirement. For this reason, five hours is sometimes referred to as *core sleep*. It is during core sleep that you engage in deep sleep and half of your REM sleep.

Over-the-counter sleep aids tend to suppress the important stages of sleep. They can also lead to tolerance buildup (that is, more of the drug will be needed to achieve the same effect) and withdrawal.

Millions of people treat their insomnia with either over-the-counter sleep drugs or physician-prescribed sleeping pills. The over-the-counter aids, such as Sominex and Excedrin PM, contain the allergy medicine diphenhydramine (Benadryl), and therefore produce some sedation. Upon wakening the next morning, you may experience grogginess and have more difficulty concentrating.

Two major surveys of hundreds of studies on the effectiveness of treatment for insomnia have shown that sleep medications are relatively ineffective. Prescription sleep medications (benzodiazepines) are half as effective as behavioral approaches. Benzodiazepines are simply not effective as a long-term treatment for insomnia. There is tolerance and withdrawal. If you take them on a regular basis, you'll experience daytime grogginess, shallow sleep, and withdrawal (making it even harder to sleep).

If you're taking a sleep medication, you should not stop abruptly but should gradually taper off. Withdrawal from benzodiazepines should be supervised by a physician. The following guidelines are important:

1. In the first week, reduce the dose by one night. It is advisable to choose an easy night, such as a weekend night.
2. In the second week, reduce the dose by two nights, but not two consecutive nights; space the nights apart.
3. Continue this pattern until you are down to the lowest possible dose for all nights.
4. Follow the same procedure until you achieve sleep with no medication at night.

Make sure that your bed is for two purposes only: sleep and sex. If you toss and turn for more than an hour, you should get up and go to another room. Getting out of bed allows your body temperature to drop and shifts the neurodynamics of lying there and thinking about the fact that you're still awake.

Don't try too hard to go to sleep. Your brain activity increases when you worry about not getting enough sleep. Research has shown that *trying* to fall asleep promotes increased muscle tension, heart rate, blood pressure, and stress-hormone production. One study offered a cash prize to the participant who could get to sleep first. The participants took twice as long as they usually did to fall asleep, because they were trying so hard.

Sleep scheduling is another way to reestablish a normal sleep pattern. By adjusting the time you go to bed—for example, by staying up considerably later than usual—you'll build up pressure to go to sleep and stay asleep through the night. This is because a sleep-deprived person will fall asleep earlier the next night to catch up on lost sleep. If insomnia has become a habit and you assign considerable importance to the problem, it's usually a good practice to establish a schedule that is commensurate with reconditioning your sleep cycle. Sleeping late in the morning, which might seem sensible, is only likely to make it more difficult for you to fall asleep the next night. Sleep scheduling, in contrast, requires that you get up in the morning at the usual time no matter how much sleep you had the previous night.

Calculate how many hours you actually sleep, on average, and then add an hour to the total. Use this formula to schedule how much sleep time you should allow yourself. For example, if you averaged five hours of sleep a night for the past month despite staying in bed for eight hours, you can allow yourself six hours of potential sleep time. If your normal wake-up time has been 6 a.m., you should be in bed at midnight. You should use this schedule for at least four weeks. Your goal will be to fill up most of your time in bed with sleep. Eventually your body temperature will adjust and the sleep pressure will build up so that you can add another hour.

This approach is useful if you have chronic insomnia, not if you have experienced a night or two of poor sleep. If you're a chronic insomniac, the task is to repair your sleep cycle. If your sleep cycle is out of sync, sleep scheduling helps you to move it back into sync and reestablish more normal neurodynamics. By practicing sleep scheduling, you'll increase sleep efficiency.

Negative sleep thoughts (NSTs) push temporary insomnia into long-term insomnia. NSTs are essentially inaccurate ideas about sleep that create a self-fulfilling prophecy. If you believe these NSTs, then you'll have more difficulty falling asleep again because of the buildup of stress. NSTs result in negative emotions such as anger and in all the biochemical changes that are associated with anger, all of which are activating rather than sedating. NSTs set off a chain of events that result in insomnia.

Identify your false thoughts and replace them with accurate information about sleep. For example, if you wake up in the middle of the night, try to interpret your wakefulness in one of the following ways:

- I might get back to sleep or I might not. Either way, it isn't the end of the world.
- This isn't great, but at least I've got my core sleep.
- If I don't get a good night's sleep tonight, I will tomorrow night.

Adopting these thoughts will, paradoxically, help you to get back to sleep. By adopting reasonable thoughts about sleep, you'll take the pressure off yourself and relax enough to get to sleep.

In addition, while you're lying in bed, use the opportunity to relax. Relaxation methods, such as deep, diaphragmatic breathing, quiet the mind. Relaxation during the daytime will help you to sleep at night. Relaxation methods work best if practiced twice daily, once during the day and once before bed. They reduce the effects of stress.

Thus, there are several techniques that can help you to achieve a healthy sleep pattern. Follow these guidelines:

1. Don't do anything in bed other than sleep and have sex. Don't watch television, balance the checkbook, discuss finances with your spouse, or argue. Reading in bed is fine and often relaxing. Associate your bed with sleep.

2. If you can't sleep, get up and go to another room.

3. Don't try too hard to go to sleep. It will increase your stress and lead to a paradoxical effect. Try telling yourself one of the three statements listed earlier. The change in expectation will free you up to be able to relax and get to sleep. The harder you try to go to sleep, the harder it will be to induce sleep.

4. Avoid drinking large quantities of liquid at night, which lowers the sleep threshold and causes you to wake up in order to urinate.

5. Avoid bright light at least a few hours before going to sleep. Don't work on the computer late in the evening.

6. Do all planning for the next day before you get into bed. If you think of something you need to remember, get up and write it down. This will help to postpone thinking or worrying about anything until the next day.

7. Avoid all daytime naps. Think of naps as stealing sleep from the nighttime.

8. Try eating a light snack with complex carbohydrates before bed. Foods rich with L-tryptophan are advisable. Don't eat anything with sugar or salt before bed.

9. Avoid protein snacks at night, because protein blocks the synthesis of serotonin and promotes alertness.

10. Exercise three to six hours before going to bed.
11. If noise bothers you, use earplugs or a source of white noise such as a fan.
12. Avoid alcohol for five hours before bedtime.
13. If you're troubled by chronic insomnia, try sleep scheduling.
14. Use relaxation exercises. These will help you go to sleep or go back to sleep if you awaken during the night.
15. Keep your body temperature cool. Don't cover yourself too heavily. Crack your window open in cool weather, use air conditioning in the summer, and make sure that your bedroom is not overheated in the winter.

7

Social Medicine

Marc came to see me after his thyroid test results came out negative. He had asked his primary care physician for the test because he thought that he might have hypothyroidism, a condition that is characterized by a low level of the hormone thyroxine. Its symptoms include low energy and mild depression.

His primary care physician thought that Marc might be depressed. He knew for sure that Marc was terribly lonely. In fact, he told me that Marc frequently went online to research medical conditions so that he could justify an appointment for a medical checkup. The real reason for the appointments was to come in and chat about the conditions. "It's like he views me as his best friend," the doctor said.

When I sat down with Marc, he acknowledged that he had no friends besides his acquaintances at work and the people he played bridge with online. Even with the latter, he never actually developed much of a relationship. At work, he never went out to lunch with people or took walks with them, and he certainly did not see them outside work. I asked him if he was lonely.

"No, no, I'm fine by myself," he said unconvincingly. Then Marc told me that he was forty-two years old, had never been married, and had dated only a few times. "Relationships are too complicated. I like to keep it simple and live alone," he insisted.

I pointed out that he went to his physician on many of his days off and that those visits were his only social contacts.

"Well, he's a good friend," he said, then realized that he had implied more than he intended.

"It sounds like you need a friend." I suggested.

"I've got all I need," he replied.

"You mean your doctor?" I asked.

"Did he complain about me?" Marc looked hurt.

"Not at all," I answered. "He's concerned about you and thinks that your loneliness is making you feel ill."

"That's nice of him to care," he said, looking comforted. "But it's not necessary." He tried to recompose himself.

"It feels good when people care about you, doesn't it?" I inquired.

Marc shrugged his shoulders, looking as if he didn't know how to answer.

I told him about the findings from a huge body of research that people who have close personal relationships experience fewer health problems, live longer, and are less depressed and anxious.

"That may be so for some people, but not for me," he claimed.

"Yet you've had some symptoms associated with having few social contacts, such as those you thought were connected to hypothyroidism," I pointed out.

His eyebrows shot up. Marc seemed more receptive to hearing more now, since he had symptoms correlated with loneliness. I suggested that one way to rule out the connection between his symptoms and the possibility that he was lonely would be to see if increasing his social contacts would reduce his symptoms.

His immediate answer was to say no. Then I told him about the parts of the brain—such as the OFC, the mirror neurons, and the cingulate cortex—that thrive on social contact. I noted that those parts of the brain, sometimes called the social brain, could help him deal with stress more effectively and boost his immune system so that he would become ill less often.

This information about his brain seemed to open the door to his at least thinking about finding out more about this connection with his health. Then it dawned on him that he might soon be encouraged to extend himself in ways that would be out of character. "Even when I was growing up, I didn't have many friends," he noted. "What am I supposed to do?" He seemed to be trying to convince me that he was unchangeable.

Marc described his emotionally distant family environment when he was growing up. His emotional attachment to his parents was avoidant, and he had few positive interpersonal experiences on which to draw. I described the process of neuroplasticity and explained how he could rewire his brain to learn to be more comfortable in social situations.

"It's never too late to develop new skills," I said.

"Just the thought of it makes me feel uneasy," he admitted.

We talked for some time about how people can make changes at any point in their lives. Despite the fact that he had a lifelong history of few intimate connections to people, it was still possible to change. After some encouraging and comforting words, I pointed out that to make gains, he must do what he didn't feel like doing.

Marc indicated that he understood it rationally and intellectually but that he still had anxiety about extending himself socially. It was too broad a jump for him to go from socializing at work to extending himself in a social situation with little structure. The thought that he could be thrust into a social situation in which people congregated for the primary purpose of getting to know one another was overwhelming. Therefore, we started by structuring time that involved doing something with other people. He registered for an activity that interested him: a computer class at the local community college.

After a few weeks, Marc acknowledged that it felt good to be with a group of people who were together by choice instead of for a paycheck, as at work. He so much enjoyed learning about computers that he bought extra books on the subject and read them.

Eventually, a few of Marc's classmates asked him for help with their computers. This motivated him to show up early so that he could be available to them. As the spring break approached, he told me that he dreaded the week away from his peers.

Then one of his fellow students, a woman named Karen, suggested that they meet at the local Starbucks with their laptops during the spring break week. This suggestion made him feel both anxious and excited. He managed to respond by saying, "No problem."

I asked why he would say "No problem," using a negative when replying in the affirmative. Instead, why not say, "Sure, that sounds great"?

Marc was surprisingly frank. "I guess I was worried that if I had sounded too positive, Karen would have thought I was hitting on her."

"Are you attracted to her?" I asked.

He blushed, then looked at his watch.

"Women don't want remoteness," I explained. "They like a man who can express his feelings. Let her know that you are enjoying the time that you spend with her."

He shifted around in the chair, looked at me sheepishly, then nodded that he would try.

At our appointment the next week, Marc looked like a different person. He was energized, there was color in his face, and he was beaming.

I asked, "So what's new?"

"Life," he responded, as if I would immediately understand.

I did. "Does Karen feel the same way?"

"I think so," he answered. "She wants to get together at Starbucks again this weekend, even though class is back in session."

Marc and Karen began meeting for coffee on a regular basis. Soon she began introducing him to her friends. Eventually he told me, "It's like a family I never had." During that month, his visits to his physician dropped to zero. I asked him about his doctor, and he said, "I don't need him. Whoops, I said that, didn't I?"

"Let's call what you're experiencing *social medicine*," I suggested.

Marc told me that not only was he enjoying his "new family," but that he also felt exhilarated with the time he spent with Karen. Yet he worried that if he told her that he felt more for her than friendship, he would lose her and all his new friends.

"Sometimes you have to take risks in relationships," I told him, "and I think you're ready."

During our next session Marc told me that they had had their first "real date" and that he would "always remember every moment of it."

My visits with Marc became sporadic after that. He told me that he would call if he needed me, then he chuckled.

Marc is not alone. Although we are frequently online, e-mailing one another, and calling on the phone, the time we actually spend with one another has decreased. Compared to just a hundred years ago— when our ancestors were socially immersed in their communities, villages, and extended families—we are in virtual communities shielded from one another but linked by our electronic devices. This lack of social connectedness leaves us starving for warmth and grasping for a vicarious version of it through TV shows and movies. Multidimensional relationships of the past have given way to one-dimensional and disconnected relationships. If you need help with your computer, you call tech support in Bhopal, India, and talk to a person who has been trained to lose his or her accent so that you will feel comfortable and trusting. Few and far between are the people who come to your home to fix whatever gadget is broken.

Despite these trends, study after study has shown that positive relationships are good for your health (particularly your immune system), whereas poor or no relationships are bad for your health. About fifteen years ago I devoted an entire section of a book to the developing field of psychoneuroimmunology (Arden, 1996). This new field details the interface among the immune system, the mind, and emotion (Cohen, 2004).

The positive effects of social medicine affect your brain as well as many other areas of your body. The following list shows the many health-related effects of social medicine:

- ↓Cardiovascular reactivity (Lepore, Allen, and Evans, 1993)
- ↓ Blood pressure (Spitzer, Llabre, Ironson, Gellman, and Schneiderman, 1992)
- ↓ Cortisol level (Kiecolt-Glaser, Rickers, George, Messick, Speicher, Garner, et al., 1984)

- ↓ Serum cholesterol (Thomas, Goodwin, and Goodwin, 1985)
- ↓ Vulnerability to catching a cold (Cohen, Doyle, Turnes, Alper, and Skoner, 2003)
- ↓ Depression (Russell and Cutrona, 1991)
- ↓ Anxiety (Cohen, 2004)
- Slowing down of cognitive decline (Bassuk, Glass, and Berekman, 1998)
- Improvement in sleep (Cohen, 2004)
- ↑ Natural killer cells (Kiecolt-Glaser, Rickers, George, Messick, Speicher, Garner, et al., 1984)

What's going on here? How do your relationships have such an impact on your body, including your brain? The answer involves the interaction between those parts of the brain that we are calling the social brain. The OFC, the mirror neurons, and the cingulate cortex thrive on social interaction. They are the brain systems that began wiring up when you bonded with your parents. If those relationships were positive, you developed an ability to control your emotions (or, in the technical jargon, gain better "affect regulation"). When your relationships are supportive, you feel comforted, and these brain systems become wired so that you can also comfort yourself. This is because these brain systems are connected to the emotional parts of the brain, such as the amygdala, and to the parasympathetic nervous system, which helps you to calm down in the face of stress.

In addition to the OFC, the mirror neurons, and the cingulate cortex, other brain systems thrive on social relationships. For example, another key part of your social brain is called the *insula*. It's not visible from the outside because it is tucked into a major fold in the cortex. The insula is involved in many social feelings and forms part of the neural basis for love and disgust. The systems of the social brain include the following:

Neurotransmitters	Brain Structures	Central Nervous System
Oxytocin	OFC	Vagus nerve
Dopamine	Amygdala	
Vasopressin	Insula	
	Cingulate cortex	
	Mirror neurons	
	Spindle cells	

These systems provide you with the opportunity to form rich and multidimentional social relationships. Consequently, there are many forms of social communication. One of the most basic is based on touch.

Touch

The skin is the largest organ in the human body. It contains two different types of receptors: (1) those that help you to locate, identify, and manipulate objects, and (2) those that help you to connect with other people through emotion. This second, socially connective function has been shown to facilitate mental and physical health and longevity.

Touching and being touched have many important evolutionary functions. In other primates, for example, mutual grooming promotes social cohesiveness and bonding. Touching expresses reassurance and affection. Partly for this reason, being touched by someone else is more pleasurable than touching yourself. Not only does it represent bonding and/or sensuality, it also feels better because it is unpredictable.

Touching and being touched promote biochemical changes in the brain. The secretion of the neurotransmitters dopamine, oxytocin, and endorphins occurs with caressing, comforting, and soft touching; this promotes closeness with a person as well as feelings of well-being. Touching has also been associated with lower levels of stress hormones and enhanced brain cell survival.

Touching has been shown to enhance the immune systems of people who are suffering from various illnesses as well as the immune systems of the people who are caring for them. For example, therapeutic back massage has been shown to enhance the immune functions of people who have cancer. Touch has been shown to positively affect the aberrant behavior of people of all ages. Depressed and/or aggressive adolescents have benefited from touch, and agitated elderly people in nursing homes are calmed by hand massages.

Touching is therefore an important way to connect with other people and produce changes in their brains as well as in your own brain. President Obama must intuitively know this, for he often adds warmth to a handshake by placing his left hand on the shoulder of the person with whom he is shaking hands.

The Effects of Nurturance and Its Deprivation

Caring for others and being cared for by others have powerful effects on the brain from the moment of birth. A graphic example of how the lack of nurturance can affect the brain occurred in Romania. After the repressive regime of Nicolae Ceausescu was overthrown in 1989, more than 150,000 children were found languishing in Romanian orphanages. They were malnourished and neglected, and many were dying of infectious diseases. Typically, one person cared for thirty or more children. The children were fed and kept clean but otherwise received minimal care.

The orphans often resorted to such primitive methods of self-stimulation as head-banging, incessant rocking, and hand-flapping. They exhibited multiple developmental delays because they missed human contact during critical developmental periods. Infants less than a year old who were placed in Romanian orphanages for more than eight months had higher cortisol blood levels (an indicator of significant stress) than orphans who were adopted within the first four months of their lives. The cortisol levels of children who were institutionalized beyond eight months continued to increase. This means that the longer they were deprived of nurturance, the greater were their stress levels during childhood.

As middle-class European, Canadian, and U.S. couples began to adopt some of these children, they were faced with the daunting problem of managing the tragic effects of early neglect. Several studies have examined how these children have adapted to their adoptive families and how they have fared in school. For example, British psychologist Michael Rutter compared 156 Romanian orphans who were adopted by age three and a half and compared them to fifty nondeprived children who were adopted before six months of age.

All the children were followed longitudinally and were examined for a variety of behavioral problems. The Romanian adoptees were more likely to exhibit behavior problems such as ADHD, autistic-like problems, and cognitive impairment. These problems were more likely to occur among children who left the Romanian orphanage after their second birthday. The children who left Romania prior to six months of age resembled the nondeprived children adopted in Britain.

The risk of developing behavioral problems increased for the children who were adopted after six months of age from a Romanian orphanage. The risk was greatest if they were adopted after age two. This study shows that during the first year of life, a baby thrives on nurturance or is stunted by the lack of it. The effects on the brain have a profound bearing on how successfully the children will adapt to the world later in life.

The British study was not the only one to illustrate the powerful effects of being deprived of nurturing, especially early in life. A similar story occurred in Canada, where children from Romanian orphanages were adopted by parents in British Columbia. The Canadian researchers found that the Romanian children who had spent at least eight months in a Romanian orphanage had significant developmental problems, whereas those who spent less than four months there did not suffer the same degree of impairment.

Similarly, the Romanian orphans who were adopted by U.S. families continue to show many of the same symptoms of their early social deprivation. They have been described as being stoic, being uninterested in playing, tending to hoard food, and having difficulty crying or expressing pain. Brain scans revealed that key parts of their social brain, such as the OFC, were underactive.

A deprivation of nurturing can also cause significant neurochemical abnormalities. Research on adult animals separated at birth from their mothers revealed persistent abnormalities in the production and normal functioning of neurotransmitters, including alterations in the following:

- The expression of dopamine transporter genes
- The dopamine-mediated stress response
- The expression of serotonin receptors
- The expression of benzodiazepine receptors
- The infant's sensitivity to morphine
- The cortisol receptors related to stress response

The extremes of deprivation described above are not common. It is far more common for mothers to be less than attentive to their babies. What if your mother was distracted and preoccupied with her own problems? The research on babies of depressed mothers has shown that these infants behave as if they too are depressed, even in the presence of nondepressed adults.

Maternal depression causes multiple deficits and developmental problems in children, including not only behavior problems but also neurological and biological problems.

For more than twenty years, Tiffany Field and her colleagues have demonstrated that infants of depressed mothers have a wide range of problems. For example, infants of depressed mothers have displayed increased aversion and helplessness and have vocalized less. They have had higher heart rates, decreased vagal tone and developmental delays at one year old.

Just as a deprivation of nurturing can damage the brain, a growing body of research shows that nurturance has a protective effect on the brain and on psychological development. For example, one series of studies showed that rat pups that were handled became more resistant to stress and lived longer.

Among the brain systems that benefit from nurturance are the hippocampus and its receptor sites for stress hormones such as cortisol. Excessive stress can damage the hippocampus through excessive exposure to cortisol, causing dendrites in the hippocampus to shrivel up, but with early nurturance, the cortisol receptors actually multiply. These receptors provide a negative feedback loop, like a thermostat. When stress hormones filter into the brain, the receptors in the hippocampus are triggered and the production of cortisol is shut down, as if to say, "I've had enough of that stress hormone; no more is needed." However, when there are too few receptors, a different response is triggered, as if to say, "Make more stress hormones!" The negative feedback loop thus keeps stress low and comfort high when you are provided with nurturance.

When you are nurtured, you are better able to nurture others. For example, the research on rat pups showed that the rats that were cared for with licking and grooming grew up to do the same for their offspring, but the rat pups that were not nurtured in this way grew up to neglect their pups. To factor out any genetic influence, the researchers had less attentive mothers raise the offspring of nurturing mothers, and vice versa. The rat pups born to the inattentive mothers but raised by attentive mothers grew up to be indistinguishable from the biological offspring of the nurturing mothers. They were significantly less fearful when put in unfamiliar surroundings, just like those who were born of and raised by nurturing mothers. The opposite occurred when the biological offspring of nurturing mothers were raised by inattentive mothers: they grew up to be neurotic and fearful adults. Thus, the genes that you were born with have less effect on you than nurturing does.

Researchers have also found that the gene that produces the glucocorticoid receptor (cortisol in humans) in the hippocampus is twice as active in rat pups raised by nurturing mothers as in those raised by inattentive mothers. It appears that receiving nurturance causes an increase in a molecule that increases production of the glucocorticoid receptors in the hippocampus (Weaver, Cervoni, Champagne, D'Alessio, Sharma, Seckl, et al., 2004). That gene produces more receptors, which provide an enhanced thermostat and resistance to stress. In other words, nurturance turns your genes on or off. This means that if you were lucky enough to be nurtured, your brain went through structural changes that helps you manage stress. This doesn't mean that you won't experience stress, of course.

It just means that you are better prepared for it than people who did not receive as much nurturance.

Despite the importance of early nurturance, you can still gain brain-based benefits from nurturance throughout your lifetime. If you were lucky to receive enhanced nurturance early in your life, it gives you a head start in gaining from all the benefits of social medicine. Through the power of neuroplasticity, you can either enhance or enjoy the benefits of the positive nurturance or, like Marc, repair the limitations you've acquired from poor nurturance.

In the next section I'll explain how having a secure relationship with your parents helps you to develop secure relationships with others. Secure relationships form the basis for good mental and physical health. If you haven't experienced those types of relationships yet, there's still time. If you are fortunate to have experienced secure relationships, you can build on them.

Bonding and Attachment

Since the beginning of your life, your emotions have functioned as a means of communication with your caregivers. Your emotions can be understood as feelings, reactions, and behaviors that arise in response to personally significant situations or events.

Bonding begins at birth, then becomes the foundation for your communication skills. Psychologists refer to these bondings as attachment relationships because they represent the degree to which you were attached to your caregivers. Early bonding begins before the development of language, and many of the basic attachment patterns are formed during the period of right hemispheric dominance, which is during the first two years. The right hemisphere continues to play a dominant role in appraising, contextualizing, and establishing the meaning of your interpersonal experiences.

The amygdala, too, plays an important role in mediating early attachment relationships. Highly connected with other brain areas, the amygdala stamps the incoming stimuli with emotional value in a very quick, black-and-white, good-and-bad manner. The amygdala does this with stimuli coming from within you as well as with the external stimuli that come in through your ears, eyes, and skin. Like the right hemisphere, the amygdala is important in appraising the meaning of facial expressions and other emotional communications that you received first from your caregivers and now in your relationships with others.

Developmental psychologists have used a variety of methods to explore how early attachment relationships play a significant role in the type and quality of your relationships later in life. For example, Mary Ainsworth devised an experimental situation called the *strange situation*. A room in the psychology department at Johns Hopkins University, where Ainsworth was working at the time, was equipped with a one-way mirror, a table and chairs, and a handful of toys. Mothers and their babies were invited into the room to play with the toys, then a stranger came in and sat down.

The researchers observed how the baby handled this change, in terms of seeking proximity to the mother or leaving her to continue exploring the toys. The mother would then leave her baby with the stranger for a few moments, returning as the stranger departed. Then the mother would leave the room again, leaving her baby completely alone. Through this method, several types of attachment behaviors that were displayed by the infants were identified, along with corresponding behaviors in their mothers.

The attachment types are secure, avoidant, ambivalent, and disorganized. (The first three were identified by Ainsworth, but the fourth was identified by Mary Main at the University of California at Berkeley.) In *secure attachment*, the child demonstrates displeasure at the mother's departure and becomes quiet as soon as she returns. The baby welcomes the mother's attempts to comfort him or her and quickly returns to exploring the environment. In *avoidant attachment*, the child seems indifferent to the mother's departure and return. In *ambivalent attachment*, the child typically shows distress when the mother leaves, relates to the stranger, greets the mother on her return with signs of anger or coldness, and is hesitant to return to play. In *disorganized attachment,* the most ominous of the four types, the child reacts to the mother's return by freezing for several seconds or rocking. The baby appears to lack an organized or coherent coping strategy.

Attachment researchers maintain that infants don't construct their attachment patterns by themselves; rather, they do it in response to their perceptions of their parents' behavior. The child's attachment behavior correlates quite well with the behavior and communication style of the mother. A mother's responsiveness to her baby can take a variety of forms, such as the following:

- Mothers of securely attached infants accurately interpret the infant's communications, responding quickly and consistently to the child's needs in a "good enough" manner.
- Mothers of children with an avoidant attachment style tend to remain unresponsive to the child's distress, discouraging crying and promoting separation.
- Mothers of ambivalently attached infants behave inconsistently, being sometimes tuned in and sometimes indifferent to the child's state of mind.
- Mothers of children with a disorganized attachment style tend to be abusive, impulsive, and depressed.

Thus, your attachment style developed in a societal context, based on the behavior of those around you. For example, certain attachment styles are more common in some cultures than in others. In northern Germany, a preponderance of avoidant attachment patterns have been reported. In Japan there is an apparent preponderance of ambivalent attachment and hard-to-soothe infants.

In northern Germany (where avoidant attachment is predominant), it is common for mothers to briefly leave their infants unattended at home or outside a supermarket. As a result of this type of parenting, the infants learn to adapt to being alone. Upon the mother's return, nearly half of the infants who were tested showed little reaction.

In Japan (where ambivalent attachment is predominant), mothers and infants are rarely separated. Babysitting is rare, and when it occurs it is generally done by the grandparents. Thus, Japanese infants rarely experience separation from their mothers. Those who were tested became considerably upset and hard to console after a separation.

You may be saying to yourself at this point, "This is all very interesting, but what does that have to do with me now?" The answer is that the attachment style you developed by the time you were a year old tends to be a highly durable personal characteristic that remains evident later in life. Longitudinal studies have shown that one's attachment style persists into adulthood 68–75 percent of the time. (Main's study put the figure slightly higher, at more than 80 percent.)

Since attachment patterns are so long-lasting, what chance is there to rewire your brain to change those patterns? In a study of the degree of rewiring that is possible even with the most deprived, Michael Rutter (whom you met earlier on the English and Romanian adoptees study team), looked at healing early attachment traumas through enriched environments. The researchers drew the cautiously optimistic conclusion that a child who is exposed to nurturing can, to some extent, overcome earlier deprivation, even in extreme cases.

If you have a poor attachment pattern and don't rewire your brain to change it, what chance is there that you will pass it on to your own children? There is growing evidence that the way a parent responds to his or her baby is based on the parent's own attachment style. Many studies have looked at the application of attachment research to adults. Mary Main created a reliable assessment of adult attachment called the Adult Assessment Interview. Its classification of the parent predicts the child's security or insecurity 75 percent of the time. This appears to hold true even when the parent is assessed before the child's birth.

If your brain was wired through a secure attachment, you have a good chance of feeling relatively secure later in life. Research suggests that 55 percent of adults fall into this category. If you grew up with a secure attachment, you are likely to feel worthy of affection and care, enter relationships with reasonable ease, become close and feel comfortable in these relationships, and expect your partner to be emotionally available and supportive in hardship. Your self-esteem is high, and you tend to be resilient, optimistic, intellectually curious, and open to new ideas. When misunderstandings result in arguments, you can more easily resist feeling rejected or insulted.

If, however, you are among the approximately 20 percent who are anxious in their adult relationships and worry that their partners don't really love them, you may feel unworthy, be clingy and prone to obsessive preoccupation, and become addicted to something. You may worry about abandonment and are prone to jealousy.

If you're among the approximately 25 percent of the adult population with an avoidant attachment style, you may be uncomfortable in intimate relationships and have a hard time trusting a partner. You might not share your feelings and might not even be consciously aware of them.

Indeed, if you had an insecure attachment experience as a child, you may tend to see the world and those around you with defensiveness and mistrust. It can be hard to maintain a sense of self-esteem, and you may be prone to pessimism. When those around you are imperfect and say or do things that are imperfect, it can be hard for you to forgive and move on.

According to a very large analysis of the Adult Attachment Inventory studies, insecure attachment is correlated with anxiety and mood disorders later in life. If you fall into this category, pay extra attention to the information and suggestions in chapters 3 and 4. In contrast, secure attachment is correlated with a lower incidence of psychiatric disorders than in the general population.

Whether or not you were securely attached as a child, you can still rewire your brain to build a sense of security that will support positive relationships. It will require that you, like Marc, feed your brain by exposing yourself to social situations that might initially feel a little risky. He did it, and so can you.

Challenging yourself to go beyond your comfort level is easier than it initially seems. In preparation for increasing your social relationships, you can imagine yourself communicating successfully with others. This will stimulate some of the same neurons that you'll be using when you actually engage in social interactions. A technique called *priming* has been used to get people to trust others when they have not trusted them in the past. For example, priming has been used successfully with Arab and Jewish students in Israel. Positive images and associations of a sense of security are primed in people before they interact with others who normally would have seemed unsafe.

You can also use priming successfully if you are anxious or avoidant by disposition. Positive attachment images and associations can be primed even by using words such as *love, fortune, hug,* and *support.* By boosting thoughts of caregiving and positive attachment, you can increase your feelings of compassion and helping while feeling less distress and greater selflessness.

To reap the gains of social medicine, you'll need to take risks like Marc and expand your sense of security in relationships. The greater your efforts, the greater your rewards. If you're lonely, think of it this way: you have nothing to lose by putting yourself out there.

Mirror Neurons and Empathy

Goal-directed behavior and planning for the future are functions of your pre-frontal cortex (PFC). It is no wonder that during evolution, the expansion of the PFC dramatically differentiated our species from other apes. Specific neurons in your PFC and in other parts of your brain are highly social. As I described in chapter 1, mirror neurons enhance your capacity for imitation and social learning.

The early work on mirror neurons involved monkeys and focused on an area of the frontal lobe that is associated with expressive movements; in the human brain, this is called Broca's area and is important in speaking. The discovery of mirror neurons in non-human primates suggests that our ability to perceive and express through gestures is a link to our common ancestor. For our species, the transition from phonetic gestural communication to actual words paralleled the expansion of the frontal lobes and the mirror neuron system. An illustration of the link between imitation and mirror neurons is that just listening to someone talk activates the listener's tongue muscles.

Mirror neurons therefore played a key role in the evolution of our species. As the social world of our evolutionary ancestors became more complex and favored more sophisticated dimensions of social situations, a more complex brain developed that supported these social skills. The cortex developed rich layered feedback loops and enhanced powers to inhibit instinctual and automatic responses to social situations. The capacity for a balanced appraisal of the social context and the complexities of each situation had tremendous survival value, not only by controlling aggression but also by increasing the chances of reproductive success in complex social settings.

During evolution the demands of communication were increased by population growth and resource competition. The mirror neurons were a complex system for communicating through hand gestures. The advantages of enhanced gestural communication, in turn, may have contributed to further social development through the imitation of gestures. Mirror neurons may also have evolved through vocal communication and sounds that emerged as a sort of protolanguage, which gave a huge competitive advantage to our species over others and vastly expanded the human potential for empathetic and intimate relationships.

Mirror neurons bestow on you the capacity for many skills. You imitate the behavior of another person on the side of your body that is the mirror image of the other person's body. That is, if someone were to move to strike you with his or her right hand, your impulse would be to block it with your left hand. This has adaptive value because it enables you to respond quickly to the threat of a physical attack.

Neuroscientists increasingly refer to mirror neurons as an important part of our ability to feel empathy for another. Mirror neurons have been found in frontal lobes, the back of the parietal lobes, the top of the temporal lobes, and the insula. Thus, the mirror neurons have a function that is far more complex than just imitation.

In addition to yawning when you observe another person yawning, mirror neurons help you to read people's intentions, get a feeling for what they are feeling, and empathize with them. Empathy is associated with the right *somatosensory cortex*, the region of the brain that is associated with integrated body mapping. Damage to the left somatosensory cortex does not result in a loss of empathy, whereas damage to the right side does.

Since mirror neurons may also be part of the neurobiology of empathy, they make you respond to a person who appears sad and dejected. You feel sad along with that person. Talented actors tap into this empathetic system, so that you can vicariously experience the trials and tribulations that the actor experiences on screen. Your attachment style is primed by exposure to attachment themes in the movies, especially when they are emotionally powerful. Your capacity for attachment also rests on the power of mirror neurons to help you understand the intentions of others.

Marco Iacoboni has postulated the existence of "super mirror neurons" that provide another layer on top of the classic mirror neurons. These super mirror neurons function to control and modulate the activity of the classic mirror neurons.

This system of super mirror neurons helps you to form a proper sense of self as well as a sense of another person from a primary sense of "us." Super mirror neurons inhibit the more classic mirror neurons so that when you see someone act, you do not impulsively imitate that action. For example, when you see a person hurt another person, you don't hurt that person, too.

Giacomo Rizzolatti, the Italian neuroscientist who led the group that discovered mirror neurons, noted that they "allow us to grasp the minds of others not through conceptual reasoning but through direct simulation; by feeling, not by thinking." Mirror neurons are an integral part of the theory of mind that each of us carries within. *Theory of mind* (ToM) is a process by which you try to understand and predict the behavior of others. The same capacity has been observed in nonhuman primates such as chimps and baboons. You probably developed aspects of it by age five. The neural foundation of this capability is the same one that you use when you are planning your future. It bolsters your capability of formulating responses to behavior that you anticipate in others.

There are several areas in the brain associated with ToM, including the amygdala, the insula, and the front of the cingulate cortex.

The right OFC decodes mental states while the left OFC reasons about those states. There are three major aspects of ToM skills:

1. Self-related mental states
2. Goals and outcomes
3. Actions

ToM skills give you insight into what another person is thinking or feeling. You can't truly communicate effectively without these skills. People differ in their level of sophistication of ToM skills, and people with autism have few or no ToM skills.

You can work at expanding your ToM skills as you cultivate the talents of your mirror neuron system. Therapists work to perfect these skills throughout their careers.

Some researchers have even proposed that experiencing empathy and compassion for others is to have compassion for yourself. Here we see "giving is receiving" as a brain-based truth. Insensitivity and selfishness are essentially bad for your brain and your mental health. Even witnessing altruism can boost your immune system. Compassion and loving relationships are therefore good for your brain and your mental health.

Also related to the capacity for empathy and insight are the OFC and the front of the cingulate cortex, which are rich in *spindle cells*. These areas are thought to be involved in our emotional reactions to others, especially the instantaneous feelings of empathy. Hearing a baby cry, for example, makes you feel empathy for that baby. These parts of your brain are also related to your capacity for love, because they activate when you find a person attractive or see a picture of a person you love.

Love

Why is falling in love so blissful? Why did Marc look so alive after he got to know Karen? Throughout history, many theories about love have contributed more to mythology than to clarity. Take, for example, the concept of the soul mate, which stems from Plato's proposal that there is another "half" out there in the universe that "completes" each of us. Although there is much debate on whether opposites attract or repel, there is a more fundamental way of understanding what happens in your brain when you are falling in love. Examining what happens in your brain does not devalue love; as I have stated several times in this book, the brain and the mind are two parts of the same picture. Whatever happens in the mind changes the brain, and vice versa. When there is chemistry between you and another person, there is actually chemistry *within* each of you when you're together. This "good chemistry" occurs because of the way you behave toward each other.

Falling in love is a blissful experience with a powerful rush of euphoria because your pleasure center is activated. For example, during the infatuation phase, your dopamine system is charged up. From the first sight of your new partner, your PFC works with the dopamine system to help you attend to this attractive person. This enhanced attention triggers your brain to release more dopamine and tells your hippocampus to remember this attractive person. The more dopamine, the greater the chance that you will probably remember the first time you saw the person.

Your attachment history and the regulation of your emotions by the OFC play a part in how connected you feel to that person. These tendencies further influence how much effort you make to reach out to him or her and enjoy a balanced relationship. Don't forget that too much right frontal lobe activity is associated with passive withdrawal. Making an effort to reach out activates the left frontal lobe and the positive feelings associated with it, enabling you to move the relationship ahead for mutual enjoyment.

The following aspects of the "chemistry of love" give you those blissful feelings:

- At first sight, the PFC says, "Pay attention! This person is attractive." This triggers your brain to discharge dopamine.
- The hippocampus records this memory of first sight.
- The nucleus accumbens (the pleasure and addiction center) is activated with dopamine. When you are separated too long

from the one you love, you experience something akin to withdrawal symptoms.

- The *septal region* (another pleasure center) is activated after dopamine triggers the excitement. This area is also activated during orgasm.
- You and your partner run the risk of developing a tolerance for dopamine. After the initial rush, there will be fewer dopamine receptors. You and your partner will have to create novelty to stimulate dopamine.

The first few dates are infused with pleasure because your nucleus accumbens is activated. This is the same pleasure center that is activated by drugs, gambling, pornography, and anything else that can become addictive. Some people don't activate the rest of their brain systems and can't move on to a more mature form of love. They are addicted to falling in love, so they move on to another relationship because they are constantly looking for that initial rush of excitement.

Since dopamine circuits thrive on novelty, you and your partner can become used to each other and not feel the same excitement; you can even become bored. To prevent the dulling of your relationship, you can charge up your dopamine system by doing novel things together like traveling and going out on romantic dates. The feelings of pleasure from the new experiences will spill over into your relationship by kindling the dopaminergic system.

When the septal region is activated, you generalize a positive feeling to other experiences. For example, when you spend time with your partner on a sunny day, that day seems gloriously full of color, fragrance, and wonderful people. Any flaw in your partner is glossed over or seen as an endearing characteristic. Everything is fused with hopeful anticipation. The things that normally bother you don't. Your brain essentially recruits memories and associations that make all experiences positive.

To maintain positive and secure attachment feelings for a long time, you'll have to stimulate the neurochemistry in your brain that fosters long-term bonding. Fortunately, your brain has the neurochemistry potential to make long-term bonding a possibility. Oxytocin and vasopressin are the two principal hormones that facilitate close relationships. Oxytocin helps to create a bond between people who are forming an intimate relationship. The oxytocin level rises when you have warm physical contact with someone you are close to and with whom you feel safe. Vasopressin rises when you recognize the person you feel close to, as if to say, "Oh, it's you!"

Oxytocin functions as a neuromodulator, which means that it orchestrates the activities of the neurotransmitters and helps to enhance or dampen the effectiveness of synaptic connections. It is sometimes called the cuddling or the commitment neuromodulator because it facilitates bonding in all mammals. Animals with a relatively high amount of oxytocin are monogamous. The classic example is the prairie vole, which mates for life. Oxytocin is released in women during labor and breastfeeding, and it is released in both sexes when nurturing children, cuddling, making love, and having an orgasm.

In romantic relationships, once dopamine triggers excitement, oxytocin triggers feelings of warmth and attachment. In one study, when people were exposed to a sniff of oxytocin, they were more apt to participate in a financial game and trust others with their money.

You can actually make the neurochemical foundation of your relationship deepen your long-term commitment. For example, when oxytocin is combined with dopamine (which occurs when excitement is rekindled through novel experiences), a long-term sense of love and commitment arises that feels exciting, safe, and fulfilling. It is my hope that this is what happened to Marc and Karen.

Use the social brain system to rewire your brain and enhance your relationships. If you make the effort to feed your brain in order to expand and deepen your social and intimate relationships, you will enjoy the vast benefits of social medicine.

8

Resiliency and Wisdom

Maria came to see me after a series of losses. First her father died. That loss was hard, and she emerged slowly from her grief six months later. Then her cat died. She had been very attached to him and had spent years holding him on her lap in the evenings. It took two months for her to move beyond the sadness. Then, when all seemed to be going well again, she was transferred to a new unit at work. She had grown very close to her coworkers, and the prospect of having to get to know an entire new group of people was daunting. Eventually, she found that this new group was as easy to get along with as her old group had been. A few months later she twisted her ankle and had to walk with crutches. This occurred just as she had begun to take a walk every evening with a neighbor.

Maria complained, "I'm just not as durable as most people. Why is it that it takes me so long to bounce back after something bad happens?"

No one in her past had ever served as a resilient role model. In fact, many members of her family were the opposite of resilient. Her father complained woefully about everything, even when things were going well. He always found a flaw in whatever was going on: his favorite restaurant was closed, or his favorite television show was being preempted by a special newscast. He sulked for hours after these minor disappointments.

Maria's mother spent much of her time trying to make sure that everything went easily for Maria's father, but she silently loathed the role. Her older brother was quite passive-aggressive, always manipulating his wife, who babied him. Thus, Maria's role models were not resilient or vibrant people. This, coupled with the fact that she married an alcoholic right after high school, meant that she entered adulthood with few durable role models. Now, thirty years old and with an eleven-year-old daughter, she was ill prepared for the general stresses of life. Even when her daughter caught a cold, it took her quite a while to adjust to taking care of her while also managing the household and going to work.

Maria told me that she was both a pessimist and a perfectionist. I noted that those attitudes set her up to react to whatever occurs in her life by making the situation worse rather than better. Her pessimism meant that she could foresee no good options and no light at the end of the tunnel. This was a prescription for despair and anxiety to return. Her neural circuitry emphasized a "worry loop" in which her amygdala triggered fear and her PFC ruminated about the possible causes of that fear. She also overactivated her right PFC and underactivated her left.

My plan to help her rewire her brain entailed inoculations of manageable periods of stress. Simultaneously, she needed to activate her left PFC, which involved taking action to kindle all the positive emotions associated with it.

I was not surprised that Maria was resistant to the plan, yet after I explained how neuroplasticity works, she indicated that she was willing to give it a try. I explained that she had to get out of the victim role. She was making herself feel as though life were nothing but a series of bad experiences over which she had no control. Instead, she needed to learn to put herself in the driver's seat by making decisions about whatever occurs in her life. Through slowly regaining a reasonable sense of control, Maria was better able to initiate the process of neuroplasticity. Rewiring her brain required that she decide to make changes rather than react to whatever occurred as if she were nothing more than a victim. To remember the steps that are required to rewire the brain, I gave her the FEED acronym as a mnemonic device.

Since Maria needed a place to practice feeding her brain, I suggested that she take initiative at work. She could, for example, volunteer to be on a committee with the new team. Her reaction was, "I just got comfortable with them. Why push it?"

"That's the point," I said. "You need to push it. Think of what you'll be doing as a sort of inoculation. You're building up your stress tolerance by expanding your comfort area." After considerable persuasion, she reluctantly agreed. I reminded her that she was still playing the passive victim by dragging herself into following through with our agreement. In fact, when she procrastinated about nominating herself, she was still playing victim in our agreement. She was not going to develop resiliency until she used the FEED plan and did what seemed to her to be against her nature.

Maria volunteered herself the next day. When she returned to see me a week later, she said that the members of the committee were pleasantly surprised and thanked her for volunteering.

After the committee assignment was completed, she asked if I thought it would be wise to "resign now because I have done my bit."

"On the contrary," I protested, "you're just getting started. Your job is to keep on expanding your comfort zone. Remember, the second *E* in FEED highlights the importance of making a continued *effort* until you find it effortless."

Maria swallowed hard but did volunteer to stay on the committee. In fact, she proposed an expansion of the last project. I complimented her on her initiative and suggested that she volunteer to chair the subcommittee. She said, "Are you kidding?"

"What do you think?" I retorted.

She nodded yes, noting that she got it.

Maria's newly developed strategy required that she generate a moderate degree of stress to promote neuroplastic changes. Later, obstacles and unfortunate situations would naturally arise on their own, but she would be prepared for them because she was inoculated by a moderate degree of stress through volunteering for projects.

That challenge came soon enough. One of her subcommittee members disagreed with one of her proposals. Although there was no way of determining his motivation for the criticism, Maria reacted as if he were being critical of her personally. I suggested that she stick to the facts and use his critique as an opportunity to examine her idea. By shifting to the content of his critique rather than wondering about its motives, she activated her left PFC. This allowed her to come up with a logical strategy to modify her idea while still retaining a moderate degree of stress. Had she remained in a defensive posture and felt overwhelmed by a presumed personal attack, she would have pushed her panic button and activated her amygdala.

The experience with her committee member and several subsequent similar experiences provided her with opportunities to rewire her brain. Maria became increasingly more resilient. She found herself craving new experiences instead of shrinking from them.

Attitude and Resiliency

Resilient people turn frustrating situations into opportunities to learn something new. Although they don't want bad things to happen, they adapt to bad circumstances by focusing on hidden opportunities. For example, you may run into financial problems and have to change your job to one that pays more. You were pretty comfortable in the old position, so switching means that you have to expand yourself in areas that you had never explored. After pushing yourself out of your comfort zone, you may actually find the new area to be more rewarding than the old one was.

Buddhists identify attachment as the root of all suffering. (The word *attachment* in this context has nothing to do with bonding.) They point out that when you become attached to a very specific outcome and it doesn't occur, you suffer disappointment. You may be lucky enough to have some approximation of your expectations occur, but when it does, do you really enjoy it? The chances are that you are too busy anticipating yet another future specific expectation. Since things generally don't occur in the way that you eagerly anticipate, you can either roll with whatever does occur or bemoan the fact that what you had expected didn't happen. In each situation, you script yourself out of being present and enjoying where you are when you are there.

It's much easier to deal with disappointment if the failed expectation was simple and within normal human experience, but what about when truly bad things happen? There are people who have experienced great trauma, yet with resiliency they have made new lives for themselves. I think of my own Armenian ancestors, who survived the genocide perpetrated by the Turks and made new, flourishing lives for themselves in the United States and France. Although they never forgot what they had endured, they didn't sit around passively waiting for better things to happen. Instead, they made things happen. They became successful in their adopted countries by crafting careers and building new families. I continue to be inspired by their resiliency.

Resiliency consists of maintaining hope in the face of adversity that things will eventually get better, while doing what it takes to make those things happen. This type of optimism forms part of what is called emotional intelligence. In fact, optimism is good not only for your mental health but also for your physical health. In one study, people who were assessed to be either pessimistic or optimistic were assessed again thirty years later for their health. Pessimism was found to be a poor risk factor for physical and mental health and blunting longevity.

Martin Seligman of the University of Pennsylvania has suggested that pessimism can have a negative effect on your health for the following reasons:

- You believe that nothing you do makes a difference.
- You have more negative life events by reacting to neutral events negatively and creating more negative events because wasted and misdirected efforts.
- It depresses the immune system.

Pessimists essentially paint themselves into a depressing corner. Their negative thinking allows them no opportunity to feel good about anything that happens in their lives.

If you focus on what something isn't, you block your perception of what it is. In such cases, you're hung up on a negative frame of reference. Let's say that you expect things to turn out a specific way and they don't turn out that way. Instead of appreciating how things turned out, you're stuck on the fact that they didn't turn out the way you hoped. This dilemma is somewhat similar to what psychologists call *cognitive dissonance,* which means that once you develop an opinion about something, it's difficult to hold an opinion contrary to it.

You can break out of these categorical mind-sets. For example, my wife and I recently drove through Elko, Nevada, on a long road trip and were struck by the number of run-down casinos and businesses there. We began to form the opinion that Elko was a sad town, and we wondered about continuing the many more miles to our destination. Then we found an interesting little gem of a restaurant called The Flying Fish. The next morning we stopped in a coffeehouse called Cowboy Joe's and were captivated by the magnificent Ruby Mountains. Thus, we experienced Elko as an interesting place not because that was obvious but because we looked deeper. If you allow yourself to be open to a wider mind-set, any place can be interesting and worth your time.

Optimism is more than just seeing the glass as half full. Cultivating an optimistic attitude might seem like a broad jump for you if you are experiencing a high degree of stress, because you might think that there is nothing to feel optimistic about. However, a sense of optimism will emerge if you look past your current situation to focus on possibilities and potentialities, thus unlocking yourself from a self-limiting attitude. A stressful situation presents an opportunity to explore new ways of doing things. By focusing on possibilities, you can see more than a potential light at the end of the tunnel. The light doesn't have to be at the end of the tunnel; it can illuminate an opportunity wherever you are.

Shifting Your Affective-Style Set Point

Richard Davidson of the University of Wisconsin is a pioneering contributor to research on cerebral asymmetry and mood. He has shown that people who overactivate one hemisphere tend to have a particular emotional style, referred to as *affective style*. For example, people whose left frontal lobe is dominant tend to be more positive, take a more active role in their lives, and embrace a more "can do" attitude than people whose right frontal lobe is dominant. In contrast, people who overactivate the right frontal lobe tend to have a more negative affective style. They tend toward anxiety, sadness, worry, passivity, and withdrawal.

These asymmetrical emotional tendencies have been shown to occur early in life. Even infants who are crying or sad show greater right frontal lobe activity, whereas infants who display approach emotions, such as happiness, show more left frontal lobe activity. Another study found that female undergraduates who rated themselves as quite shy showed right frontal lobe overactivation and left frontal lobe underactivation. Their more socially oriented counterparts, in contrast, displayed left frontal lobe dominance.

One of the key features of a positive (left frontal lobe) affective style is the capacity to neutralize negative emotions. The connections between the PFC and the amygdala play a significant role in this type of affect regulation. In other words, your stress tolerance is based on your ability to inhibit negative emotions, including the fear that is generated by the amygdala. Resilience is the ability to maintain positive emotions in the face of adversity.

The capacity to recover from negative emotional states is an important aspect of resiliency. Davidson has proposed that individuals who *practice* positive moods and well-being—for example, through mindfulness meditation—become more resilient. They easily bounce back to what may be regarded as the brain-based default mode of functioning. In one study, Davidson put a very experienced Tibetan meditator through a thorough electrophysiological assessment and found that the activity in his left PFC was associated with positive moods. This man was actually six standard deviations higher than the average Western subject in the measure. These studies indicate that the tendency toward resilience is a left rather than a right hemispheric function.

The idea of an emotional, or affective-style, set point is consistent with this research on hemispheric asymmetry and resiliency. A *set point* is a sort of emotional gravitational force. Although you might experience a great tragedy, such as the loss of a loved one, or a great fortune, such as winning the lottery, you will eventually move back to your set point after a period of adjustment.

If your set point is not as positive and calm as you want it to be, you'll have to feed your brain by inducing increased activation of positive left frontal states long enough to induce a new trait. The difference between states and traits represents two critical steps in inducing neuroplasticity. A *state* is a mood, such as happiness or sadness. Most people fluctuate among different states throughout the day, depending on what is going on in their lives. A *trait*, however, is an enduring pattern. For example, most people experience an anxious or depressed state from time to time, but not all people experience anxiety or depression as an enduring trait.

If your affective-style set point tends to be anxious or depressed, you can rewire that trait by using the FEED technique (see chapters 3 and 4) to activate the fundamental neuroplastic connection between state and trait. The more frequently you induce a particular state, such as calmness or hope, the greater is the chance that that state will become a trait. The more often you activate the neurons that represent that state, the easier it will be to induce that state again, and the more likely it will be that the feeling of calmness or hope will become a stable trait of your affective-style set point.

Shifting Your Attitude

Your attitude has a significant effect on your stress level and whether you can shift your set point. Your attitude is your way of approaching your life. To explore the range of differences in attitude, Salvator Maddi and Suzanne Kobasa, two research psychologists from the University of Chicago, identified attitudinal characteristics that help a person deal with stress. They studied busy and successful executives and identified three characteristics they had in common:

1. **Commitment:** People feel invested in what they are doing. They have energy for and are interested in their duties.
2. **Control:** People have the realistic sense that what they are doing is in their realm of control; that is, they consider themselves to be active participants in their work instead of feeling hopeless and victimized by the work conditions. This is in contrast to developing learned helplessness.
3. **Challenge:** People view change as an opportunity to act differently rather than as a crisis from which to defend themselves.

These three C's are the attitudes that can help you to stay healthy despite having to deal with high levels of stress. They are essential in developing what Maddi and Kobasa have called a stress-hardy person. By developing stress hardiness, you will be able to deal with stress that many people find unbearable.

When you cultivate stress hardiness, keep in mind that you still need social medicine in the form of the support of friends and family members. Maddi and Kobasa found that stress-hardy people tap into social support, which helps them to blunt the impact of stressful events. The social support must be directed toward caring and encouragement rather than fostering self-pity and dependence, however. It should help you to explore your options and to challenge yourself.

Consistent with the principle that a moderate degree of stress will help you to rewire your brain and inoculate you from greater stress, challenge focuses your energy on goals that require extra effort. This moderate stress activation can also keep you from becoming bored. Mihaly Csikszentimihalyi of the University of Chicago has described how people can avoid being overwhelmed with anxiety from stimulation while also avoiding boredom. By investing your energy in finding a healthy balance between the two, you can experience flow, which means enjoyment.

Your attitude not only affects how you feel about your life and how you approach stress, it also has a great deal to do with how you think and whether you believe your options are infinite. Do you invest your energy in becoming greater than you have been in the past? Such an investment can have a major bearing on your capacity to rewire your brain and respond with resiliency to stress.

Ambition and curiosity play a dynamic role in how well your brain thrives. Cultivating these two characteristics enables you to approach the future with vitality and a hunger for life. They open the door to your future and say yes to new experiences. By cultivating an insatiable curiosity, you make whatever environment you encounter an enriched environment. Enriched environments stimulate neuro-plasticity, whereas impoverished environments damage the brain.

You need the emotional fuel and the motivation to turn possibilities into actualities. This is where ambition comes into play. By cultivating ambition, you'll reach for a bright future with vast possibilities. Healthy ambition is *not* competitive or aggressive. It does not involve stepping on or over other people to attain one's goals. Healthy ambition involves curiosity and a goal-driven sense of purpose to expand beyond your current understanding.

My Father and Beethoven

My father admired and listened to Beethoven's symphonies until the last days of his life. When I spoke at his memorial service, I described how his life was similar in theme to that of his favorite composer. My father's life and Beethoven's life carried the same themes of resilience and transcendence over adversity.

For Beethoven, resiliency emerged from struggles with his family. After Beethoven studied briefly with Haydn in Vienna, his mother died, so he returned to Bonn to care for his two younger brothers. His father should have managed the responsibility of raising his children, but his alcoholism destroyed any capability for or interest in doing so. Beethoven drove his father out of town and raised his brothers by himself. After being his brothers' father figure, he returned to Vienna to launch a self-made career as the first composer who was not on the payroll of the nobility. He transformed Western music. Then tragedy hit. By the time of his Fifth Symphony, he was becoming deaf. How could a composer with such great promise lose his hearing?

Transcending this incredible limitation, Beethoven went on to write revolutionary symphonies, piano sonatas, and piano concertos. Each piece of music surpassed the last. There was only one constant: that each piece of music feel transcendent. The culmination of all his work, the Ninth Symphony, was itself about transcendence and unity. Just days before my father died, he exclaimed, "How could he write something so magnificent?"

My father, too, transcended many potentially limiting obstacles. He and his two brothers were born soon after his father and his mother fled to the United States as refugees. His parents were deeply traumatized by having barely escaped genocide. Many of their close relatives were slaughtered by the Turks—some right in front of them. My father began his life in a household with parents who spoke no English and who had experienced terrible trauma, but this did not hold him back.

After growing up during the Depression and serving in the U.S. Marine Corps in the Pacific during World War II, he became a prosecuting attorney who took two cases to the Supreme Court and convicted three people of murder even though the victims' bodies were never found. After serving as a judge, he retired and became a graduate student in art. Throughout his life he earned enough college credits for three Ph.D.s. He earned the title by which he was described in the front-page headline of the newspaper: "Superstar Judge Dies at 81."

Beethoven and my father defied limitations; they both made major efforts to activate their left PFC, transcending potentially limiting factors and pushing forward until the very end.

The characteristics of a resilient attitude will rewire your brain. If you abide by them, you'll be engaged in a strong effort to attain your goals, keep yourself from giving up, and be open to the world around you along the way.

You may say that all these concepts sound great when you have few limitations, but what if the changes that you need to adjust to include an aging body and mounting physical limitations? Does aging challenge the entire concept of resiliency? How can you bounce back if you can't become younger?

Aging Youthfully

Ponce de Leon is remembered for his futile attempt to search for the fountain of youth. He was sent on a wild goose chase in an area that is now Florida by people from the Seminole tribe. The Seminoles needed a good way to get the band of Spanish conquistadors out of their territory. They might have known that the myth of a fountain of youth emerged from a common human fear that aging brings on bad things, including death. A fountain of youth could stop the negative effects of aging from happening. Perhaps they knew that no such fountain existed, but they did know that the Spaniards would think of such a fountain as more valuable than gold.

Even though no such fountain exists, there are things you can do to slow down the aging process. Despite the fact that certain limiting changes occur in the brain with age, as I will explain, you can still minimize their effects and maximize the potential for neuroplasticity as well.

Brain Changes in Aging

During midlife, the brain goes through several structural changes in degrees, depending on how well you have taken care of your brain. Up until age thirty, the back of the temporal lobe increases in density; thereafter it decreases. This means that processing speed and remembering slowly decrease after age thirty. Between the ages of twenty and ninety, the overall processing speed for verbal tasks declines by 50 percent, whereas the speed for visual spatial tasks declines more rapidly. Language skills therefore don't slow down as quickly as visual spatial skills do. There is also a slow decrease in the density and the volume of the neurons in the PFC. This means that you can be more focused and efficient.

As you age, you also go through changes in your sleep cycle: you wake up more and spend more time in light sleep. This problem is complicated by the fact that many older people spend more time indoors and are therefore exposed to less natural light, which dysregulates their circadian rhythms. Also, when older people lose social cues, such as eating dinner at a set time, it negatively impacts the sleep cycle. These changes must be buffered by the sleep hygiene practices I described in chapter 6.

Your overall health plays a large role in how well your brain functions as you age. Body fat located at the waist appears to be particularly problematic, at least for men. Researchers have found that for men over sixty, the greater the waist circumference is, the smaller the hippocampus is. Since the hippocampus is critical for laying down memories, the inference here is that increased body fat correlates with decreased memory capacity.

A twenty-four-year longitudinal study found that people with a higher body mass index (BMI) had a higher degree of atrophy of the brain. The degree of brain atrophy was 13 to 16 percent for every one-point increase in BMI.

In an extensive study done by Kaiser Permanente, researchers examined more than ten thousand people who had been diagnosed with dementia to determine the relationship between BMI and dementia. They had been followed for twenty-seven years and were evaluated for skin-fold thickness and BMI. The results of the study indicated that men who had the highest skin-fold category at middle age had a 72 percent rate of dementia, whereas women in the same category had a 60 percent rate of dementia.

You can delay or prevent dementia by the following:

- Exercising
- Taking up a hobby, especially something creative like painting, ceramics, or gardening
- Taking a class at the local college or adult education center
- Increasing your social contacts and involvements, such as by joining a club or a social organization
- Eating a balanced diet
- Playing games or doing puzzles that are intellectually demanding, such as chess, crossword puzzles, or bridge
- Volunteering
- Spending time with young people
- Traveling
- Varying your routines

Physical exercise can slow cognitive decline and decrease the risk for dementia. For example, a Harvard University study has shown that simple walking is associated with significantly better cognitive function and the prevention of cognitive decline in older women. A University of Virginia study found that walking had the same effect in older men. Men who walked the least had almost double the risk of dementia, compared to those who walked more than two miles per day.

You can also minimize excessive stress as you age by exercising. In addition to being vulnerable to cortisol, the hippocampus can decrease in size based on the amount of oxygen it receives. Referred to as *anoxia*, a reduction of oxygen accompanies a decrease in the health and integrity of the capillaries. This decrease results in less oxygen going to the vulnerable hippocampus. Exercise is a great stress reliever and it boosts BDNF, especially in the hippocampus.

The neural networks that were the last to develop are the ones that are most vulnerable to aging. Most neuroscientists view the brain as aging from the front to the back. Thus, deficits appear first in the frontal lobe as well as in the hippocampus. A typical senior experiences symptoms that reflect frontal lobe deficits, including working memory (such as forgetting where you put your keys), and hippocampal deficits (such as forgetting what you did yesterday). The PFC is the last area of the brain to mature, so it is the first area to decline.

Other research shows that age-related deficits also occur from right to left, which means that the right hemisphere begins to lose functions before the left. You will recall that the right hemisphere is involved in spatial perception and dealing with novelty, whereas the left is involved in language and routine behaviors. Some symptoms of right-hemisphere deficits are less visual spatial perception and less ability to learn new tasks. This means that you will probably forget the directions to the furniture store before you forget the name of the store.

Brain Changes during Aging
- Loss of gray matter in the DLPFC (Raz, Gunning, Head, Dupuis, McQuain, Briggs, et al., 1997)

- Loss of gray matter in the temporal lobe (Van Patten, Plante, Davidson, Kuo, Bjuscak, and Glisky, 2004)
- Decrease of myelin in the frontal lobe (Bartzokis, Cummings, Sultzer, Henderson, Nuechtherlein, and Mintz, 2004)
- Loss of volume in the temporal lobe (Sullivan, Marsh, Mathalon, Lim, and Pfefferbaum, 1995)
- Degeneration of white matter in the PFC (Salat, Buckner, Synder, Greve, Desikan, Busa, et al., 2004)
- Hippocampus/entorhinal cortex (Bigler, Anderson, and Blatter, 2002)
- Loss of large neurons in the frontal lobe (Terry, DeTeresa, and Hansen, 1987)
- Shrinkage of the cerebellum (the bottom back part of the brain) (Raz, Gunning, Head, Williamson, and Acker, 2001)
- Preservation of the OFC (Salat, Kaye, and Janowsky, 2001)
- Shrinking of the striatum (Gunning-Dixon, Head, McQuain, Acker, and Raz, 1998)
- Decrease in length of white-matter fibers (Tang, Nyengaard, Pakkenberg, and Gundersen, 1997)
- Loss of diameter in white-matter fibers (Tang, Nyengaard, Pakkenberg, and Gundersen, 1997)
- Decrease in cerebral glucose metabolism (Willis, Ketter, Kimbell, George, Herscovitch, Danielson, et al., 2002)

The above list may seem overwhelming. There are actually many things you can do to slow down the aging process and rewire your brain so that you can enjoy your later years. You can, in effect, tap into a fountain of youth by making changes in your lifestyle. One of the things you can do is expand your cognitive reserve.

Cognitive Reserve

You can enhance your ability to weather the effects of aging by increasing your intellectual capacities. The concept of *cognitive reserve* has been used to explain why people with more education are less vulnerable to developing dementia, such as Alzheimer's disease. A person with more education has more neural networks to rely upon if he or she suffers any kind of neurological injury or disease.

Since normal aging involves cognitive decline that results from the gradual degeneration of the neurons as well as their dendrites and the biochemical mechanisms that support them, cognitive reserve builds up support for the neuronal infrastructure over a lifetime.

The more you build up this infrastructure, the more you can afford to lose and still be competent. Cognitive reserve is built up by challenging yourself educationally and emotionally while also maintaining healthy habits such as diet and exercise. These factors have been reported to shield people from even the worst types of dementia, including Alzheimer's disease.

The power of education to boost cognitive reserve and protect people from dementia was well illustrated by a study that is known as the Nuns' Study. Researchers at the University of Kentucky's Sanders-Brown Center on Aging performed autopsies on deceased elderly nuns. The most highly educated nuns (signifying greater brain stimulation) had more branches and connections between their neurons. They also seemed to have suffered the least from the symptoms of dementia.

People with more education can sustain greater neuronal damage than people with less education and still not show the symptoms of that damage. For example, one study showed that approximately 25 percent of older individuals showed no symptoms of Alzheimer's disease when they were alive, but their autopsies found that they had Alzheimer's-related brain pathology. Thus, despite the fact that their brains showed the classic Alzheimer's plaques and tangles, they functioned as well as those whose brains did not have Alzheimer's plaques and tangles.

In one of the longest and largest longitudinal studies of development, George Vaillant of Harvard University followed 824 people for several decades. The subjects came from many walks of life and included both highly educated and poor Bostonians. Despite finding some common symptoms of cognitive decline, the study showed that several elderly people developed new skills and became wiser with age. These people were less vulnerable to depression than the other older adults, and they fared better than even their younger counterparts.

One measure of neuroplasticity during aging is how you process information. As you age, your brain shifts to emphasizing different processing areas. Researchers from the University of Toronto have shown that people between the ages of fourteen and thirty tend to emphasize the temporal lobe (on both sides of the head) when performing cognitive activities. The more educated the person is, the more he or she uses this lobe. A different pattern is evident in people over sixty-five. When they are given the same cognitive tasks as younger adults, they tend to emphasize the frontal lobes. The more education they had, the more they used the frontal lobes.

Resiliency and Social Support

Support from your family and your friends plays a major role in your resiliency and your longevity. You may be so immersed in the stress of everyday life that you take your relationships for granted or have a difficult time noticing how your relationships impact your stress level. The effects of stress can build up over a lifetime. When stress is chronic, wear and tear on the body can add up to what has been called *allostatic load*. This results from chronic high levels of cortisol and norepinephrine. The health problems that can build up over a lifetime include high blood pressure, type 2 diabetes, atherosclerosis (blocked arteries), abdominal obesity, neural atrophy, cognitive deficits, anxiety, and depression.

Allostasis and Social Medicine

Allostasis is the capacity of the brain and the body to maintain stability through change. Allostatic adjustments are short-term adaptations orchestrated by cortisol, which enhances or inhibits gene transcription, the regulation of BDNF, and the regulation of amygdala activity. As noted above, allostatic load can occur when there is chronic stress.

A longitudinal study in Wisconsin illustrated that positive social relationships are good medicine. Social medicine lightens allostatic load, despite stressors such as adverse economic conditions. In contrast, those who did not receive adequate social medicine early—that is, they had to deal with abuse or neglect—experienced ongoing heavier allostatic load.

Social medicine is good for the brain as you age. Your brain needs an enriched environment in which to thrive as you age, and there is no better way to provide both emotional comfort and cognitive stimulation than with multifaceted relationships. In support of this fact, the MacArthur Study on Successful Aging found that emotional support was the best predictor of better cognitive functioning at a seven-and-a-half-year follow-up.

An aging study in Taiwan found that men between the ages of fifty-four and seventy who had had a spouse for at least six to eight years before the study had a lighter allostatic load than men who were single at the time. In both men and women ages seventy-one and older, those with close ties to friends or neighbors had a lighter allostatic load.

Elderly people who have a supportive and an engaging social life have been reported to have better cognitive abilities after seven years of follow-up than people who were socially isolated did. Social support has been shown to have a therapeutic effect on people who are suffering from various medical conditions or mental health problems. Empathy and social support are simply good for your brain, which has been built and rebuilt through relationships. Social medicine is brain medicine.

Wisdom

Aging can and often does result in gaining wisdom. A lifetime of experience can broaden your perspective so that you appreciate the complexity and interrelationships of things.

Some brain changes that occur during aging can make you wiser. There is good reason for regarding the village elders in many societies as the wise ones in their communities. Gaining wisdom is more than knowing all the ins and outs of society's traditions and beliefs. Wisdom involves being able to see the larger picture.

Neuroscience has illustrated how wisdom occurs and develops. As you move into your sixties and seventies, the balance between the amygdala and the OFC shifts to the OFC, especially when you are analyzing facial expressions. This shift is due not to the declining activity of the amygdala but rather to the maturation of the OFC, which helps to inhibit emotional impulses that can get in the way of higher levels of understanding and communicating with others. The maturation of the OFC also ushers in the emergence of grasping the bigger picture. Compared to adolescents, older adults are better able to apply their attention to problem-focused strategies rather than to emotional strategies.

There appears to be increasingly *less* asymmetry in the way the brain functions as you age. That is, one hemisphere doesn't dominate the other. I emphasize the word *less*, because there are still functions that are lateralized (dominated by one hemisphere), such as language. However, the functions that were lateralized earlier in life become less lateralized—to compensate, perhaps, for potential weaknesses or illnesses such as stroke. Like cognitive reserve, less asymmetry gives you more flexibility and potentially more resiliency in the face of illness, injury, and the effects of aging.

There is evidence that higher-functioning older adults show bilateral hemispheric activation. In contrast, lower-functioning older adults show greater activation in one hemisphere, and often with less efficiency. Thus, two hemispheres are better than one, especially as you age. The wider the activation distribution throughout your brain, the wider your perspective is and the wiser you can be.

Many people increase their knowledge and their perspective as they age. Your ability to weave a cohesive narrative increases. You can make better sense of what happened throughout your life and create a coherent story that puts it all together. Your brain undergoes neuroplastic changes throughout your later years, so you can appreciate greater complexity in the world and develop a wide-perspective narrative.

You can cultivate wisdom by rewiring your brain through the use of the FEED method. The first step is to focus on the bigger picture. Next, go beyond your traditionally held beliefs, which will recruit new neural connections. Your job is to do this enough until it becomes effortless, to rise above your personal needs and grasp your interdependence with others. The brain system for those inclusive and compassionate experiences multiplies. By being determined to stay with your efforts, you'll make your life richer.

Compassion for others is an aspect of what we might call *emotional wisdom*. Being open to modifying your beliefs based upon the perspective and needs of others cultivates wisdom and rewires your brain. In order for you to gain this aspect of wisdom, your actions should represent an empathetic and compassionate effort to consider the collective good. Incorporate the crucial insight that we are all fallible and that kindness and forgiveness are part of wisdom.

A Sense of Humor

Wisdom involves a sense of humility and the ability to laugh at yourself. As you strive to improve yourself with realistic expectations, you should not take yourself too seriously. Lighten the load by acknowledging your humanity. Humor, especially if it's self-directed, is a liberating way to transcend your attachment to the petty details that bind you to unrealistic expectations.

Cultivating a sense of humor is good for the brain and the mind. There are several physiological changes that occur, particularly in the cardiovascular system, the immune system, and the musculature. Dopamine and endorphins are released when you experience mirth.

Benefits of Laughter
- Improves cognitive function
- Exercises and relaxes the muscles
- Momentarily increases the heart rate and the blood pressure
- Decreases the cortisol level
- Increases natural killer cell activity
- Alters gene expression
- Stimulates dopamine
- Increases longevity

It's important that the type of humor you cultivate is positive. Negative humor, the kind of humor that belittles another person, is not wise, it's petty. Positive humor, the kind of humor that looks at light irony, metaphor, incongruity, and unbelievable believability, elevates rather than degrades. Cultivating positive humor enhances mental health.

Psychological Benefits of Humor

↓ Anxiety
↓ Stress
↓ Depression
↑ Self-esteem
↑ Energy and hope
↑ Sense of empowerment

Positive humor boosts the vitality of your thoughts and your emotions and enhances your self-esteem and your ability to deal with stress, anxiety, and depression.

Given all the health benefits that it provides, positive humor can be understood as an aspect of wisdom. So lighten up and be wise! Have a good laugh. It's good for your brain.

9

The Mindful Attitude

Angela came to see me after her primary care physician told her that he wouldn't schedule a return appointment unless she saw a psychologist first. He told me that he thought her problems were more psychological than physical. "She seems to look for physical problems that don't exist, then she obsesses about them."

After she sat down in my office, the first thing out of her mouth was, "I don't know what you are supposed to do for me." She then stared at me as if I had the answer.

Instead of taking the bait and providing the expected wrong answer, I told her that I wished to help her, but I, too, needed to discover how I could be helpful.

"He says that my attitude makes me sick," she explained.

When I asked for clarification, Angela told me that she went to see her doctor for any type of ailment, even when she had a cough or a skin abrasion. She added that she was an avid daytime TV talk show viewer and that she watched the talk shows to "learn what I can about how to stay healthy." After watching a television show on attention deficit disorder, she worried that she needed to be treated for it—until there was a show on fibromyalgia, and then she worried about that. She told me that she "learned" the most from medical shows like *ER*. "I go to my doctor just so I know that I'm okay. Isn't that what he's for, to provide checkups?" she inquired. "But I doubt if he's really taking me seriously."

"It sounds as if doubting all the time increases your worrying," I pointed out.

"Isn't it better to be safe than sorry?" Angela asked.

"Maybe worrying all the time causes your body to be unnecessarily stressed," I suggested, "and maybe *that* is something to worry about." It was clear that she needed to shift her attention from worrying about her health to figuring out how she could improve her overall health by changing her attitude. The question in my mind was how I could stir up the motivation in her to make that shift in attention. Since anxiety seemed to be the underlying cause of her tendency to focus on the negative aspects of her health, I tapped into that to motivate her to pay attention to something she could change: her tendency to worry excessively about one health concern after another. She needed to understand the impact that excessive worrying was having on her body and her brain. I explained that the release of cortisol damages many body systems when an increased level is extreme and prolonged.

Paradoxically, this information gave her something to really worry about: that she could be worrying too much. Her new worry was that she could be doing damage to her brain if her stress level was high enough and sustained over a long period. This motivated her to ask me about ways that she could prevent this from happening. "What about my personality would make me so susceptible to such destructive forces?" Angela wanted to know.

I told her that her problem seemed to stem from jumping from one concern to another and not using her attentional capacity to stay focused.

"I'm focused on my health!" she exclaimed, as if I hadn't heard anything she said.

"You're worried about your health, but you're not doing anything to improve it," I noted.

Angela shrugged her shoulders. She seemed to be ready to hear more, but she didn't want to come right out and say it.

We therefore started our work by addressing how she could apply her attention differently in her life. I asked her to be much more selective in what she watched on television, limiting her viewing to just a few programs.

"What's wrong with TV?" she asked, looking at me as if I were crazy.

"To begin with, it takes you away from being attentive to the present," I said. "You've become a vicarious observer rather than a participant in the world. When are you truly present?"

"What do you mean participate in the world? I'm present!" Angela insisted.

"Other than go to work and watch television, what do you do with your attention?" I asked.

"It doesn't seem like I have much time for anything else," she replied, then looked at me shyly, as if acknowledging my point that she had prevented herself from focusing her attention on anything else.

"Maybe it's time to enjoy the rest of the world," I suggested.

"I have no idea what you're talking about," she said, with an indignant look on her face.

I explained that her attention did not have to be wasted on nuisance worries that only increased her stress and adversely affected her brain. By learning to shift her attention, she could decrease her stress level and enjoy a more fulfilling life. Angela acknowledged that she did not find her life very fulfilling, and she found herself living as if on autopilot.

To break out of her autopilot mode and learn to shift her attention to being present in the world required that she break old habits. I therefore asked her to shut off the television, since it was wasted "dead time." Initially, Angela wasn't sure if she could stop watching so much TV; she said that she was addicted to it. She always felt anxious and empty after watching, yet at the same time she felt as though she hadn't gotten enough. Although Angela didn't actually have attention deficit disorder, she felt unable to sit down and focus on reading a book. It seemed like too much work, and her mind would wander by the time she reached the bottom of the page.

I explained that her frontal lobe, and specifically her DLPFC, needed some practice developing attentional skills. Her brain needed to get in shape, and she would have to rewire it by making a concerted effort to pay attention.

In the weeks to come, I taught Angela how to widen her attention span. This shift in focus helped her to develop a perspective that kindled more overall enjoyment and calmness. She learned how to practice mindfulness meditation, and this helped her to shift away from a superficial mode of attention to a broader, here-and-now focus. Mindfulness involved a new mode of attention that allowed her to savor the complete moment and not skim the surface of life.

By applying the FEED method, Angela gained ground in rewiring her attentional circuits. Several times along the way, she became distracted by real-life events. First there was a conflict at work between two coworkers who threatened to drag her into the fight. We talked about how she could focus on the positive aspects of her relationships with each party and manage to stay friends with both.

Next, a neighbor left a considerable amount of trash next to her property that became an extreme distraction every time she went outside. This served as a great opportunity to learn to see beyond the trash and enjoy the changing leaves of autumn. As other distractions occurred along the way, I helped her to get back on track and return to the FEED plan. Eventually, her life became far less complicated. Her visits to her doctor dropped dramatically, so much so that *he* actually called to check up on *her*!

Angela's case is probably more extreme than what you are experiencing, yet it illustrates how someone can become so distracted by nuisance worries that she makes herself unhealthy. To gain her health back required a focus on the here and now. It meant rewiring her PFC. By applying the FEED method, she felt not only more present but also more alive.

Awakening from Sleepwalking

Unfortunately, Angela's attention problems are all too common in our society. Many people need to rewire their PFC. Their attention skills are slipping away from a lack of rigorous use. There is an increased tendency in our society to fragment our attention.

Attention is critical for a thriving brain. Television and other modern forms of mass media have contributed to attention (and thus brain) problems. In the last thirty years, especially, these forms of media have catered to the lowest common denominator by adjusting their formatting to meet the growing attentional incompetence of their consumers. The electronic media further increase the attention problems of their viewers. When you surf the Internet, one momentary click can move you off a page that does not completely grab your attention to another site that does. We have all the necessary ingredients for an attention-deficit society.

All the flashing images in the media can wear you down. Your orientation response, which is your response to novel information, is continually exhausted by new images that flash before your eyes, giving you little time to recover. It is no wonder that after watching television, Angela felt drained yet also wanted more. These symptoms can also occur after surfing the Internet for a long time. Media addiction is no mere metaphor.

A lifetime of media consumption can take its toll. In fact, excessive consumption of television during early childhood has been shown to have long-lasting detrimental effects. For example, excessive exposure to television correlates with problems paying attention and controlling impulses years later. An important study of twenty-six toddlers found that the amount of exposure to television between ages one and three correlated with the diagnosis of ADHD by age seven. Specifically, for every hour of TV the toddlers watched each day, their chances of developing serious problems with attention increased by 10 percent.

There are too many aspects of our society that seduce you into seeing only the superficial and the sensational. Movies, television, and even the news have melted down our concerns to mediocrity.

Pictures of Angelina Jolie's babies get far more coverage in the press than the destitute in Africa do, which she tried to draw attention to.

You should try to wake up from this societal sleepwalking and break out of autopilot to pay attention to the depth and complexity below the glaze and sensation. Waking up involves paying attention to even the most routine of tasks. For example, as you drive to work each day on the same highway, you can become numb to your surroundings. You pay little attention to the houses, the fields, and the hills that you routinely pass. To break out of this autopilot mode, say to yourself that you will look for a house that you have never noticed before or a part of the topography that you have never examined. By activating your perceptual capacities and the executive control center of your frontal lobes, you can wake up and transform an experience you have taken for granted into one that is rich and multidimensional. The more you feed your brain with this attentional shift, the more it becomes your way of being present in the world.

The Grand Canyon

I am writing this section from the bottom of the Grand Canyon. A mindful attitude plays a large role in how to be present down here. When my camera fell and broke within the first hour of the hike, I was disappointed and frustrated. I was looking forward to taking photos of my wife and myself in this amazing place.

I made a deal with myself to transform the thoughts of the broken camera into a constant reminder to focus on the grandeur of the place, despite this being my twenty-seventh hike to the bottom, to try to absorb it with greater poignancy and depth than on my first time. Had I been oriented toward taking photos, I would have put most of my energy into anticipating how to compose the pictures so that we might experience the pictures later with greater awe. Instead, I transformed the disappointment into an opportunity to enhance my reverence for that which is greater than my insignificant plans. I have that sense of awe now.

Certainly this is an easy place to bathe in the wonder of the natural world. Hiking down two and a half billion years in geological time is far more than a reminder that we humans aren't even a blip on time's radar screen. As I look around me at rainbow-colored rocks that change shades throughout the day and the vast distances etched with thousands of cliff faces, I realize that this could never be captured by a camera. The picture-taking would be a nuisance and a petty distraction. The experience is far more powerful because I am focused on the present.

The Grand Canyon serves as a dramatic example of the transcending perspective. You can use it as a metaphor for how not to take petty problems seriously. Hiking the canyon provides a splash of cold water on the face, waking up to what the world has been and is now.

Focused Attention

The PFC differentiates our species from others. It is the most recent evolutionary advance of the brain and was the last to myelinate (the process of coating the axons to facilitate more efficient firing of the neurons) while you were growing up. In fact, the PFC is not finished myelinating until your mid-twenties. That means that it was not until you were in your twenties that many of the skills that your PFC provides were developed. These skills include the ability to maintain sustained attention and make complex decisions. Unfortunately, there are far too many adults who have not completely developed these skills or have lost them due to lack of use. Angela was one of those who let her attentional skills atrophy, but she worked to recover them through the FEED method.

Throughout this book I have described how activating the PFC helps neuroplasticity to occur. The first two steps of FEED activate the PFC, especially the DLPFC, which is the executive control center, or the brain's brain. The DLPFC processes working memory. Damage to or a lack of training of it results in problems in attention and working memory. Since attention starts the neuroplastic process rolling, attentional problems shut it down.

How you focus your attention plays a critical role in how you deal with stress. Scattered attention impairs your ability to let go of stress, because even though your attention is scattered, it is narrowly focused, for you are able to fixate only on the stressful parts of your experience. When your attentional spotlight is widened, you can more easily let go of stress. You can put in perspective many more aspects of any situation and not get locked into one part that ties you down to superficial and anxiety-provoking levels of attention. A narrow focus amplifies the stress level of each experience, but a widened focus turns down the stress level because you're better able to put each situation into a broader perspective. One anxiety-provoking detail is less important than the bigger picture. It's like transforming yourself into a nonstick frying pan. You can still fry an egg, but the egg won't stick to the pan.

By widening your attentional focus, you can become an observer. This is because you're watching all aspects of every experience and considering how they interrelate. It's a macro perspective rather than a micro perspective.

Biofeedback expert Les Fehmi of Princeton University has suggested that by practicing what he calls *open focus* (widened or diffuse attention), you can reverse the strains of stress. Open focus shifts your brain away from an emergency state that is characterized by a narrow focus. When he and other researchers used electroencephalograph (EEG) instruments to measure brain-wave activity, they discovered that particular patterns represent specific states of mind. When you shift to an open focus, your brain's electrical activity drops to more relaxed lower frequencies. During an open-focus state, the sympathetic part of your autonomic nervous system, which engages the fight-or-flight response, tones down, and the parasympathetic system increases its dominance. This means that by practicing open focus you activate your parasympathetic nervous system and a more relaxed state of mind.

Open-focus attention increases the efficiency of large groups of neurons that fire together. When these groups include neurons that fire for extended periods in synchrony, there is a greater potential to enhance your mental health. The term *phase synchrony* means that many parts of the brain are producing alpha waves, which are associated with a state of wakeful relaxation, and that these brain waves are rising and falling in unison (Fehmi and Robbins, 2007). This means that large numbers of neurons are firing together to produce powerful types of focused brain activity.

When you produce high-frequency, nonsynchronous beta-wave (associated with normal waking consciousness) activity, it's like the chatter of many people at a party having separate conversations. In contrast, synchronized lower-frequency brain waves are like everyone at the party singing together. It is like the fourth movement of Beethoven's Ninth Symphony: the chorus is magnificent and the experience is transcendent.

Parasympathetic Meditation

The antithesis of the fight-or-flight response is the relaxation response, which is the body's way of calming itself down. The relaxation response involves activating the parasympathetic nervous system, which promotes a slower heart rate and a slower breathing rate, whereas the fight-or-flight response is activated by the sympathetic nervous system.

During the last few thousand years, people in societies throughout the world have developed techniques to induce the relaxation response. They activated the parasympathetic nervous system without knowing of its existence. Various techniques were developed to cultivate a state of calmness and stillness. The increased feelings of tranquility gave them a sense of peace and unity with their environment. The techniques used to gain these experiences are prayer and meditation, which are facilitated by an open focus and by widened attention.

The parasympathetic nervous system can also be activated by the more recently developed methods of self-hypnosis, visual imagery, and relaxation techniques. When I was trained in hypnotherapy in the early 1980s, I noticed significant similarities with the meditation practices that I had learned in the early 1970s. All these methods promote relaxation and a sense of inner peace. Although the names and methods are different, they involve the same principles of widened attention and the same brain physiology, which I'll describe later in this chapter.

Too often we look for special differences and want to believe that our own method is more powerful, sacred, or pure than the others. Although researchers have examined one technique at time, these studies reveal many common denominators.

The methods of hypnosis, prayer, meditation, visual imagery, and relaxation all involve widened attention and the letting go of sympathetic nervous system arousal while doing things to activate the parasympathetic nervous system. The first step of each method is to focus on breathing, which serves many purposes. By breathing abdominally, you can shift from your sympathetic to your parasympathetic nervous system. This slows your heart rate, which calms you, and activates neurochemical systems that calm your amygdala. By focusing on breathing, you can also clear out the nervous chatter of worries from your mind.

Meditation combined with yoga promotes physiological as well as mental calming. Since a considerable amount of energy is wasted in maintaining muscle tension when you suffer from stress, you may feel all wound up and thus fatigued. When chronic stress builds up in the muscles, it makes the tendons thicken and shorten due to overdevelopment of the connective tissue. Stress contributes to the overactivity of the sympathetic nervous system, which results in a buildup of tension in an already taxed nervous system. A quick way to get rid of the buildup of tension and activate the parasympathetic nervous system is to stretch and breathe deeply.

The brain requires a steady flow of blood, and since the muscles are endowed with a rich blood supply, stretching can facilitate a healthy blood flow to the brain. Stretching, like exercise, promotes an energized capacity to focus combined with a feeling of relaxation. By stretching your muscles, you force or pump the used and deoxygenated blood back into your heart and lungs for refueling.

This results in the replenishment of your brain with reoxygenated blood. Stretching therefore promotes a refreshed brain, invigorates the muscles, and releases built-up tension.

Combining the practices used by yogis for a few thousand years with simple stretching synthesizes many techniques and can be called *hybrid yoga*. Hybrid yoga does not have to be a complicated routine that you engage in only when you have set aside a block of time. You can take a moment, even when you're at work, to slow your heart rate by breathing deeply, stretching, and focusing your attention on how your muscles feel as they are stretched. Try to visualize relaxing your muscles so they won't constrict your blood from flowing back to your heart for reoxygenation. After visualizing your heart revitalizing your blood, imagine how that blood flows to your brain and brings nutrients that make your brain both more relaxed and more alert.

You can do all of this in just two to five minutes. When you return to whatever task you had been trying to accomplish, you'll find that you've rid yourself of built-up stress and that you're able to engage in the task at hand with renewed vigor and a calm sense of alertness.

For example, let's say you're at work in your office cubicle or you're in the break room and you have only about five minutes to practice a little hybrid yoga. Stand with your feet separated by approximately thirty inches. Bend over and stretch your arms toward your toes. If you can touch your toes, fine. If not, don't worry about it. Feel your muscles stretch and the blood flow downward. Gradually stand up straight and raise your arms outward and upward, making a V and inhaling deeply to fill your lungs to capacity. As you are standing completely straight with your arms extended upward, hold your breath for ten seconds, then let your arms slowly drop while continuing to keep them extended. Exhale deeply and let out more air than you think you have to exhale. Once your arms have dropped to form an inverted V, repeat the entire process.

There are seven general principles to follow to activate your parasympathetic nervous system. These principles make up hybrid yoga (but are common to prayer, meditation, relaxation exercises, and hypnosis as well) and can be referred to as *parasympathetic meditation*. Think of these principles as a way to refresh your brain and feel more calm, focused, and energized. The seven principles of parasympathetic meditation are as follows:

1. **Rhythmic breathing:** Deep, deliberate, and focused breathing allows you to slow your heart rate and to calm down.
2. **Focused attention:** By widening your attention, you can focus on the here and now. This activates the PFC and enhances its ability to inhibit the overreactivity of the amygdala and the sympathetic nervous system.
3. **Quiet environment:** This will give you an opportunity to focus attention without distractions. Later, when you cannot be in a quiet environment, you'll have a head start in learning to feed your brain because you've already practiced in a quiet environment. This prepares you to avoid distractions later.
4. **Accepting and nonjudgmental attitude:** By shifting away from narrow and rigid expectations to an accepting attitude, you'll appreciate reality as it is rather than what you fear it could be. Consequently, you'll have greater resiliency in adjusting to whatever happens.
5. **Relaxed posture:** This can be achieved by sitting or by stretching.
6. **Observation:** By widening your focus and observing instead of worrying about each detail, you can detach from stress while not denying its existence. As you observe events and situations nonjudgmentally, you can simply note what is occurring at any given time. When you take the vantage point of an observer, you are no longer the victim, and you are able to detach from stress.
7. **Labeling:** Your experiences activate your left frontal lobe and its positive emotions. Labeling works if you remain in an accepting and nonjudgmental attitude as a detached observer and practice all the previous steps.

Mindfulness

A popular type of meditation derived from Buddhism is referred to as mindfulness, Vipassana, or insight meditation. Mindfulness has been used in the treatment of anxiety, depression, and other psychological problems. This technique does not utilize a mantra or prayer phrases. The focus is on breathing, observing, accepting, and cultivating a nonjudgmental attitude. Generally, mindfulness embraces the seven principles described above.

Mindfulness involves observing and accepting your thoughts, your physical sensations, and your emotions as they enter and exit your awareness. By maintaining a nonjudgmental attitude, you can take a step back from these things. You can observe them arise and fall back, like the tides on a beach. This is what I mean by a detached and nonjudgmental attitude.

Mindfulness can be practiced any time throughout the day or the evening. You can practice it even now, as you're reading this book. Sit back and feel the weight of the book in your hands. Feel the texture of the cover. As you breathe in and out deeply, feel the temperature in the room on your skin. Is it warm or cool? Random thoughts might come to mind. Simply observe and accept them as they pass by, as if they are cars going slowly by. You don't have to stop any of the "cars" to examine them; just let them pass by. Another one will soon follow. By practicing this type of observance and acceptance, you can detach from your worries and concerns. They can simply drift by, not sticking around long enough to take root.

By being in the moment, you can cleanse yourself of the nuisance worries and anxiety about what to do about something in the future that might not even happen. Being present in the here and now brings the present moment alive and allows your brain to experience the vibrancy and rich multidimensionality of the now.

You can develop a nonjudgmental attitude by maintaining an observing perspective. As you simply observe rather than react to what is occurring at any given time, you delay reacting to the situation until all the information is put in perspective. The enlarged perspective is consistent with the open-focus state. In contrast to the all-too-common narrow, rigid, and reactive state, the mindful or open-focus perspective allows you to detach from stressors because you are taking a step back and observing instead of immediately reacting to them. Mindfulness meditation develops the ability to resist automatically reacting to any stressor. Instead, you can mindfully observe and appreciate the rich complexity of each experience.

Because the mindfulness meditation and the open-focus biofeedback techniques help you to resist reacting to worries or discomfort, they have been used to treat general medical problems such as chronic pain. The highlight of these methods contains an interesting paradox about how to apply attention to pain: instead of trying to keep pain out of your mind, your task is to accept the pain. This might seem bizarre. Why accept the pain? Won't that make you feel it more? The answer is no; you'll actually experience less pain. Mindfulness training can alter how your brain works to lower your reactivity to pain. By observing and accepting the pain, you paradoxically detach from the intensity of the pain.

Mindfulness is also effective with stress, anxiety, and depression. I teach mindfulness in my anxiety class because the research supports its efficacy. Here is a brief summary of how it works:

- The process of labeling your emotions activates your left PFC, which reduces anxiety.
- There is a strong relationship between a high level of mindfulness and the neural activity in your left PFC, which tames your amygdala.
- These positive effects seem to correlate with enhancements in your neural emotional regulation pathways.

Mindfulness practice has been shown to have a positive influence on the immune system and on the reduction of anxiety and depression. It has been used successfully with people who have a great deal of difficulty controlling their emotions, people with OCD, and people with general medical problems such as chronic pain.

The benefits of the kind of detached observing that mindfulness provides can help you to cope with a wide range of potential irritants. It is no wonder that people who practice mindfulness on a regular basis have strong coping skills and are resilient in the face of adversity. Cultivating these skills can help you to rewire your brain.

The Mindful Brain

The Dalai Lama has said that if scientific discoveries conflict with Buddhist doctrine, the doctrine must evolve with these discoveries. Indeed, he has taken a big interest in neuroscience and has invited the major researchers to present their discoveries. The research on meditation has consequently flowered and has shown how mindfulness positively affects the brain.

The quality and form of attention appears to be the central issue. I have stressed throughout this book that attention is a necessary prerequisite for neuroplasticity. Mindfulness is also all about attention. Mindfulness meditation mentally engages one's concentration, which alters the connections between the thinking (cortex) and the emotional (amygdala) parts of your brain.

The parts of your brain that make it possible for you to be fully present, with reverence for each moment, have been identified by researchers at the University of Wisconsin, led by Richard Davidson. The cortical networks that involve the front of the cingulate cortex (the part of the brain that is correlated with empathy and self-awareness), the insula (the part of the brain that pays close attention to internal body states), and the somatosensory cortex (the part of the brain that senses your body in space) seem to be activated together. Also of principal importance is that the activity of the left PFC eclipses that of the right.

Using a variety of brain-imaging methods, Davidson and his colleagues examined the brains of Tibetan monks who have practiced meditation for many years. The results show a shift to relatively more activation of the left frontal lobe than of the right frontal lobe.

The monks' brain waves also showed distinct patterns. Their brain activity tied together different brain systems.

There are particular brain regions that are emphasized by practicing mindfulness meditation. The middle of the PFC is involved in self-observation and is associated with mindfulness meditation. This area has been described as the center of metacognition (thinking about thinking) or awareness. A state of positive attention made possible by the left frontal lobe combines with tactile sensations (the somatosensory cortex), decisions, empathy, and emotion (the front of the cingulate cortex).

The Tibetan monks who practice compassion meditation appear to activate their left OFC. When their brains have been examined, their left OFCs were found to be thicker than those of nonmeditators.

When the monks were asked to generate feelings of compassion, their brain activity indicated that many neural structures were firing in synchrony with one another. An increase in synchronized brain waves produces a signal at a rate of twenty-five to forty times per second, which is a rhythm known as *gamma-band oscillation*. Even during so-called resting periods, the gamma-wave activity does not die down. These increases in gamma-wave activity were some of the largest that have ever been seen.

The tendency for brain systems to fire synchronously promotes better mental health. Researchers have described the neural circuits of various styles of emotional reactivity and resilience. Mindfulness training can alter these neural functions and promote nonreactivity. Davidson has shown that a left frontal shift occurs when we focus on emotionally provocative activity. Stress tolerance increases when many brain systems fire synchronously with gamma waves and when there is an increased emphasis on left frontal lobe activity.

The following is a summation of mindfulness and the brain:

- Long-term meditators show an increased thickness of the middle of the PFC and an enlargement of the right insula.
- The process of labeling emotional states with words reduces anxiety and negative emotions.

- The middle of the PFC has been associated with self-observation and mindfulness meditation.
- A shift to the left PFC puts a positive spin on the experience.

Mindfulness meditation promotes an internal attunement that harnesses the social circuits of mirror neurons, which correlate with empathy. There is a sense of empathy for yourself that is cultivated by enhanced self-awareness, and with long-term practice there is an opportunity for greater self-regulation.

The top of the temporal lobe pays attention to breathing and then primes the brain to get ready for the next breath. This may contribute to an integration of the sense of self, which leads to harmony between the autonomic nervous system and cortical functioning. By enhancing phase synchrony, the middle of the PFC helps you to feel more present, relaxed, and in harmony with yourself and your environment.

The front of the cingulate cortex seems to be activated during mindfulness, partly because of its involvement in the attentional network. Long-term meditators show an increased thickness of the middle of the PFC and an enlargement of the right insula. The increased thickness in these brain regions may be the results of years of reflective practice, a hypothesis that is supported by several studies.

One of the many concerns that people have when I talk to them about mindfulness meditation is how to respond to the thoughts that come up as they meditate. This concern is based on the mistaken belief that they must force everything out of their minds but a mantra. However, if you try to avoid all thoughts, you will overactivate your right frontal lobe, which ironically sets the stage for the very production of those thoughts or anxious feelings that you are trying to escape. The key is to accept your thoughts and not become attached to them. If pink flamingos pass through your mind, say, "So what?" One way to accept your thoughts and detach from them is to label them as they come up: "Oh, there's another pink flamingo. It's no big deal." By practicing this method of detached labeling, pink flamingos (or whatever you are hoping to avoid) become less present in your mind.

Research suggests that labeling your emotions may be an effective way to neutralize negative ones. In fact, mindfulness-based cognitive therapy encourages the use of words to label emotional states, such as saying, "Here is anger." Labeling emotions appears to calm the amygdala. Imaging studies show that this is what happens in psychotherapy. A high degree of mindfulness also seems to correlate with enhancements in the neural pathways that regulate affect. Mindfulness practice cultivates positive feelings and has a positive influence on your immune system.

Too often, when we are with our most intimate partners, we are thinking of what we need to do or where we have to be. Since the brain thrives on relationships, and mindfulness enhances calmness and increased attentional skills, the two of you can work together on this process. Being mindfully present in each moment that you are together will enhance your relationship. By acknowledging and sensitizing your response to your mirror neural pathways, you can kindle empathy and transform your relationships, not to mention enriching your experience by sharing the world with others.

Many years ago I attempted to analyze the historical development of all the major theological systems to explore what commonalities existed among them. I was dissatisfied with the New Age belief that all theologies ultimately say the same thing. The fact is that all theologies have emerged within the cultural contexts of their historical eras and their societies. There is a wide spectrum of traditions and beliefs in the world's theologies, and I found only two common principles: compassion and unity.

These two principles make sense from a brain-based perspective. Developing compassion and an appreciation of our interdependence (unity) is good for the brain. Thus, striving to be compassionate and to appreciate your interdependence with others helps you to rewire your brain. Since compassion is one of the central tenets of all the great religions, we can say that rewiring your brain with the mindfulness principles described in this chapter is a pious endeavor.

Mindfulness, prayer, open focus, self-hypnosis—whatever you want to call the methodology that you use—can enhance your ability to stay calm and positive, thereby promoting neuroplasticity.

The more you feed your brain with these techniques, the greater the opportunity for you to rewire your brain.

All the methods and exercises outlined in this book to rewire your brain can transform your life so that you can savor each moment and thrive now and in the future.

References

1. Firing the Right Cells Together

Allman, J., Hakeem, A., & Watson, K. (2002). Two phylogenetic specializations in the human brain. *Neuroscientist, 8*, 335–346.

Doidge, N. (2007). *The brain that changes itself.* New York: Viking Press.

Dolan, R. J. (1999). On the neurology of morals. *Nature Neuroscience, 2* (11), 927–929.

Elbert, T., Pantev, C., Weinbruch, C., Rockstrob, B., & Taub, E. (1995). Increased cortical representation of the fingers of the left hand in string players. *Science, 270*, 305–307.

Frings, L., Wagner, K., Unterrainer, J., Spreer, J., Halsband, V., & Schulze-Bonhange, A. (2006). Gender-related differences in lateralization of hippocampal activation and cognitive strategy. *Brain Imaging, 17*, 417–421.

Leigland, L. A., Schulz, L. E., & Janowsky, J. S. (2004). Age-related changes in emotional memory. *Neurobiology of Aging, 25*, 1117–1124.

MacPherson, S. E., Philips, L. H., & Della Salla, S. (2002). Ages, executive function, and social decision making: A dorsolateral prefrontal theory of cognitive aging. *Psychology and Aging, 17,* 598–609.

Pascual-Leone, A., Amedi, A., Fregi, F., & Merabet, L. B. (2005). The plastic human brain cortex. *Annual Reviews of Neuroscience, 28,* 380.

Pascual-Leone, A., Hamilton, R., Tormos, J. M., Keenan, J. P., & Catala, M. D. (1999). Neuroplasticity in the adjustment to blindness. In J. Grafman & Y. Christen (Eds.), *Neural plasticity: Building a bridge from the laboratory to the clinic* (pp. 94–108). New York: Springer-Verlag.

Rosenzweig, E. S., Barnes, C. A., & McNaughton, B. L. (2002). Making room for new memories. *Nature Neuroscience, 5* (1), 6–8.

Witelson, S. F., Beresh, H., & Kigar, D. L. (2006). Intelligence and brain size in 100 postmortem brains: Sex, lateralization and age factors. *Brain, 129,* 386–398.

2. Taming Your Amygdala

Arden, J. B. (2009). *Heal Your Anxiety Workbook.* Boston: Fairwinds.

Arden, J. B., & DalCorso, D. (2009). *Heal Your OCD Workbook.* Boston: Fairwinds.

O'Doherty, J., Kringelback, M. L., Rolls, E. T., Hornak, J., & Andrews, C. (2001). Abstract reward and punishment representation in the human orbital frontal cortex. *Nature Neuroscience, 4,* 95–102.

3. Shifting Left

Davidson, R. J., Jackson, L., & Kalin, N. H. (2000). Emotion, plasticity, context, and regulation. *Psychological Bulletin, 126,* 890–909.

Goldapple, K., Segal, Z., Garson, C., Lau, M., Bieling, P., Kennedy, S., & Mayberg, H. (2004, January). Modulation of cortical-limbic pathways in major depression: Treatment-specific effects of cognitive behavioral therapy. *Archives of General Psychiatry, 61,* 34–41.

Kirsch, I. (2002, April 15). Are drug and placebo effects in depression addictive? *Biological Psychiatry, 47,* 733–735.

Lambert, K. (2008). *Lifting depression: A neuroscience hands-on approach to activating your brain's healing power*. New York: Basic Books.

Leuchter, A., Cook, I. A., Witte, E. A., Morgan, M., & Abrams, M. (2002, January). Changes in brain function of depressed subjects during treatment with placebo. *American Journal of Psychiatry, 159*, 122–129.

Mayberg, H., Silva, J. A., Brannan, S. K., Tekell, J. L., Mahurin, R. K., McGunnis, S., & Jarebek, P. A. (2002, May). The functional neuroanatomy of the placebo effect. *American Journal of Psychiatry, 159*, 728–737.

Niemi, M. J. (2009, February/March). Cure in the mind. *Scientific American Mind, 20*, 42–50.

O'Doherty, J., Kringelback, M. L., Rolls, E. T., Hornak, J., & Andrews, C. (2001). Abstract reward and punishment representation in the human orbital frontal cortex. *Nature Neuroscience, 4*, 95–102.

4. Cultivating Memory

Buchanan, T. W., & Adolphs, R. (2004). The neuroanatomy of emotional memory in humans. In D. Reisberg & P. Hertel (Eds.), *Memory and emotion* (pp. 42–75). New York: Oxford University Press.

Cohen, N. J., & Squire, L. R. (1980). Preserved learning and retention of pattern-analyzing skill in amnesia: Dissociation of knowing how and knowing that. *Science, 210*, 207–209.

Golomb, J., deLeon, M. J., Kluger, A., George, A. E., Tarshish, C., & Ferris, S. H. (1993). Hippocampal atrophy in normal aging: An association with recent memory impairment. *Archives of Neurology, 50* (9), 967–973.

Kapur, N., Scholey, K., Moore, E., Barker, S., Brice, J., Thompson, S., et al. (1996). Long-term retention deficits in two cases of disproportionate retrograde amnesia. *Journal of Cognitive Neuroscience, 8*, 416–434.

LeDoux, J. E., Romanski, L. M., & Xagorasis, A. E. (1989). Indelibility of subcortical emotional memories. *Journal of Cognitive Neuroscience, 1*, 238–243.

Milner, B. (1965). Memory disturbances after bilateral hippocampal lesions in man. In P. M. Milner & S. E. Glickman (Eds.), *Cognitive processes and brain*. Princeton, NJ: Van Nostrand.

Ochs, E., & Capps, L. (1996). Narrating the self. *Annual Review of Anthropology, 25,* 19–43.

Reisberg, D., & Heuer, F. (2004). Memory for emotional events. In D. Reisberg & P. Hertel (Eds.), *Memory and emotion* (pp. 3–41). New York: Oxford University Press.

Rudy, J. W., & Morledge, P. (1994). Ontogeny of contextual fear conditioning in rats: Implications for consolidation, infantile amnesia, and hippocampal system function. *Behavioral Neuroscience, 108,* 227–234.

Schacter, D. L. (1996). *Searching for memory: The brain, the mind, and the past*. New York: Basic Books.

Sherry, D. F., & Schacter, D. L. (1987). The evolution of multiple memory systems. *Psychological Review, 94,* 439–454.

5. Fueling Your Brain

Adams, P., Lawson, S., Sanigorski, A., & Sinclair, A.J. (1996). Arachidonic acid to eicosapentaenoic acid ratio in blood correlates positively with clinical symptoms of depression. *Lipids* (Suppl.), *31,* S157–S161.

Amaducci, L., Crook, T. H., & Lippi, A. (1980). Phospholipid methylation and biological signatransmission. *Science, 64,* 245–249.

Bayir, H., Kagan, V. E., Tyurina, Y. Y., Tyurin, V., Ruppel, R., Adelson, P., et al. (2002). Assessment of antioxidant reserves and oxidative stress in the cerebrospinal fluid after severe traumatic brain injury and children. *Pediatric Research, 51,* 571–578.

Benton, D. (2001). The impact of the supply of glucose to the brain on mood and memory. *Nutritional Review, 59* (1), S20–21.

Dittman, J. S., & Regher, W. G. (1997, December 1). Mechanisms and kinetics of hetrosynaptic depression at a cerebella synapse. *Journal of Neuroscience, 17* (23), 9048–9059.

Epstein, F. G. (1996). Mechanisms of disease. *New England Journal of Medicine, 334* (6), 374–381.

Fahn, S. (1989). The endogenous toxin hypothesis of the etiology of Parkinson's disease and a pilot trail of high-dose antioxidants in an attempt to slow the progression of the illness. *Annals of the New York Academy of Sciences, 570,* 186–196.

Farquharoson, J., Jamieson, E. C., Abbasi, K. A., Patrick, W.J.A., Logan, R. W., & Cockburn, F. (1995). Effect of diet on fatty acid composition of the major phospholipids of the infant cerebral cortex. *Archives of Disease in Childhood, 72,* 198–203.

Glen, A.I.M. (1994). A red cell membrane abnormality in a sub-group of schizophrenic patients: Evidence for two diseases. *Schizophrenic Research, 12,* 53–61.

Glueck, C. J., Tieger, M., Kunkel, R., Tracy, T., Speirs, J., Streicher, P., & Illig, E. (1993). Improvements in symptoms of depression and in an index of life stressor accompany treatment of severe hypertriglyceridemia. *Biological Psychiatry, 34* (4), 240–252.

Gustafson, D., Lissner, L., Bengtsson, C., Björkelund, C., & Skoog, I. (2004). A 24-year follow-up of body mass index and cerebral atrophy. *Neurology, 63,* 1876–1881.

Haapalahti, M., Mykkänen, H., Tikkanen, S., & Kokkonen, J. (2004). Food habits in 10- to 11-year-old children with functional gastro-intestinal disorders. *European Journal of Clinical Nutrition, 58* (7), 1016–1021.

Haatainen, K., Honkalampi, K., & Viinamaki, H. (2001). *Fish consumption, depression, and suicidality in a general population.* Paper presented at the Fourth Congress of the International Society for the Study of Lipids and Fatty Acids, Tsukuba, Japan.

Hibbelin, J. R. (1998). Fish consumption and major depression. *Lancet, 351,* 1213.

Hu, Y., Block, G., Norkus, E., Morrow, J. D., Dietrich, M., & Hudes, M. (2006). Relations of glycemic load with plasma oxidative stress marker. *American Journal of Clinical Nutrition, 84* (1), 70–76.

Jeong, S. K., Nam, H. S., Son, E. J., & Cho, K. H. (2005). Interactive effect of obesity indexes on cognition. *Dementia, Geriatric Cognitive Disorders, 19* (2–3), 91–96.

Johnson, H., Russell, J. K., & Torres, B. A. (1998). Structural basis for arachiadonic acid and second messenger signal in gamma-interon induction. *Annual New York Academy of Sciences, 524,* 208–217.

Jones, T., Borg, W., Boulware, S. D., McCarthy, G., Sherwin, R. S., & Tamborlane, W. V. (1995). Enhanced adrenomedullary response and increased susceptibility to neuroglycapenia: Mechanisms underlying the adverse effects of sugar ingestion in healthy children. *Journal of Pediatrics, 126* (2), 1717.

Joseph, J. A., Shukitt-Hale, B., Denisova, N. A., Bielinski, D., Martin, A., McEwen, J. J., & Bickford, P. C. (1999). Reversals of age-related declines in neuronal signal transduction, cognitive, and motor behavior deficits with blueberry, spinach or strawberries dietary supplementation. *Journal of Neuroscience, 19,* 8114–8121.

Kikuchi, S., Shinpo, K., Takeuchi, M., Yamagishi, S., Makita, Z., Sasaki, N., & Tashiro, K. (2003, March). Glycation—a sweet tempter for neuronal death. *Brain Research Review, 41,* 306–323.

Laganiere, S., & Fernandez, G. (1987). High peroxidizability of subcellular membrane induce by high fish oil diet is reversed by vitamin E. *Clinical Research, 35* (3), 565A.

Logan, A. C. (2007). *The brain diet.* Nashville, TN: Cumberland House.

Maes, M. (1996) Fatty acid composition in major depression: Decreased n-3 fractions in cholesteryl esters and increased C20: 4n-6/c20: 5n-3 ratio in cholesteryl esters and phospholipids. *Journal of Affective Disorders, 38,* 35–46.

Martin, A., Cherubini, A., Andres-Lacueva, C., Paniagua, M., & Joseph, J. (2002). Effects of fruits and vegetables on levels of vitamins E and C in the brain and their association with cognitive performance. *Journal of Nutrition, Health, and Aging, 6* (6), 392–404.

Morris, M. (2006, November). Docosahexaenoic acid and Alzheimer's disease. *Archives of Neurology, 63,* 1527–1528.

Murphey, J. M., Pagano, M. E., Nachmani, J., Sperling, P., Kane, S., & Kleinman, R. E. (1998). The relationship of school breakfast and psychosocial and academic functioning. *Archives of Pediatric Adolescent Medicine, 152,* 899–907.

National Institute of Alcohol Abuse and Alcoholism. (1985). *Alcohol health and research world.* (U.S. Department of Health and Human Services Pub. No. ADM 85–151.) Washington, DC: U.S. Government Printing Office.

Petersen, J., & Opstvedt, J. (1992). Trans fatty acids: Fatty acid consumption of lipids of the brain and other organs in suckling piglets. *Lipids, 27* (10), 761–769.

Practico, D., Clark, C., Liun, F., Lee, V., & Trojanowski, I. (2002). Increase of brain oxidative stress in mild cognitive impairment: A possible predictor of Alzheimer's disease. *Archives of Neurology, 59,* 972–976.

Reichenberg, A., Yirmiya, R., Schuld, A., Kraus, T., Haack, M., Morag, A., & Pollmächer, T. (2001, May). Cytokine-associated emotional and cognitive disturbance in humans. *Archives of General Psychiatry, 58,* 445–452.

Rudin, D. O. (1985). Omega-3 essential fatty acids in medicine. In J. S. Bland (Ed.), *1984–85 Yearbook in Nutritional Medicine* (p. 41). New Canaan, CT: Keats.

Rudin, D. O. (1987). Modernization disease syndrome as a substitute pellagra-beriberi. *Journal of Orthomolecular Medicine, 2* (1), 3–14.

Sampson, M. J., Nitin Gopaul, N., Isabel, R, Davies, I. R., Hughes, D. A., & Carrier, M. J. (2002). Plasma F2 isoprostanes: Direct evidence of increased free radical damage during acute hypoglycemia in type 2 diabetes. *Diabetes Care, 25* (3), 537–541.

Sano, M. (1997). Vitamin E supplementation appears to slow progression of Alzheimer's disease. *New England Journal of Medicine, 336,* 1216–1222.

Schauss, A. (1984). Nutrition and behavior: Complex interdisciplinary research. *Nutritional Health, 3* (1–2), 9–37.

Schmidt, M. A. (2007). *Brain-building nutrition: How dietary fat and oils affect mental, physical, and emotional intelligence* (3rd ed.). Berkeley, CA: Frog Books.

Sehub, J., Jacques, P. F., Bostom, A. G., D'Agostino, R. B., Wilson, P. W. F., Belanger, A. J. B., et al. (1995). Association between plasma homocystine concentrations and extracranial carotid stenosis. *New England Journal of Medicine, 332* (5), 286–291.

Simopoulos, A. P. (1996). Omega-3 fatty acids. In G. A. Spiller (Ed.), *Handbook of lipids in human nutrition* (pp. 51–73). Boca Raton, FL: CRC Press.

Slutsky, I., Sadeghpour, S., Li, B., & Lui, G. (2004). Enhancement of synaptic plasticity through chronically reduced Ca2+ flux during uncorrelated activity. *Neuron, 44* (5), 835–849.

Smith, D. (2002, April). Stress, breakfast, cereal consumption and cortisol. *Nutritional Neuroscience, 5,* 141–144.

Smith, D. (2006). Prevention of dementia: A role for B vitamin? *Nutrition Health, 18* (3), 225–226.

Sublette, M. E., Hibbeln, J. R., Galfalvy, H., Oquendo, M. A., & Mann, J. J. (2006). Omega-3 polyunsaturated essential fatty acids status as a predictor of future suicidal risk. *American Journal of Psychiatry, 163* (6), 1100–1102.

Subramanian, N. (1980). Mini review on the brain: Ascorbic acid and its importance in metabolism of biogenic amines. *Life Sciences, 20,* 1479–1484.

Tanskanen, A., Hibbeln, J. R., Hintikka, J., Haatainen, K., Honkalampi, H., & Vjinamaki, H. (2001). Fish consumption, depression, and suicidality in a general population. *Archives of General Psychiatry, 58* (5), 512–513.

Tiemeir, H., Tuijl, R. van, Hoffman, A., Kilaan, A. J., & Breteler, M.M.B. (2003). Plasma fatty acid composition and depression are associated in the elderly: The Rotterdam Study. *American Journal of Clinical Nutrition, 78* (1), 40–46.

Warnberg, J., Nova, E., Moreno, L. A., Romeo J., Mesana, M. I., Ruiz J. R., Ortega, F. B., & Sjöström, M. (2006). Inflammatory proteins are related to total and abdominal adiposity in a healthy adolescent population: The AVENA Study. *American Journal of Clinical Nutrition, 84* (3), 503–512.

Wesnes, K. A., Pincock, C., Richardson, D., Helm, G., & Hails, S. (2003). Breakfast reduces declines in attention and memory over the morning in schoolchildren. *Appetite, 41,* 329–331.

Winter, A., & Winter, R. (2007). *Smart food: Diet and nutrition for maximum brain power.* New York: ASJA Press.

Wurtman, R. J., & Zeisel, S. H. (1982). Brain choline: Its sources and effects on the synthesis and release of acetylcholine. *Aging, 19*, 303–313.

6. Healthy Habits: Exercise and Sleep

Adlard, P. A., Perreau, V. M., & Cotman, C. W. (2005). The exercise-induced expression of BDNF within the hippocampus varies across life-span. *Neurology of Aging, 26*, 511–520.

American Sleep Disorders Association. (1997). *International classification of sleep disorders: Diagnostic and coding manual*. Rochester, MN: Author.

Andreasen, N. C. (2001). *Brave new brain: Conquering mental illness in the era of the genome*. New York: Oxford University Press.

Arden, J. (2009). *Heal your anxiety workbook*. Boston: Fair Winds Press.

Bagely, S. (2007). *Train your brain, change your brain*. New York: Ballantine Books.

Beckner, V., & Arden, J. (2008). *Conquering PTSD*. Boston: Fair Winds Press.

Carro, E., Trejo, J. L., Busiguina, S., & Torres-Aleman, I. (2001). Circulating insulin-like growth factor 1 mediates the protective effects of physical exercise against brain insults of different etiology and anatomy. *Journal of Neuroscience, 21*, 5678–5684.

Cirelli, C. (2005). A molecular window on sleep: Changes in gene expression between sleep and wakefulness. *Neuroscientist, 11*, 63–74.

Cotman, C. W., & Berchtold, N. C. (2002). Exercise: A behavioral intervention to enhance brain health and plasticity. *Trends in Neuroscience, 25*, 295–301.

Fabel, K., Fabel, K., Tam, B., Kaufer, D., Baiker, A., Simmons, N., et al. (2003). VEGF is necessary for exercise-induced adult hippocampus neurogenesis. *European Journal of Neurogenesis, 18*, 2803–2812.

Farmer, J., Zhao, X., Praag, H. van, Wodtke, K., Gage, F. H., & Christie, B. R. (2004). Effects of voluntary exercise on synaptic plasticity and gene expression in the two dentate gyrus of adult male Sprague-Dawley rats in vivo. *Neuroscience, 124,* 71–79.

Ford, E. S. (2002). Does exercise reduce inflammation? Physical activity and C-reactive protein among U.S. adults. *Epidemiology, 13,* 561–568.

Frank, M. G., Issa, N. P., & Stryker, M. P. (2001). Sleep enhances plasticity in the developing visual cortex. *Neuron, 30,* 275–287.

Geffken, D. F., Cushman, M., Burke, G. L., Polak, J. F. , Sakkinen, P. A., & Tracy, R. P. (2001). Association between physical activity and markers of inflammation in a healthy elderly population. *American Journal of Epidemiology,* 153, 242–260.

Guzman-Marin, R., Suntsova, N., Methippara, M., Greiffenstein, R., Szymusiak, R., & McGinty, D. (2005). Sleep deprivation suppresses neurogenesis in adult hippocampus of rats. *European Journal of Neuroscience, 22* (8), 2111–2116.

Hauri, P. J., & Fischer, J. (1986). Persistent psychophysiologic (learned) insomnia. *Sleep, 9,* 38–53.

Jeannerod, M., & Decety, J. (1995). Mental motor imagery: A window into the representation stages of action. *Current Opinion in Neurobiology, 5,* 727–732.

Kubitz, K. K., Landers, D. M., Petruzzello, S. J., & Han, M. W. (1996). The effects of acute and chronic exercise on sleep. *Sports Medicine, 21* (4), 277–291.

Macquet, P. (2001). The role of sleep in learning and memory. *Science, 294,* 1048–1052.

Manger, T. A., & Motta, R. W. (2005, Winter). The impact of an exercise program on post traumatic stress disorder, anxiety and depression. *International Journal of Emergency Mental Health,* 7, 49–57.

Neeper, S. A., Gomez-Pinilla, F., Choi, J., & Cotman, C. W. (1996). Physical activity increases mRNA from brain-derived neurotrophic factor and nerve growth factor in the rat brain. *Brain Research, 726,* 49–56.

O'Connor, P. J., & Youngstedt, M. A. (1995). Influence of exercise on human sleep. *Exercise and Sport Science Reviews, 23,* 105–134.

Pascual-Leone, A., Dang, N., Cohen, L. G., Brasil-Neto, J. P., Cammarota, A., & Hallet, M. (1995). Modulation of muscle responses evoked by transcranial magnetic stimulation during the acquisition of new fine motor skills. *Journal of Neurophysiology,* 74 (3), 1037–1045.

Ratey, J. (2008). *Spark: The revolutionary new science of exercise and the brain.* New York: Little, Brown.

Spiegel, K., Tasali, E., Penev, P., & Van Cauter, E. (2004, December 7). Sleep curtailment in healthy young men is associated with decreased leptin levels, elevated ghrelin levels and increased hunger and appetite. *Annals of Internal Medicine, 141,* 846–850.

Strohle, A., Feller, C., Onken, M., Godemann, F., Heinz, A., & Dimeo, F. (2005, December). The acute anti-panic activity of aerobic exercise. *American Journal of Psychiatry, 162,* 2376–2378.

Swain, R. A., Harris, A. B., Wiener, E. C., Dutka, M. V., Morris, H. D., Theien, B. E., et al. (2003). Prolonged exercise induces angiogenesis and increases cerebral blood volume in primary cortex of the rat. *Neuroscience, 117,* 1037–1046.

Van Praag, H., Shubert, T., Zhao, C., & Gage, F. H. (2005). Exercise enhances learning and hipppocampal neurogenesis in aged mice. *Journal of Neuroscience, 25* (38), 8680–8685.

7. Social Medicine

Ainsworth, M.D.S., Blehar, M. C., Waters, E., & Wall, S. (1978). *Patterns of attachment: A psychological study of the strange situation.* Hillsdale, NJ: Erlbaum.

Arbib, M. A. (2002). Language evolution: The mirror system hypothesis. In *The handbook of brain theory and neural networks* (2nd ed., pp. 606–611). Cambridge, MA: MIT Press.

Arden, J. (1996). *Consciousness, dreams and self: A transdisciplinary approach.* Madison, CT: International Universities Press.

Bartels, A., & Zekis, S. (2000). The neural basis of romantic love. *Neuro Report, 11,* 3829–3834.

Bassuk, S. S., Glass, T. A., & Berekman, L. F. (1998). Social disengagement and incident cognitive decline in community-dwelling elderly persons. *Annals of Internal Medicine, 131,* 165–173.

Berns, G. S., McClure, S. M., Pagnoni, G., & Montague, P. R. (2001). Predictability modulates human brain response to reward. *Journal of Neuroscience, 21*, 2793–2798.

Chungani, H. (2001). Local brain functional activity following early deprivation: A study of postinstitutional Romanian orphans. *Neuro Image, 14*, 184–188.

Cohen, S. (2004). Social relationships and health. *American Psychologist, 59*, 676–684.

Cohen, S., Doyle, W. J., Turnes, R., Alper, C. M., & Skoner, D. F. (2003). Sociability and susceptibility to the common cold. *Psychological Science, 14* (5), 389–395.

Damasio, A. (2003). *Looking for Spinoza's joy, sorrow, and the feeling brain*. New York: Harcourt.

Field, T. (2001). *Touch*. Cambridge, MA: MIT Press.

Field, T. (2002). Violence and touch deprivation in adolescents. *Adolescence, 37*, 735–749.

Field, T. M., Healy, B., Goldstein, S., & Bendell, D. (1988). Infants of depressed mothers show "depressed" behavior even with non-depressed adults. *Child Development, 59,* 1569–1579.

Fischer, L., Ames, E. W., Chisholm, K., & Savoie, L. (1997). Problems reported by parents of Romanian orphans adopted in British Columbia. *International Journal of Behavioral Development, 20*, 67–87.

Francis, D. D., Diorio, J., Liu, D., & Meany, M. J. (1999). Variations in maternal care form the basis for a non-genomic mechanism of inter-generational transmission of individual differences in behavioral and endocrine responses to stress. *Science,* 286 (5442):1155–1158.

Fries, A. B., Ziegler, T. E., Kurian, J. R., Jacoris, S., & Pollak, S. D. (2005, November 22). Early experience in humans is associated with changes in neuropeptides critical for regulating social behavior. *Proceedings of the National Academy of Sciences, 102,* 17237–17240.

Frith, C. D., & Frith, U. (1999). Interacting minds: A biological basis. *Science, 286*, 1692–1695.

Gallese, V. (2001). The shared manifold hypothesis: From mirror neurons to empathy. *Journal of Consciousness Studies, 8* (5–7), 33–50.

Gallese, V., Fadiga, L., Fogassi, L., & Rizzolatti, G. (1996). Action recognition in the premotor cortex. *Brain, 119*, 593–609.

Goleman, D. (2006). *Social intelligence: The new science of human relationships*. New York: Bantam Books.

Goodfellow, L. M. (2003). The effects of therapeutic back massage on psychophysiologic variables and immune function in spouses of patients with cancer. *Nursing Research, 52*, 318–328.

Grossman, K. E., Grossman, K. F., & Warter, V. (1981). German children's behavior toward their mothers at 12 months and their father at 18 months in Ainsworth's Strange Situation. *International Journal of Behavioral Development, 4*, 157–181.

Gunmar, M. (2001). Effects of early deprivation: Findings from orphanage-reared infants and children. In C. Nelson & M. Luciana (Eds.), *Handbook of developmental cognitive neuroscience* (pp. 617–629). Cambridge, MA: MIT Press.

Iacoboni, M. (2008). *Mirroring people*. New York: Farrar, Straus & Giroux.

Ijzendoorn, M. H. van, & Bakerman-Kranenburg, M. J. (1997). Intergenerational transmission of attachment: A move to the contextual level. In L. Atkinson & K. Zucker (Eds.), *Attachment and psychopathology* (pp. 135–170). New York: Guilford Press.

Kiecolt-Glaser, J. K., Rickers, D., George, J., Messick, G., Speicher, C. E., Garner, W., et al. (1984). Urinary cortisol levels, cellular immunocompetency, and loneliness in psychiatric inpatients. *Psychosomatic Medicine, 46* (1), 15–23.

Kosfeld, M., Heinrichs, M., Zak, P. J., Fischbacher, V., & Fehr, E. (2005). Oxytocin increases trust in humans. *Nature, 435* (7042), 673–676.

Koski, L., Iacoboni, M., Dubeau, M. C., Woods, R. P., & Mazziotta, J. C. (2003). Modulation of cortical activity during different imitative behaviors. *Journal of Neurophysiology, 89*, 460–471.

Kuhn, C. M., & Shanberg, S. M. (1998). Responses to maternal separation: Mechanisms and mediators. *International Journal of Developmental Neuroscience, 16*, 261–270.

Lepore, S. J., Allen, K. A. M., & Evans, G. W. (1993). Social support lowers cardiovascular reactivity to an acute stress. *Psychosomatic Medicine, 55*, 518–524.

Main, M., & Goldwyn, R. (1994). *Adult attachment scoring and classification system*. Unpublished manuscript, University of California, Berkeley.

McClelland, D., McClelland, D. C., & Kirchnit, C. (1988). The effect of motivational arousal through films on salivary immunoglobulin. *Psychology and Health, 2,* 31–52.

Meany, M. J., Aitken, D. H, Viau, V., Sharma, S., & Sarrieau, A. (1989). Neonatal handling alters adrenocortical negative feedback sensitivity in hippocampal type II glucocorticoid receptor binding in the rat. *Neuroendocrinology, 50,* 597–604.

Mesulam, M. M. (1998). From sensation to cognition. *Brain, 121,* 1013–1052.

Miller, G. (2005). New neurons strive to fit in. *Science, 311,* 938–940.

Mikulincer, M., Saber, P. R., Gillath, O., & Nitzberg, R.A. (2005, November). Attachment, caregiving and altruism: Boosting attachment security increases compassion and helping. *Journal of Personality and Social Psychology, 89,* 817–839.

Mikulincer, M., & Shaver, R. (2001, July). Attachment theory and intergroup bias: Evidence that priming the secure base schema attenuates negative reactions to outgroups. *Journal of Personality and Social Psychology, 81,* 97–115.

Miyake, K., Chen, S., & Campos, J. (1985). Infant temperment, mother's mode of interaction, and attachment in Japan. In I. Bretheron & E. Waters (Eds.), *Growing points in attachment theory and research* (pp. 276–297). Ann Arbor, MI: Society for Research in Child Development.

Panksepp, J. (1998). *Affective neuroscience: The foundations of human and animal emotions*. New York: Oxford University Press.

Philips, M. L., Young, A. W., Senior, C., Brammer, M., Andrew, C., Calder, A. J., et al. (1997). A specific substrate for perceiving facial expression of disgust. *Nature, 389,* 495–498.

Remington, R. (2002). Calming music and hand massage with agitated elderly. *Nursing Research, 54,* 317–323.

Rizzolatti, G., & Arbib, M. A. (1998). Language within our grasp. *Trends in Neurosciences, 21* (5), 188–194.

Rolls, E. T., O'Doherty, J., Kringelbach, M. L., Francis, S., Bowtell, R., & McGlone, F. (2003). Representations of pleasant and painful touch in the human orbital frontal and cingulated cortices. *Cerebral Cortex, 13,* 308–317.

Russell, D. W., & Cutrona, C. E. (1991). Social support, stress, and depression symptoms among the elderly: Test of a process model. *Psychology and Aging, 6,* 190–201.

Rutter, M., Kreppner, J., & O'Connor, T. (2001). Specificity and heterogeneity in children's responses to profound institutional deprivation. *British Journal of Psychiatry, 179,* 97–103.

Saarni, C., Mumme, D. L., & Campos, J. J. (2000). Emotional development: Action, communication, and understanding. In W. Damon & N. Eisenberg (Eds.), *Handbook of child psychology: Vol. 3. Social, emotional, and personality development* (5th ed., pp. 237–309). Hoboken, NJ: Wiley.

Sabbagh, M. A. (2004). Understanding orbital frontal contributions to the theory-of-mind reasoning: Implications for autism. *Brain and Cognition, 55,* 209–219.

Sapolsky, R. M. (1990). Stress in the wild. *Scientific American, 262,* 116–123.

Siegal, D., & Varley, R. (2002). Neural systems involved in the "theory of mind." *Nature Reviews Neuroscience, 3,* 267–276.

Shaver, P. (1999). In J. Cassidy & P. Shaver (Eds.), *Handbook of attachment theory: Research and clinical applications.* New York: Guilford Press.

Spitzer, S. B., Llabre, M. M., Ironson, G. H., Gellman, M. D., & Schneiderman, N. (1992). The influence of social situations on ambulatory blood pressure. *Psychosomatic Medicine, 54,* 79–86.

Thomas, P. D., Goodwin, J. M., & Goodwin, J. S. (1985). Effect of social support on stress related changes in cholesterol level, uric acid level, and immune function in an elderly sample. *American Journal of Psychiatry, 142,* 732–737.

Wallin, D. (2007). *Attachment in psychotherapy.* New York: Guilford Press.

Weaver, I. C. G., Cervoni, N., Champagne, F. A., D'Alessio, A. C., Sharma, S., Seckl, J. R., et al. (2004, August). Epigenetic programming by maternal behavior. *Nature Neuroscience, 7,* 847–854.

Weller, A., & Feldman, R. (2003). Emotion regulation and touch in infants: The role of cholecystokinin and opiods. *Peptides, 24,* 779–788.

Wexler, B. (2006). *Brain and culture: Neurobiology, ideology, and social change.* Boston: MIT Press.

8. Resiliency and Wisdom

Abbott, R., White, L. R., Ross, G. W., Masaki, K. H., Curb, J. D., & Petrovitch, H. (2004, September 22). Walking and dementia in physically capable elderly men. *Journal of the American Medical Association, 292,* 1447–1453.

Alexander, G. E., Furey, M. L., Grady, C. L., Pietrini, P., Brady, D. R., Mentis, M. J., et al. (1997). Association of premorbid intellectual function with cerebral metabolism in Alzheimer's disease: Implications for the cognitive reserve hypothesis. *American Journal of Psychiatry, 154,* 165–172.

Allen, J. S., Bruss, J., Brown, C. K., & Damasio, H. (2005). Normal neuroanatomical variation due to age: The major lobes and a parcellation of the temporal region. *Neurobiology of Aging, 26,* 1245–1260.

Anokhin, A. P., Bibaumer, N., Lutzenberger, W., Niholaev, A., & Vogel, F. (1996). Age increases brain complexity. *Electroencephalography and Clinical Neurophysiology, 99,* 63–68.

Bartzokis, G., Cummings, J. L., Sultzer, D., Henderson, V. M., Nuechtherlein, K. H., & Mintz, J. (2004). White matter structural integrity in healthy aging adults and patients with Alzheimer's disease. *Archives of Neurology, 60,* 393–398.

Bellert, J. L. (1989). Humor: A therapeutic approach in oncology nursing. *Cancer Nursing, 12* (2), 65–70.

Berk, L. S., Tan, S. A., Nehlsen-Cannrella, S., Napier, B. J., Lee, J. W., Lewis, J. E., & Hubbard, R. W. (1988). Humor-associated

laughter decreases cortisol and increases spontaneous lympho-
cyte blastogenesis. *Clinical Research, 36,* 435A.

Bigler, E. D., Anderson, C. V., & Blatter, D. D. (2002). Temporal
lobe morphology in normal aging and traumatic brain injury.
American Journal of Neuroradiology, 23, 255–266.

Cabeza, R. (2002). Hemispheric asymmetry reduction in older
adults. The HAROLD model. *Psychology and Aging, 17* (1),
85–100.

Cabeza, R., Anderson, N. D., Locantore, J. K., & McInosh, A.
(2002). Aging gracefully: Compensatory brain activity in high
performing older adults. *NeuroImage, 17,* 1394–1402.

Cozolino, L. (2008). *The healing aging brain.* New York: Norton.

Davidson, R. J., Jackson, L., & Kalin, N. H. (2000). Emotion, plasticity, context, and regulation. *Psychological Bulletin, 126,* 316–321.

De Maritino, B., Kumaran, D., Seymour, B., & Dola, R. J. (2006).
Frames, biases, and rational decision-making in the human brain.
Science, 313, 684–687.

Deaner, S. L., & McConatha, J. T. (1993). The relationship of
humor to depression and personality. *Psychological Reports, 72,*
755–763.

Fry, W. F. Jr. (1992). The physiological effects of humor, mirth, and
laughter. *Journal of the American Medical Association, 267* (4),
1874–1878.

Gunning-Dixon, F. M., Head, D., McQuain, J., Acker, J. D., & Raz, D.
(1998). Differential aging of the human striatum: A prospective MR imaging study. *American Journal of Neuroimaging, 19,*
1501–1507.

Gustafson, D., Lissner, L., Bengtsson, C., Björkelund, C., & Skoog, I.
(2004). A 24-year follow-up of body mass index and cerebral
atrophy. *Neurology, 63,* 1876–1881.

Hayashi, T., Urayama, O., Kawai, K., Hayashi, K., Iwanaga, S.,
Ohta, M., et al. (2006). Laughter regulates gene expression in
patients with type 2 diabetes. *Psychotherapy and Psychosomatics,
75,* 62–65.

Kuhn, C. C. (1994). The stages of laughter. *Journal of Nursing
Jocularity, 4* (2), 34–35.

Lawrence, B., Myerson, J., & Hale, S. (1998). Differential decline on verbal and visual spatial processing speed across the adult life span. *Aging, Neuropsychology, and Cognition, 5* (2), 129–146.

Levine, B., (2004). Autobiographical memory and the self in time: Brain lesion effects, functional neuroanatomy, and lifespan development. *Brain and Cognition, 55,* 54–68.

Maddi, S. R. & Kobasa, S. C. (1984). *The hardy executive.* Homewood, Ill: Dow Jones-Irwin.

Martin, R. A., Kuiper, N. A., Olinger, L. J., & Dance, D. A. (1993). Humor, coping with stress, self-concept, and psychological well-being. *Humor: International Journal of Humor Research, 6* (1), 89–104.

Maruta, I., Colligan, R. C., Malinchoc, M., & Offord, K. P. (2002). Optimism-pessimism assessed in the 1960s and self-reported health status 30 years later. *Mayo Clinic Proceedings, 77,* 748–753.

McEwen, B. S. (1998). Stress, adaptation, and disease: Allostasis and allostatic load. *Annals of the New York Academy of Science, 8,* 840–844.

McEwen, B. S., & Stellar, E. (1993). Stress and individual-mechanisms leading to disease. *Archives of Internal Medicine, 153,* 2093–2101.

McEwen, B., & Wingfield, J. C. (2003). The concept of allostasis in biology and biomedicine. *Hormones and Behavior, 43,* 2–15.

Mobbs, D., Greicius, M. D., Abdel-Azim, E., Menon, V., & Reiss, A. L. (2003). Humor modulates the mesolimbic reward centers. *Neuron, 40,* 1041–1048.

Morrison, J. H., & Hoff, P. R. (2003). Changes in cortical circuits during aging. *Clinical Neuroscience Research, 2,* 294–304.

Pearce, J. M. S. (2004). Some neurological aspects of laughter. *European Neurology, 52,* 169–171.

Raz, N., Gunning, F. M., Head, D., Dupuis, J. H., McQuain, J., Briggs, S. D., et al. (1997). Selective aging of the human cerebral cortex observed in vivo: Differential vulnerability of the prefrontal gray matter. *Cerebral Cortex, 7,* 268–282.

Raz, N., Gunning, F. M., Head, D., Williamson, A., & Acker, J. D. (2001). Age and sex differences in the cerebellum and the ventral pons: A prospective MR study of healthy adults. *American Journal of Neuroradiology, 22,* 1161–1167.

Reuter-Lorenz, P. A., Stanczak, K. L., & Miller, A. C. (1999). Neural recruitment and cognitive aging: Two hemispheres are better than one, especially as you age. *Psychological Science, 10,* 494–500.

Richards, M., & Deary, I. J. (2005). A life course approach to cognitive reserve: A model for cognitive aging and development? *Annals of Neurology, 58,* 617–622.

Salat, D. H., Buckner, R. L., Synder, A. Z., Greve, D. N., Desikan, R. S. R., Busa, E., et al. (2004). Thinning of the cerebral cortex in aging. *Cerebral Cortex, 14,* 721–730.

Salat, D. H., Kaye, J. A., & Janowsky, J. S. (2001). Selective preservation and degeneration within the prefrontal cortex in aging and Alzheimer's disease. *Archives of Neurology, 58,* 1403–1408.

Schmidt, L. A. (1999). Frontal brain electrical activity in shyness and sociability. *Psychological Sciences, 10,* 316–321.

Seeman, T. E., Lusignolo, T. M., Albert, M., & Berkman, L. (2001). Social relationships, social support, and patterns of cognitive aging in healthy, high-functioning older adults. *Health Psychology, 4,* 243–255.

Seligman, M. (2001). Optimism, pessimism and mortality. *Mayo Clinic Proceedings, 75* (2), 133–134.

Singer, B., & Ryff, C. D. (1999). Hierarchies of life histories and associated health risks. *Annals of the New York Academy of Sciences, 896,* 96–116.

Snowden, D. (1997). *Aging with grace: What the Nun Study teaches us about leading longer, healthier, and more meaningful lives.* New York: Bantam Books.

Sowell, E. R., Peterson, P. M., Thompson, P. M., Welcome, S. E., Henkenius, A. L., & Toga, A. W. (2003). Mapping cortical change across the human life span. *Nature Neuroscience, 2,* 850–861.

Sterling, P., & Eyer, J. (1988). Allostasis: A new paradigm to explain arousal pathology. In S. Fischer & J. Reason (Eds.), *Handbook of stress, cognition, and health* (pp. 269–249). Hoboken, NJ: Wiley.

Sullivan, E. V., Marsh, L., Mathalon, D. H., Lim, K. O., & Pfefferbaum, A. (1995). Age-related decline in MRI volumes in temporal lobe gray matter but not hippocampus. *Neurobiology of Aging, 16*, 591–606.

Sullivan, R. M., & Gratton, A. (2002). Prefrontal cortical regulation of hypothalamic-pituitary-adrenal function in the rat and implications for psychopathology: Side matters. *Psychoneuroendochrinology, 27*, 99–114.

Takahashi, K., Iwase, M., Yamashita, K., Tatsumoto, Y., Ve, H., Kurasune, H., et al. (2001). The elevation of natural killer cell activity induced by laughter in a crossover designed study. *International Journal of Molecular Medicine, 8*, 645–650.

Tang, Y., Nyengaard, J. R., Pakkenberg, B., & Gundersen, H. J. (1997). Age-induced white matter changes in the human brain: A stereological investigation. *Neurobiology of Aging, 18*, 609–615.

Taylor, S. E., Kemeny, M. E., Reed, G. M., Bower, J. E., & Gruenewald, T. L. (2000). Psychological resources, positive illusions, and health. *The American Psychologist, 5*, 99–109.

Terry, R. D., DeTeresa, R., & Hansen, L. A. (1987). Neocortical cell counts in normal human adult aging. *Annals of Neurology, 21*, 530–539.

Tessitore, A., Hariri, A. R., Fera, F., Smith, W. G., Das, S., Weinberger, D. R., et al. (2005). Functional changes in the activity of brain regions underlying emotion processes in the elderly. *Psychiatry Research: Neuroimaging, 139*, 9–18.

Vaillant, G. E. (2002). *Aging well: Surprising guide points to a happier life from the landmark Harvard study of adult development*. Boston: Little, Brown.

Van Patten, C., Plante, E., Davidson, P. S. R., Kuo, T. Y., Bjuscak, L., & Glisky, E.L. (2004). Memory and executive function in older adults: Relationships with temporal and prefrontal volumes and white matter hyperintensities. *Neuropsychologia, 42*, 1313–1335.

Whalley, L. J. (2001). *The aging brain*. New York: Columbia University Press.

Whalley, L. J., Deary, I. J., Appleton, C. L., & Starr, J. M. (2004). Cognitive reserve and the neurobiology of cognitive aging. *Aging Research Reviews, 3*, 369–382.

Willis, M. W., Ketter, T. A., Kimbell, T. A., George, M. S., Herscovitch, P., Danielson, A. L., et al. (2002). Age, sex, and laterality effects on cerebral glucose metabolism in healthy adults. *Psychiatry Research Neuroimaging, 114*, 23–37.

Wilson, R. S., Beckett, L. A., Barnes, L. L., Schneider, J. A., Bach, J., Evan, D. A., et al. (2002). Individual differences in rates of change in cognitive abilities of older persons. *Psychology and Aging, 17*, 179–193.

Wooten, P. (1996). Humor: An antidote for stress. *Holistic Nursing Practice, 10* (2), 49–55.

Wueve, J., Kang, J. H., Manson, J. E., Breteler, M.M.B., Ware, J. H., & Grodstein, F. (2004, September). Physical activity, including walking, and cognitive function in older women. *Journal of the American Medical Association, 292*, 1452–1461.

Yoder, M. A., & Haude, R. H. (1995). Sense of humor and longevity. Older adults' self-ratings for deceased siblings. *Psychological Reports, 76*, 945–946.

Yovetich, N. A., Dale, J. A., & Hudak, M. A. (1990). Benefits of humor in the reduction of threat-induced anxiety. *Psychological Reports, 66*, 51–58.

9. The Mindful Attitude

Arden, J. (2003). *America's meltdown*. Westport, CT: Praeger.

Aron, A. R., Robins, T. W., & Poldrack, R. A. (2004). Inhibition and the right inferior cortext. *Trends in Cognitive Sciences, 8*, 170–177.

Baxter, L. R. Jr., Schwartz, J. M., Bergman, K. S., Szuba, M. P., Guze, B. H., Mazziotta, J. C., et al. (1992). Caudate glucose metabolic rate changes with both drug and behavior therapy for obsessive-compulsive disorder. *Archives of General Psychiatry, 46*, 681–689.

Cahn, B. R., & Polich, J. (2006). Meditation states and traits: EEG, ERP, and neuroimaging studies. *Psychological Bulletin, 132* (2), 180–211.

Christakis, D. A., Zimerman, F. J., DiGiuseppe, D. L., & McCarty, C. A. (2004). Early television exposure and subsequent attentional problems in children. *Pediatrics, 113* (4), 708–713.

Cresswell, J. D., Way, B. M., Eisenberg, N. I., & Lieberman, M. D. (2007). Neural correlates of dispositional mindfulness during affective labeling. *Psychosomatic Medicine, 18,* 211–237.

Davidson, R. J., Jackson, L., & Kalin, N. H. (2000). Emotion, plasticity, context, and regulation. *Psychological Bulletin, 126,* 890–909.

Davidson, R. J., Kabat-Zinn, J., Schumacher, J., Rosenkranz, M., Muller, D., Santorelli, S. F., et al. (2003). Alterations in brain and immune function produced by mindfulness meditation. *Psychosomatic Medicine, 65,* 564–570.

Fehmi, L., & Robbins, J. (2007). *Open focus brain: Harnessing the power of attention to heal the mind and the body.* Boston: Trumpter.

Hariri, A. R., Bookheimer, S. Y., & Mazziotta, J. C. (2000). Modulating emotional responses: Effects of a neocortical network on the limbic system. *NeuroReport, 11,* 43–48.

Kabat-Zinn, J. (1990). *Full catastrophe living: Using the wisdom of your body and mind to face stress, pain, and illness.* New York: Delta.

Kalisch, R., Wiech, K., Critchley, H. D., Seymour, B., O'Dohery, J. P., Oakley, D. A., et al. (2005). Anxiety reduction through detachment, subjective, physiological and neural effects. *Journal of Cognitive Neuroscience, 17,* 874–883.

Kuber, R., & Csikszentimihalyi, M. (2002, February 23). Television addiction is no mere metaphor. *Scientific American, 286*(2), 79–86.

Lazar, S. W., Kerr, C. E., Wasserman, R. H., Gray, J. R., Greve, D. N., Treadway, M. T., et al. (2005). Meditation experience is associated with increased cortical thickness. *NeuroReport, 16* (17), 1893–1897.

Lieberman, M. D., Eisenberger, N. I., Crockett, M. D., Tom, S. M., Pfeifer, J. H., & Way, B. (2004). Putting feelings into words: Affective labeling disrupts amygdala activity in response to affective stimuli. *Psychological Science, 18* (5), 421–428.

Linehan, M. (1993). *Cognitive-behavioral treatment of borderline personality disorder.* New York: Guilford Press.

Lutz, A., & Davidson, R. (2004). *A neural correlate of attentional expertise in long-term Buddhist practitioners.* Slide presentation at the Society for Neuroscience, Cambridge, MA.

Lutz, A., Greischar, L. L., Rawlings, N. B., Richard, M., & Davidson, R. J. (2004, November 6). Long-term meditators self-induce high-amplitude gamma synchrony during mental practice. *Proceedings of the National Academy of Sciences, 101,* 16369–16373.

Niebur, E., Hsiao, S. S., & Johnson, K. O. (2002). Synchrony: A neuronal mechanism for attentional selection? *Current Opinion in Neurobiology, 12* (2), 190–195.

Ochsner, K. N., Bunge, S. A., Gross, J. J., & Gabrieli, J.D.E. (2002). Rethinking feelings: An fMRI study of the cognitive regulation of emotion. *Journal of Cognitive Neuroscience, 14,* 1215–1229.

Segal, Z. V., Williams, J. M. G., & Teasdale J. D. (2002). *Mindfulness-based cognitive therapy for depression.* New York: Guilford Press.

Siegel, D. J. (2007). *The mindful brain: Reflection and attunement in the cultivation of well-being.* New York: Norton.

Index

About the Author

John Arden has published eleven other books: two on the neurodynamic study of consciousness, six self-help books, one critique of contemporary society, and two books on brain-based therapy.

His first book, *Consciousness, Dreams, and Self,* was awarded the 1997 Outstanding Academic Book Award by *Choice,* a publication of the American Library Association. An international panel of jurists nominated his second book, *Science, Theology, and Consciousness,* for the Templeton Prize award funded by the Templeton Foundation.

His six self-help books are *Surviving Job Stress, Improving Your Memory For Dummies, Stop Spoiling That Man, Conquering Post-Traumatic Stress Disorder* (with Dr. Victoria Beckner), *Heal Your Anxiety Workbook,* and *Heal Your OCD Workbook* (with Dr. Daniel DalCorso). His book *America's Meltdown: Creating the Lowest Common Denominator Society* explored the degradation of the fabric of American society. John is also the lead author (with Lloyd Linford) of *Brain-Based Therapy with Adults* and *Brain-Based Therapy with Children and Adolescents.*

Arden has a background in neuropsychology and is the Director of Training in Mental Health at the Kaiser Permanente Medical Centers. In this capacity, he oversees one of the largest mental health training programs in the world, which operates in twenty-four medical centers throughout Northern California. He also practices part-time at Kaiser Permanente in Petaluma and San Rafael, and he served for several years as the chief psychologist at Kaiser Vallejo. He has taught in colleges, professional schools, and universities.